A comparison of British and German industries' reaction to the opportunities and threats offered by the single European market (SEM) is presented here. The book outlines the effect that SEM was expected to have
on the two countries and contrasts this with actual progress, based
on published data and a detailed study of four industries: retailing,
pharmaceuticals, insurance and machine tools. It shows that while indeed the single European market has had an impact, many measures
have had a far weaker effect than expected. The existence of other
barriers not tackled by the SEM programme – weakened measures,
poor implementation, global business trends and the recent recession –
helps dominate the impact of the SEM. Nevertheless it stands out as one
of the most striking influences on British and German industries for
many years. Germany, with its geographical advantage, longer-term
approach and stronger manufacturing, seems the better placed to benefit overall. But the less regulated and, in some respects, more flexible
UK economy may have competitive advantages as the pressures increase.
It is no accident that it has been chosen so frequently as the best site
within the EC for investment by firms from non-EC countries.

THE NATIONAL INSTITUTE OF ECONOMIC AND SOCIAL RESEARCH

Occasional Papers
XLVII

THE SINGLE MARKET PROGRAMME AS A STIMULUS TO CHANGE
COMPARISONS BETWEEN BRITAIN AND GERMANY

THE SINGLE MARKET PROGRAMME AS A STIMULUS TO CHANGE
COMPARISONS BETWEEN BRITAIN AND GERMANY

DAVID MAYES
AND
PETER HART

WITH DUNCAN MATTHEWS AND ALAN SHIPMAN

CAMBRIDGE
UNIVERSITY PRESS

Published by the Press Syndicate of the University of Cambridge
The Pitt Building, Trumpington Street, Cambridge CB2 1RP
40 West 20th Street, New York, NY 10011-4211, USA
10 Stamford Road, Oakleigh, Melbourne 3166, Australia

© The National Institute of Economic and Social Research 1994

First published 1994

Printed in Great Britain at the University Press, Cambridge

A catalogue record for this book is available from the British Library

Library of Congress cataloguing in publication data

Mayes, David G.
    The single market programme as a stimulus to change: Britain and Germany/David
Mayes and Peter Hart, with Duncan Matthews and Alan Shipman.
        p. cm.– (Occasional papers:47)
    Includes bibliographical references and index.
    ISBN 0 521 47156 7
    1. Great Britain –Industries. 2. Germany (West)–Industries.
    3.Industry and state–Great Britain. 4.Industry and state–Germany (West) 5. Europe
1992. I. Hart, P.E. (Peter Edward)
    II. Title. III. Series: Occasional papers (National Institute of Economic and Social
Research): 47.
    HC256.6M385 1994
    338.4'0941–dc20   94–21348 CIP

ISBN 0 521 47156 7 hardback

Contents

Tables

Charts

Preface

This book is the result of a joint project with the IFO Institut für Wirtschaftsforschung in Munich, financed by the Anglo-German Foundation for the Study of Industrial Society. The idea for the study emerged from three strands of previous work by the authors. David Mayes had recently participated in a study of the impact of 1992 on European industry, financed by the European Commission and since published as Mayes, D.G. *et al.*, *The European Challenge: industry's response to the 1992 programme*, by Harvester Wheatsheaf in 1991. In this it was clear that the single market programme had had a substantial effect on European industry already, but one which was rather different from that envisaged in the 1988 Cecchini Report, *1992: The European Challenge*, and one that varied very considerably across countries. In particular Britain and Germany seemed to be differing in their responses, with the latter already having a more 'European' structure to its industry and showing a more collaborative response in industry to the challenge posed. British industry on the other hand appeared still to have international rather than European strategies and responded far more by foreign direct investment and mergers and acquisitions.

Peter Hart and Alan Shipman were in the final stages of collaborative work with the IFO Institute on a project on skill shortages in Britain and Germany, also financed by the Anglo-German Foundation. There was therefore a ready channel for putting together a joint comparative project.

Furthermore, a few years earlier David Mayes had completed a study of companies in the UK that had sharply improved their performance (Grinyer *et al.*, 1988). One of the principal conclusions of this work had been not only that firms respond much more readily to threats than they do to opportunities but that such threats or opportunities have to be major if they are to elicit a response. The 1992 programme seemed to be an unusual example which would fit that bill as it offers both threats and opportunities. As response was substantially affected by individual circumstances, including the culture of the business, it is likely that responses would differ strikingly between Britain and Germany in the case of 1992.

Our German collaborators, Uwe Täger and Günter Weitzel, were interested in particular mechanisms which can be used to further competitiveness in the single market. One was the role of trade fairs, which we did not include in our study, but the second was the use of patents, particularly European patents, as a means of gaining market share in Europe.

We therefore explored this route in addition to the traditional breakdown of the means of growth in the European market, that is, internal or 'organic' growth, external growth by merger or acquisition and restructuring of the cost base by relocation. The problem is a very large one so we restricted consideration to some economy-wide issues relating to differences in industrial structure, economic institutions, regulation and corporate governance. We then considered four industries in more detail – pharmaceuticals, machine tools, insurance and retailing – all of which were expected to be affected fairly markedly by the single market. The industries are important in both countries but sometimes of contrasting characteristics, so while communalities in behaviour could be expected so could differences.

This book is largely the result of the work undertaken by the NIESR team. The IFO team has produced two reports. The first of these considers retailing (Günter Weitzel), a brief assessment of insurance (Arno Städtler) and a study of the legal framework for mergers and acquisitions (Ulrich Immenga with Andreas Fuchs, Birgit Hellberg, Karin Nissing and Daniel Zimmer). The second deals directly with the issue of patents, *Entwicklung der Patentaktivitäten von in- und ausländischen Unternehmen in Deutschland und Grossbritannien* (Uwe Täger with W. Bockenfeld).

The NIESR team was led by David Mayes, who organised this book. However, Peter Hart took responsibility for the comparison of productivity between the two countries, the study of internal and external growth of firms and the work on the pharmaceutical and insurance industries and therefore has made a major contribution. Although the book is a joint effort, Peter is the primary author of chapters 4 and 5. Initially the team was joined by Alan Shipman who assisted with the work on productivity and was the first author of chapter 3. After he left the Institute his place was filled by Duncan Matthews, who helped complete the work on machine tools and provided the first draft of chapter 6. Günter Weitzel helped organise the interviews in Germany and contributed a study of retailing which is incorporated in chapter 3. Chapter 2 also draws on some previously published work by Mary O'Mahony at NIESR (O'Mahony, 1992), which considered differences in the average levels of productivity in the two countries.

The work, as could be expected, was affected by German unification, which raised many crucial economic issues which needed immediate attention. It has therefore been somewhat delayed and altered in format.

We take this opportunity to thank those who have contributed to its success: first those in companies and organisations whom we visited in the two countries (listed below), secondly our colleagues who took the trouble to comment on the text and in particular to Rita Charlton and Sarah Leeming who typed parts of it, and finally to the Anglo-German Foundation whose finance made the work possible and in particular to its two research directors, Nicholas Watts and Ray Cunningham, who encouraged and advised us throughout. Many people have helped us in many ways in the preparation of this study. It is a pleasure to record our thanks but this does not imply that they are responsible in any way for our findings.

Profesor J. Badenhoop, Sir James Ball, Dr T. Brinkman, Mr P. Brook, Sir John Cuckney, Dr M. Burstall, Professor R.L. Carter, Mr R. Chew, Dr W. Cloos, Dr R. Davies, Mr M. Digby, Dr A. Faller, Mr T. Ginty, Dr J. Griffin, Mr J. Brian Griffin, Mr I. Harcus, Mr R. Heath, Dr M. Hekeler, Mr M. Hesketh, Mr J. Holmes, Mr R. Jones, Mr J.M. Keane, Mr P. Lumley, Ms M. Lustman, Mr N. Matthews, Mr R. Moore, Mr S.C. Moore, Mr Edgar Müller-Gotthard, Mr A. Paish, Mr C. Preston, Mr H.M.J. Ramshaw, Professor B. Reuben, Mr W.R. Rowland, Mr A.P. Sanden, Professor G. Teeling Smith, Dr A. Treadgold, Dr J. Zech, the Department of Trade and Industry Insurance Division, MTTA, Tesco, the OXIRM library.

1 Routes to change

Introduction

Our objective in this book is to explore how the advent of the single European market, as set out in the European Commission's White Paper of 1985, *Completing the internal market*, has thus far acted as a stimulus to change. Our focus is principally on industry and on the institutions and regulations which govern its behaviour. The analysis is restricted to the UK and Germany both to get a better idea of the range of possible responses than would be available from a single country study and to provide a basis of comparison against which to judge the importance of the effects in the two countries.

In this chapter we begin the analysis with a brief survey of the changes entailed by the single market measures and the types of impact they could be expected to have. By examining what we have described as 'routes to change' we set the basis for exploring how firms and the institutions which affect their behaviour are reacting to the changes imposed on them and how those measures are themselves implemented and enforced.

The chapter begins with an assessment of what the stimulus to change was. Here we are not just dealing with a list of some 300 measures outlined in the White Paper but the perception by firms as to what those measures would mean for the conduct of their business. Thus we are not dealing with a mere description of what measures were actually implemented and a careful analysis of their likely impact but a review of what the single market measures were expected to achieve as viewed during the period 1986–9. We thus explore what the measures were intended to be and what information was available to firms about their likely impact.

This information base would have been used by firms in making their initial responses during the period of our analysis, which ends in 1992, by which time the measures in the White Paper were supposed to be implemented. The final impact will of course take much longer to come through and in our opinion is unlikely to be complete even by the end of the century.

The next section of this chapter therefore explores the nature of the expected stimulus in the two countries – its size, the industries and regions which were expected to be most affected – and it is followed by an examination of how firms might react. Chapter 2 considers what characteristics of the German and British economies and their industrial organisation might lead to differing responses. This then completes the background to our research which compares these preconceptions with the reality of experience during the period 1986–92, focussed on four industries, retailing, pharmaceuticals, insurance and machine tools, that are widely spread across industrial activity. Chapters 3–6 cover these four industries in turn before the last chapter draws conclusions from the experience.

We therefore turn first to the single market programme and what it was expected to achieve.

The stimulus to change

The nature of the stimulus

Europe's single market programme was envisaged as providing a major stimulus to economic growth in a Community whose momentum had slowed in the years following the first oil crisis in the mid-1970s. Europe appeared to be stalling in its progress towards catching the US, even though the US had its own problems and was at the same time finding itself being passed rapidly by Japan. It was therefore clear from the US and Japanese examples that higher levels of GDP per head could be achieved and that faster rates of growth were possible. Although the finger might be justifiably pointed at European industry for failing to take many measures necessary for greater competitive success, many other structural factors affect economic performance, only some of which are readily alterable by public or private action. Nevertheless it was clear that the fragmentation and complex regulation of the European economy encouraged a host of havens in which less competitive behaviour could persist with adequate profits.

By concentrating a major step in the programme of market integration envisaged in the Treaty of Rome into just a few years, Europe's political leaders intended not a change in direction but an acceleration in pace. It has long been recognised that sustained faster growth in an economy is not just a matter of taking new actions but of changing the culture or climate of economic behaviour (Barnett, 1986). The rapidly industrialising countries in East Asia and ASEAN are the most striking examples. Reaganomics in the US, the Thatcher revolution in the UK and the various stabilisation and restructuring programmes encouraged by the IMF and the World Bank in the third world are other recent examples, several of which show that attempting such cultural change is no guarantee of success. Perhaps the most obvious cultural change is the transformation of central and eastern Europe from state planning to market driven systems since 1989. These programmes have one element in common. They offer the hope of great opportunity in the future, combined with the reality of harsh market pressures in the present. Although change is a necessity rather than an option for most organisations, rapid and wholesale change has attendant dangers (Popper, 1950). Wiping the slate clean may induce chaos rather than improvement.

It is an unfortunate feature of market economies that firms seem to respond much more weakly to opportunities than they do to threats. It is thus difficult to induce favourable change without the concomitant risk of causing substantial harm. In a previous study of twenty-five companies that had indeed made a vigorous and sustained improvement in their performance Grinyer, Mayes and McKiernan (1988) found few examples where companies had voluntarily chosen to change largely because they saw a new opportunity. Big shocks could do this, like the discovery of North Sea oil which stimulated the John Wood Group to move from fishing into support services, or the discovery of fashion leisurewear in the US which stimulated Ellis and Goldstein into starting DASH. However, more normally it was downside shocks, either from a general economic downturn or from specific events, which stimulated change, like the loss of their major customer in the case of Macallan-Glenlivet or major losses on a large project for Low and Bonar. These are, of course, only twenty-five out of the many thousand companies in the UK, however, they are all chosen from the best fifty performing companies among those publicly quoted in the UK and so can be thought representative of this group (Grinyer et al., pp. 151–2).

The single market programme thus *prima facie* provides an example of an ideal combination of the stick and the carrot because both the threats and the opportunities occur in the future. Since the legislative programme was scheduled for completion over a six-year period (and implementation over the succeeding years) there was time to prepare rationally. Most importantly it was not necessary to get into financial difficulties first before realising the need for change. Most turnarounds fail (Slatter, 1984) because the process of achieving change requires substantial investment. Only strong companies either have the resources themselves to invest or the credibility to raise the funds to do so from others. A weak company has to make extreme cuts and sell off assets before it can generate the breathing space to organise a recovery. While the process of reorganisation may result in an increase in unemployment for the member states in the early stages of the transition, there is no reason why this should entail any permanent loss in output for the firms undertaking reorganisation. Indeed it may even increase profitability as companies can eliminate inefficient facilities which had previously been necessary to ensure market access to some parts of the Community. Thus one could envisage a process of change whereby each step released the resources for the investment in the stages which were to follow by reducing costs and increasing profitability. Crucial in this would be the opportunity to change before the pressures of increased competition reduced profit margins.

The single market programme would thus encourage early action, providing just the sort of stimulus to advance the process of change that the member states were looking for.

The single market programme

Although the single market programme is well known, it is worth summarising very briefly the nature of the stimuli to it which engendered change, because there is no single uniform impulse applying equally to the whole of European industry (see table 1.1). The White Paper explaining the programme identified a set of physical, fiscal and technical barriers to the 'completion' of the internal market involving the free movement of goods, services, capital and labour (CEC, 1985). It went on to outline a set of nearly 300 measures, which when implemented in detail should eliminate those barriers. The general idea was to try to remove those aspects of national regulations which discriminated between goods, services, capital and labour according to whether they were domestic or came from another member state. Thus, for example, subsidies were included as well as trade barriers because subsidies favour domestic production.

Table 1.1   *The main features of the single market progamme*

Taking a wide view of the various steps involved the 1992 Programme calls for action in six main areas.

---

1. *Unified market in goods and services* Removal of barriers to trade in financial and other services, and of remaining non-tariff barriers to visible trade. Simplification of customs procedures and elimination of vehicle checks. Harmonisation of technical standards and health/safety regulations, with mutual recognition of certification. Closer alignment of VAT and excise duties.
2. *Unified factor market* Free movement of capital, with removal of exchange controls. Alignment of savings taxes. Free movement of labour, with mutual recognition of qualifications.
3. *Promotion of competition* Common rules on regulation, takeovers, state assistance to industry, patents and copyrights, company accounting and disclosure of information. Opening up of public procurement of competitive tender. Reduced intervention in agriculture.
4. *Monetary integration* Exchange rate alignment (via ERM). To be followed by adoption of a single currency and creation of a European central bank.
5. *Social protection* Adoption of a Social Charter incorporating freedom of movement, fair wages and conditions of employment, vocational training, collective bargaining, consultation over technological change and company restructuring, protection of children, elderly and disabled people.
6. *United response to external challenges* A common external tariff. Infrastructure projects, especially high-speed rail and road links and integrated telecommunications. Cooperative R&D, especially in microelectronics and information technology. A common energy policy.

Source: adapted from Mayes *et al.* (1991), chapter 1
Note: a narrow view of the single market might restrict it to the first three headings but the three others are necessary to paint the full picture of proposed measures affecting firms.

Firms taking decisions on how to respond to this programme had to evaluate what the new regulations might mean in practice. This was a heroic requirement because the detail was not known. Firms therefore had to make a complex series of guesses, such as:

• whether any particular measure would in fact be agreed,
• what form that agreement might take,

- how it might be implemented in their own member state and in those of their markets,
- how their competitors might decide to respond to it,
- how it might be enforced in the event of non-compliance.

In technical areas where opinions were well known and agreement would take the form of a voluntary standard through the European standards bodies, CEN, CENELEC or ETSI,[1] it might be possible to make an intelligent guess. In most areas, however, understanding in the early stages was very sketchy and considerable scepticism was voiced over whether the Community would actually be able to achieve these steps when previous progress had been so slow.

As the single market programme has progressed, the form and content of the new directives, regulations, standards and other rules has become steadily clearer and by the end of 1992, the scheduled completion date, most had been agreed. In some respects the timetable is rather slower than was originally envisaged with some measures not coming into effect until later in the decade (as discussed in more detail in our later chapters on pharmaceuticals and insurance, for example). Some of the measures are rather more diluted than might have been originally expected. Many measures still await transposition into national law and the way in which they will operate is still to be observed. Reactions by firms therefore were taken in the face of considerable uncertainty. The stimulus was hence rather more muted in some respects than might be inferred from the general statements of the time. By the time the information programme in the member states was in full swing in 1988, there were few firms of any great size which had not given some thought to the single market. Nevertheless the diffusion of the ideas among smaller firms about what was intended was quite a slow process. However, given the uncertainty, some firms will also have held considerably exaggerated views about what was likely to happen, or had expectations that the single market would lead to the establishment of more effective external commercial barriers round the Community. The idea, commonly labelled 'Fortress Europe', held considerable sway in the early years (Dell and Mayes, 1989). The European Roundtable of Industrialists had put forward their own plan for a single market to come into force by 1990 and some may have been influenced by the discussions which went into producing this document rather than the official White Paper, whose detailed proposals are rather opaque for many readers.

Early assessment of the likely impact of the single market

Although firms want to act on the basis of 'facts', they still have to take decisions on whatever information is available – not acting is itself still effectively a decision. The initial stimulus to change was therefore heavily larded with beliefs. All it is possible to do is to review such evidence as there is about the nature of those beliefs and forecasts and estimates which were available at the time. Subsequently expectations have been updated as legislative progress has been made and new evidence and estimates have come to light. This has been a strongly evolutionary process. In drawing up the detailed proposals the Commission has relied heavily on industry, on existing practice in the member states and on a number of independent experts. Lobbying from both inside and outside the EC has affected the final form of the measures (Mayes *et al.*, 1993). There is therefore no clean stimulus followed by clearly defined reactions to observe, rather it has been a process of development heavily overlaid by the other changes in market behaviour which have influenced industry over the past six years.

While the far-sighted might have been able to forecast further progress towards economic and monetary union, there were no suggestions that the prospects for change in central and eastern Europe were on anything like the scale that has been observed. More predictable changes in the form of the continuing development of information technology, advanced manufacturing and production management techniques and the globalisation of markets have also continued to sweep through industry. Few firms would want to say that they have not reacted to 1992 but it is clearly a very difficult task to separate the individual impact of the single market programme from all the other influences.

The impact of the removal of the various physical, fiscal and technical barriers varies by industry, by country and by firm. Clearly, the less the tradeability of the product then the less important are any existing barriers to trade for the future structure of the industry. Industries where there are already strong international standards, such as for railway rolling stock that crosses borders, have little to gain from further technical harmonisation. Firms in countries whose existing regulations are close to the new EC directives will need to make few adjustments. Thus, for example, where public procurement is already relatively open, as in various instances in the UK, domestic firms will not find themselves subject to as great a change in purchasing behaviour. How much an individual firm is affected will depend very much on its segment of the market, its size and its previous strategies. Industries defined by the Standard Industrial Classification are not homogeneous, major motor car manufacturers may be in the same industry as small firms producing specialist parts for augmenting performance and the range of EC legislation which affects them is likely to be totally different.

It was very difficult to assess beforehand what the nature of the likely impact might be and the European Commission, which undertook the most thorough assessment through its massive programme of work, 'The costs of non-Europe', that provided evidence to support the Cecchini Report (Cecchini, 1988), was illustrative rather than exhaustive in its approach. Indeed, its major concern is over what the Community loses by having barriers preventing a single market; it does not actually claim that all the costs will be recouped by the single market programme. The Commission adopted the view that two sorts of evidence were available, first of all the subjective opinion of firms as to the importance of the potential impact and secondly empirical evidence on the extent to which the market which existed in 1986 differed from what one might call a 'single' market – for example the extent that prices for relatively homogeneous products varied markedly across countries. This second set of information was published in 'The impact of the internal market by industrial sector: the challenge for the member states' (*European Economy*, special edition 1990).

THE SUBJECTIVE EVIDENCE FROM FIRMS

The survey evidence, compiled by Gernot Nerb and his colleagues at IFO (Nerb, 1988) was obtained from some 11,000 firms across the Community. They were asked to say whether removal of each of the following eight barriers currently fragmenting the EC market would be important for their company: standards and technical regulations; public purchasing; administrative barriers (such as customs);[2] frontier delays and costs; differences in VAT and excise taxes; transport regulations; capital market restrictions; and implementation of EC law.

The overall results are difficult to interpret and show considerable variation, both by country (chart 1.1) and by industry (chart 1.2). The main reason why these results are so difficult to use for our purposes stems from the phraseology of the question, which does not ask whether the actions proposed in the White Paper will have a major impact on the firm, but whether they are 'important'. For example, technical harmonisation is placed top of the ranking in chart 1.2 by the motor vehicle industry. It is indeed widely accepted that technical harmonisation is extremely important to the industry (Salvadori, 1991) but most of the

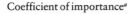

Coefficient of importance[a]

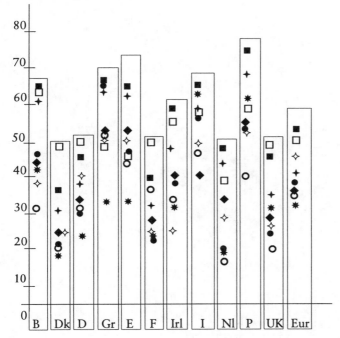

☐ Standards, technical regulations   ✳ Public purchase
■ Administration barriers (customs)   + Frontier delays, costs
○ Different VAT, excise taxes   ◆ Transport regulations
● Capital market restrictions   ✧ Implementation of EC law

Chart 1.1 Importance of barriers by country

Source: Nerb (1988)

[a]The coefficient ranks responses from 0 (all companies consider a particular reason to be of little or no importance) to 100 (all companies consider a particular reason to be very important).

relevant measures have already been agreed and the single market has relatively little further to offer on the subject.

Secondly, they present merely a summing of the views of firms, not any individual firm's ranking or a quantitative assessment. Clearly views could differ markedly if they are weighted by firm size rather than summed, as the latter will reflect the views of smaller firms. The survey is also limited to the manufacturing industry and does not cover

Coefficient of importance[a]

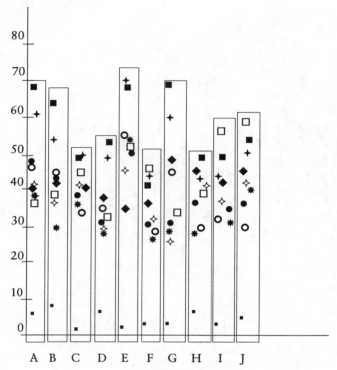

Key:
A Textiles   B Footwear, clothing
C Timber, furniture   D Paper, printing, publishing
E Leather, leather goods   F Plastics
G Mineral oil refining   H Production of metals
I Non-metal mineral products   J Chemicals

Notes:
□ Standards, technical regulations   ✳ Public purchase
■ Administration barriers (customs)   ✚ Frontier delays, costs
○ Different VAT, excise taxes   ◆ Transport regulations
● Capital market restrictions   ✧ Implementation of EC law
▪ Other barriers

Chart 1.2 Importance of barriers by industry

Source: Nerb (1988)
[a]The coefficient ranks responses from 0 (all companies consider a particular reason to be of little or no importance) to 100 (all companies consider a particular reason to be very important).

Coefficient of importance[a]

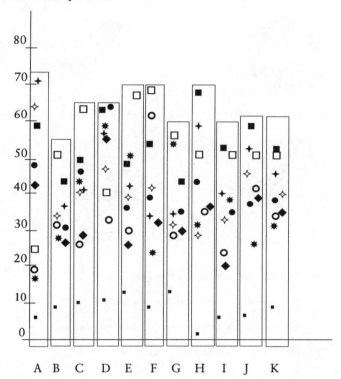

Key:
A Man-made fibres   B Metal articles
C Mechanical engineering   D Office and data equipment
E Electrical engineering   F Motor vehicles
G Other transport equipment   H Rubber products
I Precision engineering, optics J Food, drink and tobacco
K All sectors

Chart 1.2 *continued*

the whole economy. Given that the opening up of the market for services is one of the major steps in the programme this omission is rather
unfortunate. The UK and Germany are shown by the comparison to
hold similar views about the importance of the changes, not just in terms
of the proportions holding those views but the ranking of the various
barriers. They also stand somewhat below the average for the Community as a whole. Standards and administrative barriers are clearly top of
the list. While public purchasing is thought to be of least importance in

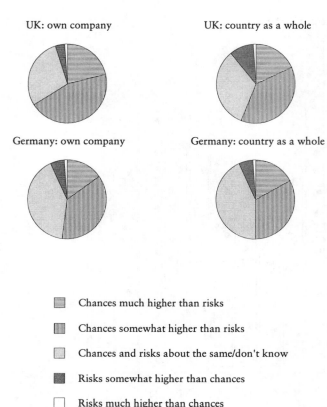

Chart 1.3 Opportunities and risks of the internal market[a]

Source: Nerb (1988)
[a] Per cent share of company responses.

Germany, as it is in the Community-wide ranking to some extent, this may reflect the industry mix (public purchasing is most important in the other transport equipment sector for example). However, to some extent rankings will reflect differences between the perceived position elsewhere in the Community and that at home. Nevertheless, we cannot argue readily on the basis of these results that those who have been most successful in foreign trade rate the barriers of least importance.

Chart 1.3, however, shows that UK firms were considerably more bullish about the prospects for their own enterprise than their German counterparts, although the firms' views about the economy as a whole were much more similar in the two countries. Nevertheless, there is a clear majority in each case that the chances for gain offered by the single market programme exceed the risks. Most importantly few think that risks for them are much higher than the chances for gain being offered. This therefore supports the view that in general the stimulus to change from 1992 is more likely to have come from the positive rather than the negative.

EVIDENCE FROM EMPIRICAL STUDIES

Although the 'Costs of non-Europe' included some illustrative studies of industries, such as clothing, textiles, pharmaceuticals, cars, foodstuffs and construction, there is no comprehensive assessment. The main aggregate results relate to inferences drawn from these examples and are set out in Catinat *et al.* (1988), shown here as table 1.2.

The estimation strategy they used had two main steps, beginning with what they described as a microeconomic assessment of the immediate gains from lower costs. These microeconomic effects were then used as inputs to a macroeconomic model (a combination of two models called HERMES and INTERLINK) which was simulated over a six-year time horizon. Such an exercise is subject to enormous qualification at all stages – calculation of input shocks, specification of the model and assumptions behind the base run (see Davies, Kilpatrick and Mayes, 1988, for an example of what has to be sorted out even for a simple case). However, whatever the criticisms which could be made about this particular exercise by the Commission, this was the only quantitative assessment about the potential impact on the UK and Germany, which was available at that time, on which firms could base their own judgements.

What is immediately apparent from table 1.2 is the degree of similarity between the UK and Germany. After six years both countries are expected to gain about 4 per cent of GDP by elimination of the barriers, fractionally less than the 4½ per cent for the EC as a whole. The impact is progressive but builds up relatively quickly, only giving one or two years in which employment falls (unemployment rises). Price effects are quite substantial, with a reduction in the price level of some 5–8 per cent after six years. Given that UK inflation rates have tended to be higher than those in Germany and closer eventual convergence is likely in a single market, particularly with monetary union, the disinflationary impact needs to be greater for the UK, as is shown in the table.

Table 1.2 *Completion of the internal market: aggregation of main macroeconomic results*

	Year 1	Year 2	Year 3	Year 4	Year 5	Year 6
Percentage differences			EUROPE 12			
GDP	1.13	2.31	3.16	3.64	4.10	4.52
Private consumption price	-1.58	-2.68	-3.71	-4.66	-5.49	-6.16
GDP deflator	-1.68	-2.93	-4.04	-5.02	-5.84	-6.45
Real wage rate	0.77	0.80	1.11	1.48	1.86	2.22
Labour productivity/head	1.57	2.35	2.72	2.81	2.95	3.04
Employment	-0.44	-0.03	0.45	0.83	1.16	1.47
Absolute differences						
Employment ('000)	-533	-40	552	1043	1462	1866
Budget surplus % GDP	0.13	0.72	1.19	1.57	1.89	2.22
External balance % GDP	0.30	0.39	0.63	0.76	0.86	0.95
Percentage differences		FEDERAL REPUBLIC OF GERMANY				
GDP	1.22	1.97	2.57	2.89	3.52	4.20
Private consumption price	-0.74	-1.46	-2.30	-3.52	-4.90	-6.16
GDP deflator	-0.45	-1.09	-1.74	-2.82	-4.10	-5.20
Real wage rate	0.44	0.91	1.44	1.87	2.48	3.14
Labour productivity/head	1.53	1.84	2.07	2.08	2.32	2.51
Employment	-0.31	0.14	0.50	0.80	1.19	1.68
Absolute differences						
Employment ('000)	-78	34	129	208	311	438
Budget surplus % GDP	0.13	0.55	0.77	0.95	1.18	1.52
External balance % GDP	0.49	0.53	0.69	0.73	0.68	0.70
Percentage differences		UNITED KINGDOM				
GDP	0.81	2.44	3.29	3.59	3.79	4.00
Private consumption price	-2.55	-4.33	-5.57	-6.39	-6.96	-7.43
GDP deflator	-2.52	-4.72	-6.26	-7.14	-7.66	-8.06
Real wage rate	0.94	0.65	1.12	1.83	2.40	2.71
Labour productivity/head	1.79	2.95	3.10	2.93	2.89	2.91
Employment	-0.64	-0.08	0.65	1.07	1.26	1.39
Absolute differences						
Employment ('000)	-157	-16	167	285	342	385
Budget surplus % GDP	-0.06	0.71	1.32	1.61	1.69	1.80
External balance % GDP	-0.33	-0.32	-0.02	0.28	0.49	0.61

Source: Catinat *et al.* (1988)

For the EC as a whole a range of outcomes is quoted, approximately 1½ per cent either side of the point estimate of the 4½ per cent increase in GDP quoted above. If firms believed these numbers, or indeed had heard about them, they might have been expecting a modest increase in demand over six years of between ½ per cent and 1 per cent a year in real terms over and above their forecasts before the single market seemed likely. However, these figures are merely estimates. They are a product of the estimation method and the model applied and have been questioned. The technique was to identify a series of impulses to the system from four sources of change identified by the Commission, namely: the removal of customs barriers, the liberalisation of public procurement, financial liberalisation and 'supply' effects. These are detailed in table 1.3.

For any one economy the removal of customs barriers was expected to reduce the cost of imports, by about 1½ per cent in total, to reduce employment requirements for exporters, customs clearance agents and customs officials. This latter employment reduction would also take the form of a cost reduction for exporters, thus increasing their competitiveness. There is therefore an important difference in viewing these impulses from the point of view of the firm and from the point of view of the economy (to say nothing of the point of view of those losing their jobs in the short run). For an importer/exporter costs are reduced. For a domestic producer foreign competitors' costs are reduced, while for those involved with the transactions themselves there may be dramatic changes in their businesses. More trade will mean more work for freight forwarders, for example, even if some of the complexities of individual transactions are decreased. From an economy-wide point of view we have to consider the consequences of the increased unemployment and the impact this may have on the pattern of demand and public sector spending. (Not everything is modelled, of course. Presumably VAT will become more complicated to operate thereby increasing public sector employment in another quarter.)

The public procurement impulse is broken up into three components in the analysis, although the second two have been combined in table 1.3. In the first line of panel II, an assessment is made of the degree to which the market is out of equilibrium, in the sense that, without domestic preference, more goods and services would have been imported from other member states. Those foreign supplies would tend to be of lower price (although some of the reasons for preferring them may reflect non-price factors, like flexibility of supply, payment terms, quality, maintenance arrangements, and so on). Here there is a distinct

Table 1.3 *Main shocks introduced in the Hermes and Interlink models for macroeconomic simulations*

Description	Germany	UK	Eur12	Shock as % of Eur12 GDP
I. Customs barriers				
Decrease in intra-EC import prices (in %)	1.53	1.58	1.70	-
Employment decrease (thousands):				
- exporting firms	Distributed pro rata according to corres- ponding employment		17.53	-
- customs clearing agents	figures by country		40.03	-
Govt employment decrease (in %):				
- customs officials	0.06	0.07	0.11	-
Total shock I (% GDP)	-	-	-	0.26
II. Public markets				
Increase of import penetration rate of public markets (% points)	8.50	3.90	5.60	0.22
Price decrease of equipment goods on public markets (in %):				
- government	0.13	0.12	-	0.28
- public enterprises				
energy	1.50	1.10	-	
transportation & telecom.	7.80	7.20	-	
Total shock II (% GDP)	0.50	0.67	-	0.50
III. Financial markets				
Decrease in interest rate margins (% points):				
- short-term households	2.20	1.90	1.90	-
- long-term households	0.30	0.00	0.20	-
- long-term firms	0.20	0.40	0.50	-
Decrease in price of financial services (in %):				
- private consumption	3.40	2.80	7.90	-
- intermediate consumption of firms	8.00	3.90	10.40	-
Total shock III (% GDP)	0.55	0.79	-	0.65

Source: Catinat *et al.* (1988)

difference between the UK and Germany. German public procurement markets are thought to be relatively closed, while those of the UK were relatively open even at the start of the single market programme.

However, all this assumes that there are no price changes. Increased competition would itself be expected to lower prices of domestically produced goods, simply through eroding profit margins. Secondly the domestic and foreign industries could be expected to respond to the changes in demand and market openness by restructuring their production, generating economies of scale through concentrating production in a smaller number of plants, reducing X-inefficiency through improved practices, increasing productivity and so on which will lead to further price decreases. These are combined in the table but this presents a problem as it confuses impulses and the results they have on behaviour. The impulse in the case of public procurement is the increase in competition because new players are allowed into the market and existing sellers from other member states no longer have an extra hurdle to surmount. The other impulses described are in fact first or second order effects.

For the economy as a whole these shocks amount to ½ per cent of GDP (approximately twice as important as the removal of customs barriers) but their impact is much more concentrated on those involved in public supply contracts. In some cases the impact could be dramatic rather than marginal and it would not be unreasonable to expect some local suppliers to go out of business as a result. Unfortunately, although the authors do simulate each of these shocks separately, this effect is not distinguished. In each case the losses to domestic producers from foreign competition are more than offset by a combination of their own success in entering public procurement markets in other member states and in the real increase in purchasing power for the government or the taxpayer which is achieved.

In the case of financial liberalisation, the third panel in the table, the main forces for change come from increased competition, leading both to a fall in interest rates in many instances and also to a fall in the price of various financial services. The nature of the changes is on the basis of lower prices available elsewhere in the Community. No change in the underlying longer-term real interest rates was assumed other than convergence towards the lower rates. The main changes will, therefore, occur in nominal rates. It is immediately apparent that substantial price decreases are expected. These calculations were, of course, undertaken before German unification pushed up interest rates generally.

Outside the financial services industries themselves this particular change is likely to have a rather more even impact on companies across the Community although the larger and more heavily trading/multinational companies probably have the least to gain as they have cross-border access to many of these services already. It is noticeable in this instance, however, that while the knock-on effect of the impulse in the UK is very limited, there is an effective multiplier of about 1½ in Germany after six years. (There is some variation between the values recorded in tables 1.2 and 1.3 and that in the discussion in the document.)

The remaining category of 'supply' effects has itself been divided into three by Catinat *et al.* They have been rather limited by the industry coverage of the 'Costs of non-Europe' and for those industries for which detailed assessments were made can distinguish direct and indirect reductions in costs from increases in market size and competition. The former take the form of decreased input prices while the latter reflect the adjustment of firms and include productivity gains from restructuring and from economies of scale. As a percentage of GDP this impulse alone is more important than any of the previous three. For the remainder of industry a simple assessment has been made of the unexploited economies of scale and the gains which would be made if the plants in each of the sectors moved up to the minimum efficient scale of operation. Again this implies an impulse of about 1 per cent of GDP for the Community as a whole. Lastly, an attempt is made to estimate the size of what can be described as a 'competition effect' which drives down prices by removing opportunities to earn monopoly profits and drives out other sources of inefficiency from companies previously insulated from some of the pressures of the market (X-inefficiences in the Leibenstein terminology – see Mayes, Harris and Lansbury, 1994, for a discussion of these various sources of inefficiency).

These impulses again amount to around 1 per cent of GDP or a quarter of the total, thus taken together these 'supply effects' form the lion's share of the total impulse. This is rather unfortunate as they are the least well defined and, with the exception of the first category, do not vary across the member states. This latter assumption is clearly false as the degree of inefficiency is likely to be higher in the more protected and the smaller markets. Indeed one of our main hypotheses is that in spite of the degree of openness there may be more persistence of inefficiency in British industry than in its German counterpart.

All these results tend to mask the extent to which individual firms could be affected as a 10 per cent price reduction might be accompanied by a 30 per cent reduction in the number of firms. They also tend to be either completely aggregate, economy-wide conclusions or, if more detailed, restricted largely to manufacturing industries.

Variations in the stimulus across industries

Only one study in the 'Costs of non-Europe', that by Smith and Venables (1988), makes any serious attempt to assess how the structure of industry might change. They look at ten industries (NACE code in parenthesis): cement, lime and plaster (242); pharmaceutical products (257); artificial and synthetic fibres (260); machine tools (322); office machinery (330); electric motors, generators, and so on (342); electrical household appliances (346); motor vehicles (350); carpets, linoleum, and so on (438); and footwear (451). They break the EC into five: France, Germany, Italy, the UK and the rest. Their study is therefore illustrative rather than painting a comprehensive picture but the nature of the illustration itself shows the dangers of generalisation and the need for views of the likely impact to be reviewed at a detailed level. Assumptions such as 'price equalisation' are clearly a step away from the variety which persists for many consumer goods, even within small markets.

The results, shown below in table 1.4 for the two industries we have drawn from this list for our detailed comparisons, namely, pharmaceuticals and machine tools, show widely differing results. The individual numbers are subject to various reservations but the point to notice is that if trade costs are reduced (in this case by 2½ per cent) the impact is much more limited if the ability to segment markets remains (case S) than if prices are equalised after allowing for transport costs (case I) in the case of pharmaceuticals. For machine tools, however, there is little difference. This reflects the high segmentation of the pharmaceutical industry at the start of the single market programme. In extreme cases the number of firms might fall by a third.

Since the publication of the 'Costs of non-Europe' other assessments of the impact of 1992 have tended to be rather lower, quite simply because the authors do not believe that many of the gains suggested will be realised (see Gasoriek *et al.*, 1992; and Mayes, 1990, for example), with figures nearer the 1½–2½ per cent of GDP range being suggested. At this level, the aggregate 1992 effect would tend to be swallowed up by other sources of variation in year-to-year behaviour. Even so the effect on the composition of industry could be considerable and we have no particular means of assessing what firms expected might happen on the basis of their own analysis and this limited data. However, al-

Table 1.4 *Impact of reduction in trade barriers*

Country	Pharmaceuticals					Machine tools				
	% change in output		No. of firms	No. of changes		% change in output		No. of firms	No. of changes	
	S	I		S	I	S	I		S	I
France	0.6	1.6	135	0	-10	-18.4	-16.2	79	-15	-15
Germany	0.4	1.8	71	0	-10	18.6	18.4	204	38	39
Italy	-0.4	3.5	88	-1	-10	-4.5	-5.6	115	-6	-10
UK	0.3	-0.4	46	0	-10	-6.5	-5.4	186	-13	-12
Rest EC	0.4	5.8	50	0	-5	-29.5	-28.2	62	-19	-20
EC	0.3	2.1	298	-1	-47	2.5	2.9	556	-15	-18

Source: Smith and Venables (1988)
Note: S = segmented markets I = integrated markets.

though there are many negative features, particularly at the sectoral and regional level, it has not been suggested that the overall effect would be negative, either for the EC as a whole or for the UK and Germany in particular.

The Commission (Buigues and Ilzkowitz, 1988 and *European Economy*, 1990) itself continued the analysis by identifying forty sectors where the changes were, *prima facie*, expected to be largest (table 1.5). (These changes may be positive or negative.) The individual authors in Commission (1991b) then explore how well this pattern is repeated within each member state. It is worth reflecting on this assessment as the methods used would have been familiar to analysts within firms. They looked at three main features: an assessment of the height of non-tariff barriers to be removed, the degree of price dispersion and the degree to which the industry was already exposed to foreign trade.

Other things being equal, the higher existing barriers, the greater price dispersion and the lower exposure to trade then the greater the chance that the single market will have a considerable impact. Burridge and Mayes (1993b) classified the UK's industries at the input-output level of disaggregation (approximately one hundred industries) according to this three dimensional scheme (Chart 1.4) and used this as the input to a simulation of the impact with the Oxford Economic Forecasting (OEF) disaggregated industry model.[3]

The industries whose output is most affected are shown in table 1.6. The absolute magnitudes reflect the authors' assumptions but the rela-

Table 1.5 *The industrial sectors most affected by the internal market*

NACE Codes	Sector	Dispersion prices net of taxes	Share in value added	Share of intra-EC imports in demand	Share of extra-EC imports in demand	Extra-EC export/ import ratio
	High technology public procurement sectors					
	Group 1 (a)					
330	Office machines	7.44	2.45	30.91	36.30	57
344	Telecommunications equipment	8.89	4.29	22.44	28.76	117
372	Medico-surgical equipment	21.12	0.38	31.48	31.38	139
	Traditional public procurement or regulated markets					
	Group 2 (a)					
257	Pharmaceutical products	32.65	2.48	10.61	6.40	248
315	Boilermaking, reservoirs, sheet-metal containers	22.12	1.00	2.54	1.10	1108
362	Railway equipment	21.74	0.35	4.97	3.48	680
425	Wine and wine-based products	15.88	0.34			
427	Brewing and malting	20.94	1.21	3.27	0.20	2047
428	Soft drinks & spa waters	24.87	0.53	4.56	0.33	721
	Group 3 (a)					
341	Electrical wires & cables	8.89	1.40	11.21	8.79	163
342	Electrical equipment		3.42	17.91	13.04	182
361	Shipbuilding		0.78	7.75	21.72	178
417	Spaghetti, macaroni etc	8.86	0.14	6.72	0.38	1038
421	Cocoa, chocolate & sugar confectionery	10.12	0.72	12.98	2.83	214
	Sectors with moderate non-tariff barriers					
	Group 4 (b)					
	Consumer goods					
345	Electronic equipment	7.65	1.84	19.71	28.80	63
346	Domestic-type electrical appliances	7.67	0.88	22.68	11.37	130
351	Motor vehicles	10.61	7.21	22.82	10.44	201
438	Carpets, lino, floor covering	15.76	0.23	44.85	23.65	122
451	Footwear	14.28	0.81	44.65	36.84	106
453	Clothing	10.17	1.98	13.43	18.37	57
455	Household textiles	13.42	0.21	26.05	31.68	59
491	Jewellery, goldsmiths' & silversmiths' wares	22.06	0.27			157
493	Photographic & cinematographic labs	10.12	0.16	15.99	10.23	128
495	Games, toys & sports goods	12.07	0.26	23.95	43.41	48
	Capital goods					
321	Agricultural machinery & tractors	8.30	0.66	19.75	5.40	442
322	Machine tools for metals	10.73	1.22	17.91	16.25	191
323	Textile and sewing machines	10.97	0.53	34.96	23.26	369
324	Machines for foodstuffs ind.	12.26	1.28	31.45	14.63	400
325	Plant for mines, etc.	18.06	1.68	29.40	14.81	342
326	Transmission equipment		0.73	23.79	13.48	178
327	Other specific equipment	12.92	0.76	38.66	20.92	330
347	Lamps and lighting equipment	15.70	0.36	31.84	12.70	252
364	Aerospace equipt, manufacturing & repairing	17.10	2.20	18.05	24.25	121
	Intermediary goods					
247	Glassware	21.46	1.11	21.29	7.39	213
248	Ceramics	21.46	0.90	20.93	8.62	255
251	Basic industrial chemicals		4.81			
256	Other chemical products for industry		1.81	30.39	11.41	249
431	Wool industry	23.02	0.62			
432	Cotton industry	23.02	0.94			
481	Rubber industry	17.85	1.48	20.45	8.43	175

Sources: *Panorama of EC Industry*, and estimates from Commission services

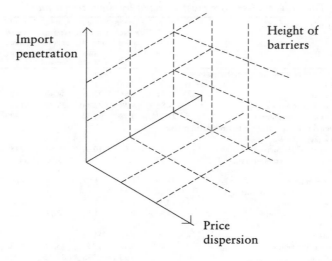

Chart 1.4 Classification of industrial sectors by potential for impact

tive size of the impact provides a useful indicator of not just the initial shock but also the consequences when those shocks feed right through the economy. The correspondence with table 1.5 is relatively limited because the level of disaggregation is different and the simulation included all industries, not just those in manufacturing. The major point to note from the simulation is that industries involved in the process of change are the main gainers. Thus it does not matter if firms over-estimate the effects, the construction and investment goods industries still benefit, as do the service industries involved in the transactions, finding and investigating acquisitions or new sites for direct investment.

Variations in the stimulus across countries

The rather simplified analysis of potential sources of variation in the stimuli across industries can be replicated in the second dimension of variation across the member states and indeed for finer divisions of location across the Community. Clearly those countries which had either already abandoned the barriers which were to be removed as part of the single market programme or had domestic rules in place which were similar to those likely to be implemented by the Community were likely to be least influenced in terms of increased competition and the need to change in their own markets. On the other side of the coin they

Table 1.6 *Implications of the single European market for UK industry[a]*

Industrial category	Ave % change in output	Industrial category	Ave % change in output
Coal extraction	1.3	Metal packing	1.3
Electric & nuclear fuels	1.0	Machine tools	1.6
Aluminium	2.0	Mining & construction equpt	1.0
Other non-ferrous metals	2.0	Other mechanical engineering	2.0
Stone & clay	4.0	Insulated wires & cables	2.3
Structural clay products	5.5	Industrial electrical appliances	1.5
Cement etc	4.0	Other electrical/electrical equpt	10.0
Concrete etc	4.0	Shipbuilding & repair	2.5
Glass	1.4	Soft drinks	2.3
Refractory & ceramic goods	6.0	Clothing & fur	2.0
Inorganic chemicals	3.4	Household & other textiles	1.6
Organic chemicals	3.0	Timber processing & wood	1.5
Fertilisers	1.5	Pulp, paper & board	1.2
Synthetics, rubber, plastics	2.7	Paper & board products	1.7
Paints & dyes	1.8	Rubber products	1.7
Specialised chemicals	1.5	Processing of plastics	1.1
Pharmaceutical products	3.0	Construction	6.2
Metal casting	2.2	Business services	1.5
Metal doors	5.0		

Source: Burridge and Mayes (1993b)
[a]Projected changes smaller than 1 per cent are not shown.

could expect that their competitors might have higher costs of change and that they as exporters would have more to gain in foreign markets, which had previously been more closed to them, either as a result of deliberate discrimination, say through public purchasing, or indirectly because the rules with which they had to comply were different.

It is difficult to assess the difference in the height of these barriers by country now, let alone from the standpoint of the first few years after the publication of the White Paper, as the nature of the changes to be implemented through legislation and the form of the compromise in finding new harmonised standards and other measures was yet to be worked out. The simplest method would be to use the same material explored in table 1.5 and chart 1.4 and to aggregate it by country, exploring, for example, the number of instances where a country had prices which were near or a long way above the lowest values observed elsewhere in the EC. Coupled with the information about the extent of current import penetration (and export performance) it would be possible to form a view about the likely relative extent of change in one country compared with another.

The aggregate figures suggest that the scope for change in the UK and Germany was relatively similar in terms of diversion from the lowest prices in the Community for manufactured goods. At a more dis-aggregated level (see Appendix table 1A.1) it appears that the UK prices tend to be lower than those in Germany. However, it was relatively rare for either country to have the highest or lowest prices in the EC. This scope for resultant change is to be distinguished from the nature of the regulations to be changed or the degree of compliance that has been observed with them. It is clear that the general level of regulation in German industry tends to be greater than that in its UK counterpart. In some cases German regulation of an area is more complex or harsher in its requirements. For example, shop hours are much more highly regulated in Germany and the 'environmental' requirements of various forms of packaging are harsher. In other cases the difference is that some areas of activity are not subject to regulation in the same way. There are no similar controls over the terms of insurance policies in the UK for example. Furthermore, self-regulation by industries is more common in the UK, particularly in service industries and in the professions. Membership of trade associations may be compulsory in Germany with consequent restrictions on the activities of their members.

Regional variation and the problems of location

The extent of the stimulus also reflects the extent of the pre-existing responses to market forces. This in part is a reflection of the location of industry as much as a reflection on the regulations which apply to it. Peripherality is the simplest concern. Some local markets have been protected effectively by relatively low barriers as these barriers have a cumulative effect – the relatively small size of the market is exacerbated by greater transport costs. Hence all the other non-tariff barriers may make entry unlikely, whereas market entry into the largest markets in Germany and also into the south-east of England might very well have occurred already despite non-tariff barriers of a similar height.

Our IFO colleagues (Nam and Reuter, 1991) were responsible for a separate study undertaken for the European Parliament, which showed very clearly that the least-favoured regions of the EC, particularly those which were most peripheral, were likely to lose rather than gain from the single market (this discussion is amplified in NIESR, 1991).

The main line of argument runs that these smaller, more peripheral markets, primarily concentrated in Ireland, Portugal, Greece, Spain and the south of Italy, do not have sufficient size to sustain many of their existing industrial activities when markets are opened up and do not provide a sufficient attraction to newer investment through lower cost labour, infrastructure, the network of business services and the availability of workforce skills. This implies that the process of integration is likely to be centripetal rather than centrifugal on the regions of the Community. It is immediately obvious that in this sense the UK is likely to be more adversely affected than Germany, for with the exception of the former DDR, little of Germany can be regarded as peripheral (and will be even less so as the European Economic Area develops and Austria and the Scandinavian countries become full members of the Community).

These highly peripheral regions which in general have a GDP per head less than 80 per cent of the EC average (Objective 1 regions in the parlance of the Community's structural funds, see NIESR, 1991) are not the only parts of the EC which might be differentially affected. The Nam and Reuter study also considers the declining industrial (Objective 2) regions. Here the prospects are much better as on average it is expected that these regions will benefit. The main reason is that these regions are in general nearer the core regions of Europe, have substantial populations of their own, skilled workforces, a good infrastructure and an experienced network of business services. It is somewhat worrying that two of the only three European regions that are exceptions to this conclusion lie in the UK.

We cannot, however, take these conclusions without modification, because a large portion of the point of the EC's structural policies is to try to offset these difficulties. As a result the structural funds were doubled in 1988 and the agreement on the new budgetary perspective for 1993 onwards at the Edinburgh Summit means that there will be a redoubling before the end of the century. Firms have to take account of both effects and form a view of their joint outcome. This will to some extent depend on the effectiveness of the policies for recovery at the local level. Previous evidence suggests that the impact of these forms of structural policy is very varied (NIESR, 1991). Hence discussions of the net stimulus will also have to be undertaken at a fairly disaggregated level.

Concluding remark

Taken together, therefore, firms faced a rather limited set of information about the likely changes which would be imposed and the way in which they might have a variable impact across industries and across the member states. Our analysis hence has to build on rather general hypotheses which will need considerable modification when considered at the detailed level. We felt therefore that our analysis should have two main ingredients, first of all a study of the differences in the characteristics of German and UK industry and secondly an illustrative analysis of some industries in detail. But before discussing these this chapter reviews the likely routes of response to the stimulus we have just discussed and then concludes with a brief exposition of our main line of argument in the rest of the book.

The possible routes of response

The previous section has outlined the form of stimulus that has been applied to UK and German industry by the 1992 programme. As a result of previous work for the Commission (Mayes et al., 1991) we expected the response to be concentrated in three main types of mechanism: reorganisation (particularly through relocation), external growth (takeovers, mergers and so on) and internal growth.

The 'Sharpbenders' book was largely concerned with internal reorganisation and growth, not because external growth was considered unimportant but because the companies had been deliberately chosen as those which remained independent throughout the process. Nevertheless it was noticeable that many of the companies divested themselves of more peripheral businesses in order to generate the funds to reorganise their core activities.[4] Secondly it is clear that the sharpbenders indulged in far less merger and acquisition activity than the less successful control companies also considered in the study. However, as Grinyer and McKiernan (1993) have observed, the sharpbenders themselves seem to have since been subject far more to takeover than the average in the UK economy – not so much because they were underperforming but because of their greater potential, not properly reflected in their stock market price.

The case of the single market is different. The existing shape of European industry has not been suboptimal because of lack of previous action by managers to improve it but rather because of the external constraints. As these are removed the range of possible changes opens up and managements are able to refocus their firms in a way they would have liked to follow in more open circumstances. However, we anticipated that the stimulus would not only be more than the mere release of frustrated action, but also an injection of new ideas by allowing actions which were previously not available.

Relocation was thought likely simply because the various member state markets often required production facilities either to meet local technical requirements or to increase the chance of getting public purchasing contracts. It is common to operate below the maximum economies of scale technically achievable because there are other costs of distance from customers. The simplest is the speed of delivery, the need for local repair, installation and maintenance. Furthermore there has been a great deal of emphasis in recent years following the work of Peters and Waterman (1982) for example, on the importance of maintaining close contact with customers, which is aided by having a local plant. Hence the sorts of calculation as to the full extent of the changes possible, discussed by Pratten (1988) and others in the background papers to the 'Costs of non-Europe', are likely to be overestimates of the extent of the reorganisation. In any case if it is expected that the single market will result in an increase in the rate of growth and hence in the size of the market to be served, it may be worthwhile to maintain what is currently a somewhat below-scale operation.

However, it is not just a matter of the reorganisation of plants into larger single sites which are better suited for serving the EC as a whole but the reorganisation of each of the stages in the production process (table 1.7). Low skill production processes may be best located in lower labour cost parts of the Community, whereas R&D laboratories might best be located in areas of high skill where there are many other similar laboratories. Skilled labour itself is likely to move more readily to these locations in the single market. This form of clustering, or exploitation of external economies to use the economists' more normal terminology, has become an increasing feature of economic development. The Silicon Valley, Route 128 and Silicon Glen examples are among the best known but this also applies to more traditional industries (as we show later in the case of machine tools). The clusters can be in industrial terms not just geographic ones as Porter (1990) has pointed out; mutual gains can be reaped from related activities. Software services can assist the development of hardware, packaging and the development of precooked single portion meals, to give just two examples.

Table 1.7 *Impact of 1992 on the stages of production*

	Component of value added:	Possible nature of the impact:
1	Research & development	Growth in the number of joint projects More homogeneous environment at European level
2	Supplies	Wider range of suppliers Lower prices
3	Logistics	Lower transport costs Relocation of storage facilities (better adapted to an integrated market)
4	Production	Increased production at each plant Reduction in the number of production plants
5	Marketing & distribution	Centralisation of product management at European level Community-wide marketing campaigns
6	Consumers	Availability of a wider range of products Increased demand (growth effect) and lower product prices

Reorganisation of location takes place not just within companies but between them as well. Access to different resources and markets may very well come much more readily from an alliance or from acquisition than from setting up a new 'greenfield' activity or expanding existing resources. If we accept the basic premise behind the single market, we must expect that there is considerable inefficiency within European industry and hence surplus capacity for current production if only it could be reorganised. This would imply a preference for links and reorganisation rather than the creation of new capacity.

A study of the reaction to the single market by manufacturing industry across the whole Community (Mayes *et al.*, 1991) showed that mergers and acquisitions were the most common single response (chart 1.5) while other forms of cooperation in R&D or in sales and services organisations covered about half of the industries studied.

This is one area where we expect to see a striking difference between behaviour in the UK and in Germany. In the UK shares in most sizeable public companies are actively traded, so voluntary alliances can be replaced by unsuccessfully contested takeovers if agreement cannot be reached. In Germany on the other hand the hostile takeover is virtually

	Airlines	Aero-space	Machine tools	Railway equip-ment	Micro-electronics semi-conductors	Micro-electronics consumer goods	Metal goods	Cars	Trucks	Basic chemicals	Pharma-ceuticals	Fibres	Textile products
1992 measures and opportunities													
Scale/scope economies from SEM		X			X	X		X		X			
R&D cooperation (via EC progs)		X			X								
Open public procurement		X		X	X						X		
Removal of subsidies				X			X	X					
Environmental standards	X							X		X			
Deregulation, competition policy	X							X	X				
Technical harmonisation		X	X	X				X	X				
Common external tariff and protection from NICs					X	X	X	X				X	X
Responses													
Merger/joint ventures (via rationalisation)		X	X		X	X	X	X	X	X	X		X
R&D cooperation		X	X	X	X			X					
Sales/service cooperation	X							X	X				
Scale/scope economies via joint ventures		X		X	X			X	X				
Greater product differentiation		X	X			X		X	X		X		X
Restriction to speciality niche markets	X		X			X	X	X	X		X		X
Cost-cutting to compete on price			X			X	X					X	X
Diversification to service industries				X		X	X					X	X

Chart 1.5 The 1992 programme and responses to it by industry
Source: Mayes *et al.* (1991)

unknown (Hart, 1992a). Shares are not so readily available and major shareholders usually act to try to restructure a company or build alliances without the need to change ownership.

Merger and acquisition activity has indeed increased during the 1980s (*European Economy*, 1990) (chart 1.6) but this has been part of a worldwide boom, only some of which can be ascribable to the single market. Unfortunately, chart 1.6 does not distinguish between agreed and hostile takeovers; although takeover activity remains higher in the UK than in Germany, there has been a strong rise in both countries in recent years.

One of the main reasons for expecting a surge in acquisitions is the extension of the European market to services from its previous concentration on manufacturing (and agriculture). 'Retail' services in particular require extensive local networks. As we show in the studies of retailing and insurance, the routes open for market entry are relatively limited. Licensing or franchising may provide openings but setting up a new distribution network is prohibitively expensive or a long-term operation (Mayes *et al.*, 1991, explains this for the cases of motor cars and trucks). Buying an existing network or combining networks provides a substantial entry at a stroke.

Since the sharpbending companies were facing somewhat different stimuli their experience will not necessarily be a good guide. Six features stood out in the main measures they took (see table 1.8): reduction in production costs, changes in management, exploitation of windfall opportunities, stronger financial controls, new product market focus, and improved marketing.

These relate entirely to internal measures. We would expect, in the case of the single market, that reducing production costs and altering the product market focus will form the key features of the changes. Stronger financial controls and improved marketing are likely to be the sorts of features that distinguish the most successful responses to the single market from the others. As is clear from table 1.8, the control companies also took quite a large range of steps; however they were less well coordinated and focussed.

Looking at the sharpbenders' results in detail shows further discrepancies from what we might expect on this occasion. (Changing the chief executive, which was the most important feature, scarcely seems likely to be so crucial.) However, where the changes required involve internationalising or 'Europeanising' the 'culture' of the company the sharpbenders' experience has prime relevance. Attempting to establish new alliances, make mergers work and enter new markets are

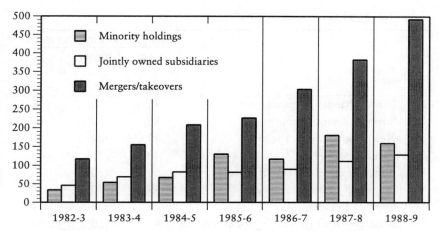

Chart 1.6 Number of takeovers, acquisitions of minority holdings and new jointly owned subsidiaries: situation for the 1,000 largest European industrial firms

Source: Commission services

all high-risk activities involving the ability to come to terms with differences between existing cultures. One of the reasons why so many joint ventures fail is simply because the partners are too different and have divergent objectives when it comes to making the project work. Eden (1992) has shown the importance of a reasonable correspondence of what is dubbed the 'cognitive maps' of the two entities – the objectives they have, the means they want to use to achieve them and their general philosophy of doing business. To this must be added simple physical problems of linkage, from incompatible computer systems to transport networks.

In the sharpbenders study we noted that the process of change was not one of simple comparative statics, of moving from one orientation of the market to another with a similar form of activity in the two states, but a transformation of the company towards a much more dynamic and action-oriented form of behaviour. The line of argument is simply that the increased performance required behaviour which continues to improve on that of competitors, otherwise market share will again level off. In the case of the single market the position is somewhat different as competitive conditions will be worsened and firms will tend to lose if they do not take action. In this case even protecting existing positions will involve an increased level of action, hence requiring a change in

Table 1.8 *Steps taken by sharpbenders (controls)*

| | | % of firms citing this factor | | |
		Sharp-benders (A)	Controls (B)	% difference (A - B)
I	Major changes in management(a)	85	(30)	55
II	Stronger financial controls	80	(70)	10
III	New product market focus	80	(80)	0
IV	Diversified	30	(70)	-40
V	Entered export market vigorously	50	(30)	20
VI	Improved quality and service	55	(50)	5
VII	Improved marketing	75	(30)	45
VIII	Intensive effort to reduce production costs (a)	80	(30)	50
IX	Acquisitions	50	(80)	-30
X	Reduced debt	50	(80)	-30
XI	Windfalls	85	(70)	15
XII	Other	25	(20)	5

Source: Grinyer *et al.* (1988)
(a) 50 per cent of the Sharpbenders took at least four steps in this category.

continuing behaviour, not a one-off step change. These arguments are reflected in the work of Baldwin (1989, 1990), who argues that the Commission has tended to underestimate the impact of the single market because it has not allowed for this dynamic impact which increases the rate of investment (in both human and physical capital) and innovation.

Taking these facets together, the impact for any one industry will depend upon the specific single market measures that are to be implemented and on the degree to which they are to be enforced. Within that market the response in individual member states will depend upon the structure of their existing legislation and behaviour compared with that intended within the single market. To some extent then this is very much a question of industrial structure. However, once one considers the role of firms within the industry, specific issues become important. Not only does reaction depend upon the sector of the industry in which the firm is located and its market focus but also on its previous performance. Those which have recently had difficulties and are heavily laden with debts will be far less likely to be able to respond than those which are cash rich. (Such features may apply to a member state's whole industry if it has been going through a largely domestically induced downturn.)

Own performance is not the only important factor as firms will also respond to the actions of competitors. Indeed their own actions in most imperfectly competitive industries will be taken in the light of the actions or responses they expect from their competitors. Even though it may be obvious to the outside spectator that there is over-investment in an industry leading to excess capacity, each individual company is likely to feel that it has to invest to maintain or increase its share of the new more open market. While some will inevitably lose, it is difficult to identify them beforehand and most firms tend to be over optimistic when estimating whether it is they or their competitors who will lose out.

However, the single market is but one of the forces affecting the decision-making of companies and in some cases it will be by no means the most important. It is thus necessary to fit the single market measures into their context of other forces for change in the industry, such as those emanating from changes in technology or changes in demand. Mayes *et al.* 1991 (reproduced here as table 1.9) sought to suggest how the single market measures fitted in with the general trend of current industrial activity. Some of those trends have now changed. The rate of Japanese investment has slowed but the issues remain the same. It is still the case that in many respects non-EC firms find themselves at a relative advantage because either as recent entrants or as new entrants they are investing to serve the EC market as a whole and merely have to develop their strategy beyond the previous emphasis on exporting to one of production inside the EC. Unlike domestic firms or long-standing foreign entrants they do not have an existing network of plants based on the previous divisions in the European market. Incumbents thus face two costs, the first is the closure of existing misaligned facilities and the second the investment in the new plant. New entrants from outside the EC have only the second cost. Exit costs may be high not just in terms of redundancies but because in such a general realignment there may be no good market for the second-hand equipment.

Surprisingly, the degree to which market trends and the single market fail to pull in the same general direction is relatively limited. This reinforces our hypothesis that the single market programme may act as a stimulus to change, simply because it is the last push needed to make firms commit themselves to the sorts of changes they had already envisaged.

Table 1.9 *Complementarities and inconsistencies between the internal market measures and market trends*

Trend	Complementary measure
New technology leads to reduction in minimum efficient scale through flexible manufacturing systems	Unified market enables greater access to new market areas but with substantial differences in buyers' requirements likely to remain
Japanese surplus looking for reinvestment abroad	Incentive for Japanese to invest in Europe to get inside external tariffs and reap full advantage of single market
R&D scale economies and advantages of collusion at the pre-competitive stage of R&D	Large cooperative R&D programmes in pre-competitive areas (IT, telecoms innovation dissemination)
Scale economies, scope economies and competition incentives made available through cross-border ownership market	Capital-market deregulation and new legal framework making cross-border acquisitions easier
Growth of oligopolies within EC, prevent competition but unchallenged by domestic competition policy	European-level merger control to prevent anti-competitive concentration
Pressure for standardisation of technical/ safety/environmental regulations, to reduce cost of modification before a product becomes exportable	Harmonisation, and removal of non-tariff barriers
Concern about the environment	Stronger environmental standards and regulations
Contracting-out and privatisation as means to control public spending and increase revenue	Opening-up of public procurement, restriction of state subsidies to firms
Competition in concentrated markets requiring ease of entry/exit and reduced sunk costs (for contestability)	Single market providing greater scope for potential entry and redeployment of fixed-cost resources to other uses
Fall in transport costs relative to pro- duction costs	Single market allowing producers to locate in lowest cost regions: infrastructure projects which further reduce costs

Trend	Related measures
Shift to knowledge-intensive production requiring higher skilled more autonomous workforce	Social Charter and structural funds providing for vocational training, participation
Increased external effects of national macro policies and interdependence of main macro instruments	Move towards common monetary and fiscal policies, economic union
Increased trade requiring exchange-rate stability to reduce costs of hedging/ exchange risk	Completion and hardening of ERM

Trend	Inconsistent measure
Use of product differentiation to reduce competition and achieve market power	End to national standards as a basis for product differentiation
Restructuring/reallocation/building-up of new sectors requiring state intervention	Restriction of state aid to industry
Innovation for competitiveness with non-European firms requires collusion to protect monopoly rents, or subsidy to compensate for their loss	Competition promoted, collusion reduced, state subsidy restricted
Opening up of Eastern Europe as source of low production costs and direct investment opportunities	Attempts to attract inward investment and achieve higher investment within the EC
(In some member states) Return to free labour market with weak trade unions, flexible wages	Social Charter conditions for union power, minimum wages, etc.

Source: Mayes *et al.* (1991)

The structure of the analysis

In the pages which follow we begin our analysis by looking at the structure and performance of the UK and German economies as a whole. We then examine the characteristics of the two economies which might lead them to behave differently in the face of the single market programme. Afterwards, the analysis proceeds to four studies of individual industries: retailing, pharmaceuticals, machine tools and insurance, before drawing conclusions. These four case study industries cannot hope to give a comprehensive picture but they have been picked because *prima facie* they are industries in which large-scale changes could have been expected from the single market programme. They are also industries which are important in the UK and Germany but have different structures. This provides a helpful basis on which to make the comparison.

Table 1A.1 *The Community market: prices of consumer and investment goods, Germany and the UK*

	Prices with indirect taxes (1985)		
Products	UK	Germany	EC Lowest
Textiles, clothing, footwear			
Outer garments, sportswear, industrial	83.0	104.6	83.0
Children's underclothing & knitwear	89.2	100.1	78.3
Ladies' underclothing & knitwear	73.6	105.2	61.2
Materials & drapery	85.5	115.3	75.3
Men's & children's footwear	86.1	105.3	83.2
Women's footwear	73.6	92.1	73.6
Household textiles	99.4	105.9	85.6
Durable goods			
Furniture & furnishing accessories	103.2	88.6	87.5
Refrigerators, freezers, washing machines	91.9	99.5	79.3
Cookers, heating appliances	98.4	92.8	86.0
Cleaning equipment, sewing machines	87.1	97.3	84.5
Glassware & tableware	134.3	110.8	64.7
Other household utensils	114.3	101.7	78.5
Motor vehicles, cycles, motorcycles	109.6	87.4	74.8
Radio sets, record players	81.4	88.5	81.4
Photographic equip't, musical instruments	93.7	83.2	83.2
Records, tapes, cassettes, flowers	95.3	117.3	78.5
Other manufactures			
Floor coverings	93.0	83.6	78.6
Non-durable household articles	93.7	104.8	85.6
Medical & pharmaceutical products	90.6	156.6	65.9
Therapeutic appliances & equipment	47.0	119.0	47.0
Tyres, inner tubes, parts & accessories	105.5	97.0	81.5
Petrol & lubricants	90.3	99.0	82.4
Books	90.0	101.7	54.6
Newspapers, periodicals, other printed	73.8	110.4	73.8
Toiletries, perfumes, cosmetics	93.5	91.2	86.4
Jewellery, watches, alarm clocks	93.6	132.7	51.5
Cigarette lighters & travel goods	107.7	99.9	85.5
Writing, drawing equipment & supplies	112.8	96.1	78.2

Table 1A.1 continued

Products	Prices without indirect taxes (1985)		
	UK	Germany	EC Lowest
Textiles, clothing, footwear			
Outer garments, sportswear, industrial	82.8	105.9	82.8
Children's underclothing & knitwear	100.2	98.6	85.0
Ladies' underclothing & knitwear	79.8	106.5	65.4
Materials & drapery	83.6	115.9	78.5
Men's & children's footwear	87.4	106.3	80.6
Women's footwear	74.2	93.2	74.2
Household textiles	102.8	108.4	82.6
Durable goods			
Furniture & furnishing accessories	105.6	92.3	86.5
Refrigerators, freezers, washing machines	98.0	105.3	81.2
Cookers, heating appliances	103.0	100.2	82.2
Cleaning equipment, sewing machines	91.2	102.6	86.1
Glassware & tableware	141.3	114.5	63.5
Other household utensils	117.2	104.2	82.4
Motor vehicles, cycles, motorcycles	122.0	105.8	78.9
Radio sets, record players	90.0	96.6	73.8
Photographic eqpt, musical instruments	96.1	87.4	87.4
Records, tapes, cassettes, flowers	100.1	124.3	77.7
Other manufactures			
Floor coverings	98.3	84.8	75.9
Non-durable household articles	98.1	108.7	85.5
Medical & pharmaceutical products	91.9	155.7	66.1
Therapeutic appliances & equipment	51.3	116.2	51.3
Tyres, inner tubes, parts & accessories	108.9	99.6	81.2
Petrol & lubricants	95.7	103.4	95.7
Books	95.9	104.4	53.3
Newspapers, periodicals, other printed	76.1	107.8	76.1
Toiletries, perfumes, cosmetics	95.5	94.4	90.8
Jewellery, watches, alarm clocks	94.4	135.7	56.7
Cigarette lighters & travel goods	110.0	104.7	86.3
Writing, drawing equipment & supplies	113.9	99.1	79.1

Table 1A.1 continued

Products	Prices without indirect taxes (1985)			
	UK	Germany	EC	Lowest
Equipment goods				
Structural metal products	101.7	94.7		89.9
Products of boilermaking	71.6	93.8		71.6
Tools & metal goods	92.2	101.0		87.6
Agricultural machinery & tractors	110.1	100.1		85.8
Machine tools & metal-working	118.7	98.0		87.4
Textile machinery & sewing machines	91.6	103.2		86.7
Machinery for food, chemicals, rubber	81.5	96.3		81.5
Mining equipment	120.0	89.7		86.4
Machinery for working wood, paper	108.2	111.6		82.4
Other machinery & mechanical equipment	105.5	112.0		84.3
Office & data-processing machines	107.9	86.9		86.9
Wires & cables, electrical equipment	91.3	93.9		91.3
Telecommunications equipment, meters	91.3	93.9		91.3
Electronic equipment, radio, televisions	96.4	101.4		91.8
Optical instruments, photographic equipment	87.9	123.5		81.3
Motor vehicles & engines	106.1	88.6		79.7
Ships, warships	105.9	85.9		85.9
Locomotives, vans and wagons	125.6	96.4		83.0
Cycles, motorcycles, invalid carriages	107.1	84.7		84.7
Aircraft, helicopters, aeronautic equipment	91.6	77.7		77.7

Source: Emerson, M. *et al.* (1988), *The Economics of 1992*, Oxford, Oxford University Press.
Note: EUR 9 = 100.

2   The UK and German economies

It really depends on your point of view whether you regard the UK and German economies as being very similar or being very different. They are both north-western European advanced industrial economies with similar populations (57 vs 62 million before unification), sharing similar roots. However, they also have considerably different economic structures – manufacturing industry, for example, represents 30 per cent of GDP in Germany compared with 22 per cent in the UK[1] – and the legal and regulatory systems have different bases. Germany is a country characterised by low price inflation, high levels of training and, until recently, a consistently higher rate of economic growth (table 2.1). At the outset of the single market programme, Germany was characterised by a considerable surplus in its balance of trade while the UK faced a substantial deficit (in 1987 the UK's trade balance was –$1.985 billion whilst Germany's was $5.459 billion). After the recent devaluation of the pound, GDP per head in the UK at $13,723 compares rather unfavourably with Germany at $24,404 but in purchasing power parity terms the two countries have been much closer – $14,985 for Germany compared with $14,345 for the UK in 1989.

We can therefore expect that while Germany is similar enough to the UK to make comparison of the two countries' responses to the single market meaningful, it is different enough to lead us to expect considerable variety in those responses.

In this chapter we focus on some of the major differences in structure and performance which characterise the two economies to help provide the basis for our comparison of responses to '1992'. However, before going any further we need to acknowledge that while the UK and Germany may have gone into the single market on a similar basis, by 1989 the whole position had changed. The 1992 programme was designed without any

Table 2.1   *Average rates of growth of GDP and prices in the UK and Germany, 1971–90 (per cent, per annum)*

	1971-80		1981-90	
	UK	Germany	UK	Germany
GDP (a)	2.1	2.7	2.9	2.3
Consumer prices (b)	14.2	5.1	6.0	2.3

Source: OECD Historical Statistics
(a) 1985 prices.   (b) UK RPI, Germany CPI.

thought to the changes which have happened in eastern and central Europe. Suggestions made in 1986 that Germany would be unified within five years would have been ridiculed. Unification has, however, come to dominate the German economy and while the single market might have been top of the agenda at the outset it has clearly been displaced and will continue to be so. However, the impact of unification is not restricted to Germany and the progress of European integration as a whole has been substantially affected.

Our concern in this chapter is to paint the picture of why UK industry might be expected to respond differently from that in Germany to the impulses from the 1992 programme. Our approach is to consider the differences in structure and resources available and then the factors which affect how they are used. This is in a sense analagous to growth account-ing in advance of the process of change. One of the best known ap-proaches to explaining differences in economic performance is the Struc-ture, Performance, Conduct model (Schmalensee, 1989), and we there-fore follow this framework.

Comparing structure and performance

We begin with the structure of industry and trade in the two countries. Comparisons of performance in different industries (Prais, 1981; Prais *et al.*, 1989; NEDO, 1985) normally consider the contribution which is made by a series of factors relating to the conditions of supply: the ex-tent and quality of capital available including the technologies avail-able; the quality and availability of purchased inputs; the nature and quality of the labour force; the structure of output; the organisation of industry; and the organisation of production and management within the individual firm. We go somewhat further than this by expanding the consideration of the supply-side factors beyond just physical capital to

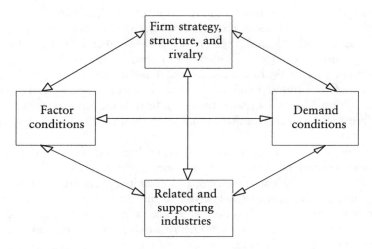

Chart 2.1   The determinants of national advantage
Source: Porter (1990)

the availability of financial capital, the regulatory framework in which firms operate and the characteristics of demand that the two sets of industries face. Location forms an important element of the nature of both demand and supply as firms have to have access to networks of supplies as well as to the potential purchasers.

Porter (1990) has a helpful way of characterising these forces by using four major sources of influence on performance, three acting externally and the fourth the nature of competition in the market itself (chart 2.1). From this one can see the importance of externalities (spin-offs from one activity on another) both from up and down the supply chain and from the behaviour of competitors. It is thus essential to understand the framework in which firms operate in order to assess the strengths of the economy. Strength comes from the four facets of the 'diamond' in chart 2.1 reinforcing one another. Porter regards Germany and the UK in different lights as a result of this analysis. Germany is seen as having developed a 'broad and deep national competitive advantage' again in the postwar recovery, while Britain has continued to slide from its position of pre-eminent importance in the 19th century. The special feature of German manufacturing is that so many industries (345) had a share of world trade exceeding 10 per cent in 1985, while the top fifty industries only represented 40 per cent of export value compared with the much greater concentration in the US (50 per cent) and over 60 per cent in Japan. German strength thus comes from a broad front of manufacturing. The characteristic of many of these industries of strength is that German production is specialised and segmented, with product differentiation being the major strategy followed by firms. The particular areas of German success lie in chemicals and related industries (including plastics and associated machinery), metals, metal-working and associated machinery. The two manufacturing industries we have to study in detail, pharmaceuticals and machine tools, come from each of Porter's two main clusters.

Four further areas of strength are identified for Germany: transportation equipment, parts and machinery; printed materials and printing machinery; health care products; and machinery related to food processing and textiles and clothing. Even so this does not cover all areas of strength, which extend to optical products, household goods and appliances. By contrast there are weaknesses in electronics, services, steel, coal, shipbuilding and clothing.

The UK on the other hand derives its strength from its accumulated wealth, with high foreign investment and success in service industries. British exports are characterised by their breadth rather than particular areas of strength. The identified strengths lie in food, drink and tobacco, household furnishings, retailing, financial services, petroleum and chemicals. Our other two industries used in detailed study come from these clusters: retailing and insurance. Other significant areas of strength include pharmaceuticals, entertainment and leisure products, publishing and information, aerospace and other defence goods.

German industry's strength comes not from natural resources, which are now relatively poor, but from 'a pool of high-wage but highly educated skilled and motivated workers', which gives 'a deep scientific and technical knowledge base.' Links between industry and research institutes have helped transform this base into product improvements and a demand for high standards has encouraged this process. Nevertheless, Porter points to a number of danger signs which suggest that the strength may be slipping – productivity growth has slowed markedly since the late 1970s. New industries have not emerged to replace those in decline, domestic competition has tended to decline and be replaced by collaboration.

In Porter's opinion Britain's weaknesses lie very much in similar fields to those in which Germany is strong: the poor quality of the general (as opposed to the élite) education system, the lack of emphasis on technical subjects and poor industrial training.[2] The linkages between industries outside areas like financial services are relatively weak so that there is a lack of reinforcement in the process of development. The weakness of the economy has had a progressive effect leading to low government revenue growth and the need to cut public services. Unlike Germany there has been no jolt to change behaviour, although that may have been provided after 1979 by the striking change in government policy. The single market is perhaps a second jolt but the recent recession is likely to have muted its effect. We therefore go on to explore in more detail how and why the two countries differ, beginning with their location and the natural advantages they possess.

Structure

Location

It is a rather obvious truth that there are important differences between the geographical location of the UK and Germany but nevertheless this is a significant contributor to the differences between the German and British responses to the single market. We have already noted that the response of firms in the two countries will vary even if the single market legislation is successful in creating some sort of 'level playing field' of competition within the Community on a reasonably equal basis, because the two countries do not start from the same regulatory position. The 1992 programme is thus not an equal shock. In each individual case the shock reflects the changes which are necessary for each industry in each country to reach the common position, the single market. In this chapter we are concerned with the ability to respond to these shocks irrespective of their differing nature. We leave the assessment of the combination of the shocks and responses to the chapters on our four case study industries after establishing this framework, as it is very difficult to generalise across the whole Community.

The most important distinction between the two countries stemming from their location lies in the links with other countries. Germany has land borders with five other member states including four of the five other original EC countries. Its land borders extend to four other countries including Austria which is part of the European Economic Area and expected to join the Community as a full member shortly. More than that it is the main route for trade with Sweden. Primarily it is a central European country in the sense that in whatever direction you turn you have to pass through or by other European countries.

Not only does this centrality relate to the existing EC and the EEA but to the former CMEA countries as well. A large portion of trade with

Table 2.2 *EC/EFTA trade with Germany and the UK, 1991*

	Germany		UK	
	% exports to	% imports from	% exports to	% imports from
Austria	39.0	43.0	3.7	2.8
Belgium/Luxembourg	23.7	23.6	7.6	8.3
Denmark	20.8	21.9	9.7	8.1
Finland	14.8	17.1	10.0	7.8
France	18.7	17.8	8.9	7.5
Germany	-	-	7.6	6.6
Greece	22.2	18.2	6.7	4.5
Ireland	12.9	8.2	32.1	41.5
Italy	20.7	21.3	6.5	5.6
Netherlands	28.8	25.2	8.9	8.3
Norway	11.7	15.4	26.5	7.6
Portugal	18.8	14.6	10.6	7.3
Spain	16.4	16.2	7.8	7.6
Sweden	14.5	18.0	1.8	8.0
Switzerland	23.7	33.0	6.5	5.6
United Kingdom	14.0	14.9	-	-

Source: OECD Foreign Trade by Commodities (1991)

these last countries comes overland to or through Germany even if they do not have a direct border with it. The centrality is shown by the trade pattern, first of all, for Germany looking outward, 54 per cent of Germany's exports go to other member states and 52 per cent of imports come from them. Secondly, Germany is the most important trade partner for nine of the other member states and the second most important partner for the remaining two (table 2.2).

In these terms the UK is clearly more peripheral. Not only does the mainland have no land borders with other member states but it is central only for the Irish Republic. Only three other countries, Norway, Finland and Portugal, part of the original EFTA partnership, have even 10 per cent of their trade with the UK, while there is only one case where trade with Germany is less than 10 per cent. The large figure for Norwegian exports to the UK is because of North Sea oil and gas. The EC represents a very similar proportion of trade (52 per cent of the UK's exports go to other member states and 50 per cent of imports come from them). This question of land versus sea borders is not trivial. It has long been

known from gravity models of trade flows (Aitken, 1973) that a land border encourages trade markedly over and above the effect of distance
between countries. However, in practical terms it means that firms in
one country can distribute, supply, source and market in 'border' regions of other member states in the single market as if it were part of
their own. The clearest example of this occurred in one of the firms we
examined in detail in the Stuttgart area which had a plant in Strasbourg.
Stuttgart would by almost any definition be considered part of the heart
of Germany yet this Strasbourg plant could be reached far more quickly
than most locations in Germany.

There is of course the fact of the opening of the Channel tunnel in 1994
but this will still not substitute for a land border. The costs of taking a
lorry through the tunnel to the nearest part of France and back for the day,
for example, although feasible in terms of time, will be considerably
greater than supplying anywhere in the Netherlands from north-western Germany even though the distance may be similar. Most of UK industry is not near enough to the tunnel to make this pattern of supply
feasible even if it made economic sense.

It is, of course, mistaken to focus just on trade in goods. Trade in
services is much more important for the UK than for Germany (exports
of services are about 30–35 per cent of exports of goods in the UK compared with 15–20 per cent of exports of goods in Germany). Many
services do not require physical presence to be transacted, some financial
services, for example. However, most 'retail' services, with the obvious exception of mail order shopping, do require a physical presence, as our chapters on retailing and insurance reveal very clearly. The emphasis on
services is thus a reflection of the UK's traditional comparative advantage stemming from its relative peripherality in European terms and
access to the open sea. However, there are limits to this advantage as
services tend to follow goods. In our discussions with Royal Insurance
it was explained how the international structure of the company had
followed British seaborne trade in the nineteenth century. Similarly, in
a related study of the leasing industry (Matthews and Mayes, 1993), it is
clear that a large portion of cross-border deals in both the UK and
Germany had been driven by the needs of established domestic clients.

This element of history is an important facet of the influence of location. The UK's empire was outside Europe and the current trading and
cultural links reflect this. The change round occurred in the sixteenth century when the last foothold on the continent was lost and the first attempts
at colonisation in America began. The UK has strong cultural links with
North America, Australasia, the Indian subcontinent, Africa, Latin

Chart 2.2 Comparison of distribution of total inward FDI in the EC, 1980–9
Source: European Commission (1991)

America (particularly the Caribbean) and parts of Asia-Pacific. Germany's history, however, has been almost entirely within Europe, with ethnic Germans spread across Poland, Russia, Belarus, the Ukraine, Czechoslovakia, Hungary and further afield. Austria and part of Switzerland are also German speaking. Much of this European influence goes back to the middle ages and even earlier, with the Hanseatic league round the Baltic. It has been argued that part of the origin of the tale of the Pied Piper of Hamelin reflects the organisation of colonisation programmes further east.

A second major facet of locational difference is that, with the exception of the creation of the Irish Free State, the borders of the United Kingdom have been the same since the Act of Union in 1707. Germany on the other hand has only had its current borders for three years. Its borders were changed radically in 1945 following a previous radical change after the First World War, itself an important contribution to the Second World War. The country had been characterised by loose coalitions of independent states even into the second half of the last century. We return to the organisational and cultural implications of these developments later in this chapter but in terms of the present discussion of location this difference in history reflects a radically different view of centrality within Europe.

This difference is also reflected in the pattern of overseas investment. The location of the UK encouraged seaborne trade followed by colonisation which was a major factor leading to a tradition of foreign overseas investment. Although the UK was the world's largest overseas investor in the nineteenth century, aided by earlier industrialisation, much of that original investment has either been lost or sold. Nevertheless,

Table 2.3 *Inward direct investment in EC countries, million Ecu*

	1986	1987	1988	1989
United Kingdom	7364	12073	13889	29173
Germany	1215	1649	1160	5389
France	2800	4008	6098	8670
Netherlands	1980	2030	3448	5620
Spain	2068	2261	3737	5154
Rest of EC	1386	6747	12135	11156

Source: CEC (1991)

since the Second World War the UK has built up a new stock of overseas assets second only to those of the United States. Although overtaken by Japan in 1988, the UK remains third in the world for new overseas investment each year. In 1991 only 27 per cent of that investment was in Europe; 54 per cent went to North America. Thus, although the focus has moved towards Europe, non-European countries are still more important. This importance of non-European investment is also seen in Germany (45 per cent), although not to such a marked extent. The discrepancy between the UK and Germany is shown up clearly by the figures for the stock of overseas investment as opposed to the net additions to it. In 1991, 42 per cent of the stock of UK overseas investment was in North America whereas the equivalent figure for Germany was only 22 per cent. Thus in relative terms the switch towards North America was even greater for Germany than for the UK. Amongst the G7, Germany's stock of overseas assets is the fourth highest but is substantially lower than that of the US, Japan and the UK.

However, there is an added complication in that this high outward direct investment by the UK is matched by high inward flows (chart 2.2 and table 2.3). The UK has been receiving around 40 per cent of inward investment in the EC, over six times as much as that going to Germany. In part this is because the UK is more attractive to investors outside the EC, 75 per cent of funds have come from non-EC countries, virtually 50 per cent from the US (CEC, 1991), compared with 65 per cent for Germany with a third coming from the US.[3]

There is thus much more to the attractiveness of locations to external investors than the simple geographic concerns which we have outlined up to this point. Nam and Reuter (1991) present a typical diagram of such factors (chart 2.3) for the various parts of the EC. Some of these fac-

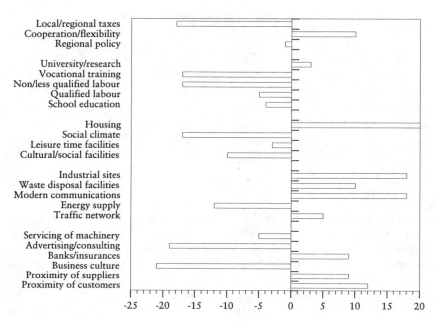

Chart 2.3   Infrastructure endowment in the Objective 1 regions – companies'
assessment
Source: Nam and Reuter (1991)

tors relate to other aspects of the structure of the economy such as business culture or social climate, which are relatively difficult to alter, others, however, are largely regulatory in character, particularly those
which relate to the incentives given to inward investment. Many of
the other facets are also changeable but those relating to infrastructure, education and training will take a long time and major investment
to change. The UK has actively encouraged inward investment; even if
the financial inducements have been relatively limited the environment
has been much more welcoming than in some other member states. However, direct investment takes a number of forms and dealing with it in
aggregate confuses new investment in greenfield sites with domestically
retained profits of overseas owned companies and acquisitions of existing companies. The relative magnitudes suggest that the UK is much
more open to both greenfield investment and acquisitions. Since mergers
and acquisitions are such an important route of response to the single
market we return to them later in this chapter.

The most important feature of the Nam and Reuter (1991) analysis is the fact that the impact of the 1992 programme is uneven on a regional basis, not just a national one. As we mentioned in chapter 1, Nam and Reuter emphasise that most peripheral regions can expect to be losers from the single market as the centripetal forces will tend to outweigh the centrifugal ones stemming from easier access to lower costs. But it is not clear whether these losses will be absolute or merely relative. Regional and social policy can be used to ensure that they are only relative in countries like the UK and Germany where the aggregate effects are expected to be positive (NIESR, 1991). The main implication for our comparison of the UK and Germany is that, whereas Germany as a whole is part of the core of the European economy, a large part of the UK economy shows characteristics of peripherality.

In the southern member states it is suggested (*European Economy*, 1990) that this relative difficulty may be offset to some extent by traditional inter-industry trade rather than the intra-industry trade which has tended to characterise the development of the European Community. In these cases the less favoured regions can exploit both their lower labour costs and their locational advantages for tourism and retirement. This is not an attractive recipe because other countries outside the EC can play the card of lower labour costs much more effectively, as has been demonstrated by the rapidly growing economies in Asia-Pacific and is likely to be followed by central and eastern Europe. In any case this is a temporary phase. The point of the specialisation in these other countries is to raise incomes and hence eventually change to becoming a 'northern style' economy.

However, this low labour cost/locational advantage option is even less open to the peripheral regions of the UK, first of all because they do not have the climatic advantages of southern Europe and second because they already have relatively high incomes per head. Clearly tourist potential is already being exploited, particularly in Scotland, but a full response will have to include a much wider range of industrial development for which the UK does not have a locational advantage and where the protection of local markets simply by distance is falling. Location therefore is an important contributor both to the existing differences in industrial structure in the UK and Germany and to their potential response to the single market.

The structure of industry

As was indicated earlier, the German economy is much more heavily oriented towards manufacturing than the UK (table 2.4). North Sea oil

Table 2.4 *Structure of German and UK economies*

| | % share of GDP (employment) 1991 | |
	Germany	UK
Agriculture, etc	1.6 (3.3)	1.5 (1.3)
Energy, water, mining	3.2 (1.6)	8.2 (2.0)
Manufacturing	29.7 (31.1)	22.1 (21.6)
Construction	4.8 (6.6)	6.0 (4.3)
Services	56.0 (52.9)	62.2 (70.8)
traded	28.8 (22.1)	-
non-traded	17.1 (16.0)	-
government	10.1 (14.8)	-
distribution, hotels, repair, transport, communication	-	20.3 (27.2)
financial	-	18.3 (12.2)
other	-	23.6 (31.4)

Source: OECD Economic Surveys

adds an emphasis on raw materials to the UK structure which Germany does not possess. However, it is Germany which stands out among the European countries for the large size of its manufacturing share rather than the UK for the smallness of its sector.

SERVICES

Germany's high share of activity in manufacturing has its counterpart in a rather lower share in services activity than the UK (table 2.4). The UK has a substantial trade surplus in services while Germany has a defi-cit.[4] However, unlike the rest of the EC, Germany has been experi-encing similar growth in productivity in services and manufactur-ing industries, 1.3–1.4 per cent a year between 1980 and 1990. This is largely because its performance in manufacturing is low. The UK recorded manufacturing productivity growth of 4.6 per cent a year over the same period but 1.8 per cent for services. In relative terms the UK only shows higher levels of services productivity in banking and insurance although the unfavourable gap in distribution, transport and communications is smaller than the average (table 2.5).

The UK is characterised by a share of value-added in banking and insurance nearly three times that of Germany in services within the country. This is reflected in trade performance where the UK has a 36

Table 2.5 *Relative productivity in 1990 (EC average = 100)*

	West Germany	United Kingdom
Transport	107	95
Hotels and catering	82	53
Banking and insurance	92	126
Distribution	97	84
Communications	115	99
Other services	157	46
Market services	123	78

Source: *European Economy*

per cent share of intra-EC trade in banking compared with 9 per cent for Germany. The UK also has the larger share in communications, 27 per cent compared with 24 per cent for Germany. Construction is the only sector where Germany's share is markedly larger than that of the UK.

Sutherland *et al.* (1993) suggest a two way assessment of the likely impact of 1992 on services.

		Impact of EC–1992	
		HIGH	LOW
Impact of	HIGH	Banking	Telecoms (basic)
technological		Telecoms (value-added)	
change			
	LOW	Airline	Business services
		Insurance	Construction
		Road transport	Distribution
			Hotels

The UK has strengths in most of the high impact sectors with the possible exception of road transport. Insofar as merger and acquisition activity is an indicator of change, the UK has made nearly six times as many purchases (1,392 compared with 246 in Germany) involving companies valued as being five times as large ($bn41.5 compared with $bn8.7). Acquisitions in the UK were fewer in number than in Germany (593 compared with 709) but involved a much larger value ($bn30.5/7.5). The UK was involved in nearly half the mergers and acquisition activity in services in the Community as a whole whether in purchases or sales. (We explore the reasons for this later in this chapter.)

Table 2.6   *Shares of employment and sales by industry branch*

	Employment share		Sales share	
	UK	Germany	UK	Germany
Metal manufacture	3.3	4.6	5.1	5.6
Non-metallic mineral products	4.5	3.6	4.2	3.4
Chemicals	6.9	9.0	11.8	12.0
Metal products	6.4	7.5	4.7	5.9
Mechanical engineering	12.0	17.4	10.2	14.5
Electrical engineering	13.5	16.9	11.4	14.0
Vehicles	12.8	13.7	12.2	15.4
Instrument engineering	1.8	2.1	1.2	1.3
Food, drink & tobacco	13.4	7.1	20.6	12.7
Textiles	5.1	3.4	3.1	2.7
Clothing, footwear, leather	7.0	3.5	3.2	2.3
Timber and furniture	3.7	3.3	3.4	2.8
Paper and board	3.5	2.3	3.6	2.8
Rubber, plastics & other	6.1	5.8	5.2	4.7

Source: O'Mahony (1992)

MANUFACTURING

The major distinguishing feature of the structure of UK manufacturing
compared with its German counterpart is the importance of food, drink
and tobacco (table 2.6). In terms of sales it forms just over 20 per cent
of manufacturing compared with 13 per cent in Germany. Many other
lower value-added activities like clothing, textiles, footwear, timber and
furniture and non-metallic mineral manufactures also have somewhat
higher weights. By simple arithmetic this entails that higher value-
added activities like engineering, vehicle manufacture and chemicals
have a lower weight. The UK's strengths are not concentrated in the higher
growth, higher value-added activities, although there are well-known
counter examples such as pharmaceuticals – one of the reasons why we
selected it for a case study (table 2.7).

The potential for structural change as a result of '1992'

We must be careful not to draw the simplistic inference that just because
current industrial structures exist '1992' will result in little change in the

Table 2.7 *Position of industries likely to be affected by the single market*[a]

NACE Group code		Sector	Intra-EC export/import ratio 1985-87	Intra-EC SI 1985-87	Extra-EC SI 1985-87	Production specialisation 1985	Score
		Above-average performers					
330	1	Computers & office equipment	1.11	2.16	1.58	1.32	4
344	1	Telecommunications equipment	1.16	2.28	1.51	1.64	4
372	1	Medical & surgical equipment	0.94	1.41	1.27	1.05	3
257	2	Pharmaceuticals	1.23	1.85	1.42	1.12	4
362	2	Railway equipment	1.09	0.62	1.12	1.83	2
361	3	Shipbuilding	0.78	1.31	0.76	1.93	2
256	4	Industrial & agricultural chemicals	1.09	1.36	1.24	1.64	4
325	4	Mining & related plant	0.62	1.23	1.16	1.01	2
326	4	Transmission equipment	0.73	1.06	0.90	0.93	1
328	4	Other machinery	0.71	1.15	1.15	1.32	3
345	4	Other electronic equipment	0.70	1.27	1.06	1.01	1
371	4	Measuring equipment	0.99	1.49	1.44	2.23	4
373	4	Optical instruments	0.76	1.64	0.93	0.95	2
491	4	Jewellery	3.69	3.39	1.28	0.33	2
494	4	Toys, games & sports goods	1.01	1.58	1.07	0.53	1
		Average performers					
341	3	Insulated wires & cables	0.48	0.79	1.29	3.29	0
342	3	Electrical plant & machinery	0.64	0.95	1.15	0.53	0
421	3	Chocolate & sugar confectionery	0.44	0.80	1.42	1.11	0
248	4	Ceramics	1.16	0.87	1.01	0.91	0
251	4	Basic industrial chemicals	0.83	1.06	0.82	0.96	0
321	4	Agricultural machinery	0.57	1.13	1.43	0.72	0
431	4	Woollen goods	0.66	0.75	1.14	0.98	0
455	4	Household textiles	0.90	0.69	0.63	2.31	0
		Below-average performers					
315	2	Boilermaking	0.59	0.84	0.65	0.90	-3
427	2	Brewing	0.41	0.83	0.76	1.58	-2
428	2	Soft drinks	0.23	0.33	0.51	1.16	-2
247	4	Glass	0.37	0.60	0.76	0.73	-4
322	4	Machine tools	0.56	0.91	0.80	0.88	-3
323	4	Textile machinery	0.46	0.75	0.53	0.41	-4
324	4	Food processing & chemical mach.	0.46	0.85	0.70	0.99	-3
327	4	Wood, paper & leather machinery	0.43	0.97	0.81	0.94	-2
346	4	Domestic electrical appliances	0.21	0.43	0.39	0.85	-4
347	4	Lighting	0.41	0.66	0.68	1.41	-2
350	4	Motor vehicles	0.31	0.60	0.68	0.87	-4
432	4	Cotton goods	0.26	0.49	0.68	0.46	-4
438	4	Carpets	0.30	0.58	0.93	1.22	-1
451	4	Footwear	0.25	0.33	0.19	0.62	-4
453	4	Clothing	0.69	0.80	0.75	0.83	-3
481	4	Rubber goods	0.82	0.98	0.88	0.88	-1

Source: *European Economy*, Special Edition (1990)
Notes: Intra-EC export/import ratio only: ratio below 0.60 = −1; ratio between 0.60 and 0.72 = 0; ratio above 0.72 = 1. Other measures: ratio below 0.90 = −1; ratio between 0.90 and 1.10 = 0; ratio above 1.10 = 1. SI = Balassa specialisation index. Extra-EC SI = (UK share of Community exports of industry *i* to rest of world/UK share of Community exports of manufactures to rest of world). Production specialisation = (Share of Community production of industry *i*)/ (Share of Community manufacturing production).
[a]The classification into three groups (above-average, average and below-average) is made using a composite score of 0 as a threshold.

Table 2.8 *Median plant size, UK and Germany, 1987*

	Number of employees		Germany/UK
	UK	Germany	
Metal manufacture	482	1900(a)	3.94
Non-metallic mineral products	195	97	0.50
Chemical, man-made fibres	503	1600(a)	3.18
Metal products	95	184	1.94
Mechanical engineering	181	370	2.04
Electrical engineering	483	752	1.56
Vehicles	2000(a)	6000(a)	3.00
Instrument engineering	149	60	0.40
Food, drink and tobacco	359	31	0.09
Textiles	178	232	1.30
Clothing, footwear, leather	129	71	0.55
Timber and furniture	63	37	0.59
Paper and board	201	258	1.28
Rubber, plastics and other	137	183	1.34
Total manufacturing	260	341	1.31

Source: O'Mahony (1992)
(a) The median size fell within the upper size band; estimated by logarithmic extrapolation from smaller size bands.

pattern in the future. Clearly it depends whether the single market programme will have a disproportionate effect on what are currently high or low growth industries. A major feature of the arguments put forward in the explanation of the rapid productivity growth in the UK relative to Germany in the 1980s (Matthews and Feinstein, 1990) was that it reflected catching up. This catching up could be achieved merely by emulating German methods, whether this involved improving physical capital, technology, work organisation and management, innovation or human capital through training. There is some evidence of a general reduction in discrepancy among the OECD countries (Dowrick and Nguyen, 1989) which would confirm convergence models along the lines of Abramovitz (1986) and Baumol *et al.* (1988). However, Barro and Sala-i-Martin (1991, 1992) indicate that these arguments may not be completely convincing.

The simplest example of this potential for convergence lies in economies of scale (and indeed scope). Although minimum efficient plant size may be falling as a result of flexible manufacturing systems and other advances from the IT revolution, despite the simultaneous increase in dif-

Table 2.9 *Country distribution of top 100 EC firms*

	1989		1983	
	Number	% of turnover	Number	% of turnover
United Kingdom	29	23	34	30
Germany	28	30	28	22
France	24	21	21	20
rest	19	26	17	28

Source: CEC (1991)

ferentiated demand which is restricting the size of some markets, it is nevertheless abundantly clear that the UK has a smaller average scale than in Germany (table 2.8). Although the median size of plant is some 30 per cent higher in Germany, the ratio varies considerably across industries.[5] Several of the industries which have a higher weight in UK manufacturing production also have a higher median plant size: non-metallic mineral products, clothing, footwear and leather, timber and board, for example. However, the most striking difference lies in food, drink and tobacco, where the median size in the UK is ten times as large as in Germany. Not only does the UK have a number of very large plants in the industry but it lacks the long tail, despite the fact that whisky distilleries, which are an important element in this sector, actually have rather small workforces. However, in the main engineering and vehicles industries where the principal economies of scale are thought to lie (Pratten, 1988) the UK has a median size one third to two thirds that of its German counterparts.

This distinction in plant size has more than one implication. On the one hand it suggests that the known scope for improvement in efficiency is greater in the UK than in Germany, while on the other it could be taken to imply that smaller inefficient UK plants will be unable to compete in the single market. It is one thing for there to be scope for improvement, it is another to have the resources or ability to achieve it.

It is important to draw a distinction between plant size and firm size. In 1989 (table 2.9) the UK had twenty-nine out of the top one hundred largest firms in the EC compared with twenty-eight in Germany. However, the UK share was some 8 per cent lower in terms of turnover. Moreover, while average UK productivity was improving, the UK's share of the largest firms was falling. It is, however, important to note the sectoral distribution of these largest enterprises (table 2.10). Of the UK

Table 2.10 *The largest UK and German groups in the Community in 1989*

Rank-ing	Company name	Country	Turnover (bn Ecu)	Employees ('000s)	Sector
2	British Petroleum	UK	44.9	119	Oil
4	Daimler-Benz	D	38.8	368	Automobiles
7	Volkswagen	D	31.5	250	Automobiles
8	Siemens	D	29.6	365	Electrical engineering/electronics
9	Deutsche Bundespost	D	27.2	567	Services
13	BASF	D	22.9	136	Chemicals
14	VEBA	D	22.6	94	Oil
15	Hoechst	D	22.1	169	Chemicals
17	BAT Industries	UK	21.3	311	Agro-alimentary(a)
20	Bayer	D	20.8	170	Chemicals
22	ICI	UK	19.8	133	Chemicals
23	The Electricity Council	UK	18.4	131	Energy
24	RWE	D	16.7	78	Energy
25	British Telecom	UK	16.6	244	Services
26	Thyssen	D	16.6	133	Metallurgy
28	Robert Bosch	D	14.7	174	Automobiles
33	British Aerospace	UK	13.5	125	Aeronautics
34	Grand Metropolitan	UK	12.9	152	Agro-alimentary(a)
35	BMW	D	12.7	66	Automobiles
37	British Gas	UK	11.7	80	Energy
38	Ruhrkohle	D	11.2	124	Extraction
41	Mannesmann	D	10.7	125	Metallurgy
42	Hanson	UK	10.7	89	Agro-alimentary(a)
44	BTR	UK	10.4	109	Engineering
47	Deutsche Bundesbahn	D	10.1	254	Transport
48	GEC	UK	10.1	145	Electrical engineering/electronics(a)
49	Metallgesellschaft	D	9.7	24	Metallurgy

companies which lie in the top thirty, one is an oil company (Shell is treated as Dutch owned and is the EC's largest company on this basis), the second a tobacco based conglomerate, the third is ICI and the remaining two are utilities. Germany on the other hand has eight major manufacturing companies in the top thirty. Six of the remaining twenty-

Table 2.10 *continued*

Rank-ing	Company name	Country	Turnover (bn ecu)	Employees ('000s)	Sector
52	RTZ	UK	9.1	77	Non-ferrous metals
53	Krupp	D	8.5	63	Engineering
55	MAN	D	8.3	62	Engineering
56	Preussag	D	8.1	65	Oil
58	British Steel	UK	7.8	55	Metallurgy
61	SmithKline Beecham	UK	7.2	62	Pharmaceuticals
62	Degussa	D	7.1	33	Metallurgy
64	British Coal	UK	6.8	105	Mining
66	P&O Navigation	UK	6.8	64	Transport
67	Saatchi & Saatchi	UK	6.6	18	Services
70	British Airways	UK	6.4	50	Transport
71	Lufthansa	D	6.3	51	Transport
72	Allied-Lyons	UK	6.2	81	Agro-alimentary
73	Bertelsmann	D	6.0	43	Publishing
76	British Post Office (1988)	UK	5.8	200	Services
78	BICC	UK	5.6	46	Electrical engineering/ electronics
80	Henkel	D	5.6	38	Chemicals
82	Hillsdown Holdings	UK	5.4	40	Agro-alimentary
85	Ladbroke Group	UK	5.4	51	Transport
87	Thorn EMI	UK	5.2	65	Electrical engineering/ electronics
88	Salzgitter	D	5.2	39	Metallurgy
90	British Railways Board	UK	5.1	135	Transport
91	Tate & Lyle	UK	5.1	18	Agro-alimentary
92	Hoescht	D	5.1	44	Metallurgy
93	Bass	UK	5.1	90	Agro-alimentary(a)
94	Tarmac	UK	5.0	32	Construction
95	VIAG	D	5.0	34	Mining
96	Trafalgar House	UK	4.9	27	Construction
97	Ruhrgas	D	4.8	8	Energy
99	Feldmuehle Nobel	D	4.7	35	Paper

(a)Heavily diversified.

four UK companies in the table have been classified in the food, drink and tobacco sector, two are in transport, two in construction, one in utility and two in services, leaving only eleven manufacturers. Thus the UK's concentration at the very largest end of the market may not be quite as large as it first appears.

However, larger firms have an absolute ability to draw on resources to implement change so firm size can be an indicator of the potential to respond to the challenge of '1992'. Company size alone can actually be a disadvantage (Prais, 1981) where this does not reflect single plant or system economies of scale. Furthermore, according to the league table shown in the January/February 1993 issue of *International Management*, the number of UK firms in the largest one hundred by turn-over has fallen to twenty-two, only eight of which are in manufacturing other than food, drink and tobacco, while that of Germany is now thirty-one, eighteen of which are in mainstream manufacturing.

Taken together therefore it does appear that the UK has a rather different economic structure from that in Germany. Insofar as the single market has a greater impact on services industries, then the UK appears to have current relative strengths in these industries, aided by greater openness to international competition before the single market started. This is also the case in utilities and public services, which have been rather more open. Hence to an extent some of the adverse adjustment in terms of increased imports has already occurred. How much this advantage can actually be translated into a deliverable gain within the single market is a different matter. The much more open insurance industry does not seem set to make major gains in the UK despite the restrictions in the German system. Indeed what we may see is a growth in products for the German consumer and an expanded market where the major beneficiaries (at least in terms of market size if not perhaps profits if margins are reduced) will be German companies. Similarly in retailing, although the UK industry is concentrated and well organised, the scope for cross-border activity seems distinctly limited. Existing exposure and international competitiveness may actually be reflected in lower profit rates and hence a lower ability to benefit from the new opportunities available.

We therefore now turn to the resources available to implement change as the single market develops.

Investment and capital

It is very difficult to make comparisons of the capital available at a national level in order to draw conclusions about the ability of German and UK industry to respond to the challenges of the single market. Neither country makes direct surveys of the physical capital available in firms (Mayes and Young, 1993) and hence any comparisons have to be made either on the basis of accumulated investment or at a very disaggregated plant level when detailed statistics have been derived for specific purposes (Prais, 1984). Just knowing how much has been spent on capital or knowing its replacement cost is not enough. We would normally want to assume that a considerable portion of the productive potential of physical capital depended upon its age. To quite an extent technological advance is 'embodied' in the equipment used and although it is possible to devise new techniques to employ capital better and to 'retrofit' some new improvements into existing equipment, by and large newer equipment tends to be more productive and, through the advent of IT, more flexible.

Any assessment of the capital available therefore has to take into account its vintage. While there have been some elaborate attempts to do this for the UK (Ingham and Ulph, 1992) the main comparison available comes from O'Mahony (1993), who has reworked estimates of the capital stock of the main OECD countries using similar assumptions to achieve comparability. The major assumption required to apply the perpetual inventory method (PIM) of estimating the (gross) capital stock is to decide how long assets last. Hence assets can be entered into the stock when they are purchased (investment) and removed from it when they are deemed to have been scrapped (or exported). There is no equivalent information to investment on these losses from the stock so their value has to be estimated from a model of behaviour. The calculated capital remaining of each particular vintage then needs to be revalued using a price index to express it all in the prices of a common year. Otherwise it will be estimated on the accountants' conventional historic cost basis, which has little economic meaning. (Calculating the net capital stock requires an additional assumption about the rate of depreciation but we use gross values here.)

Table 2.11, drawn from O'Mahony (1992) assumes that equipment and vehicles last for fifteen years and buildings for forty years on average in the two countries. This is rather closer to the German assumptions used in the official statistics (Mayes and Young, 1993) than to their UK equivalent. Actual asset lives are assumed to be uniformly distributed over a range ± 20 per cent of the average. DM values are converted to sterling by using 1985 PPPs for machinery and industrial buildings (Eurostat, 1988). We could argue that better assumptions should be made, or indeed that average asset lives are not likely to be the same in the two countries, but the table illustrates the point. German capital per worker (per man-hour) and capital–output ratios are larger than in the UK by a factor of

Table 2.11 *The contribution of physical capital*

	Germany	UK	Germany/ UK ratio
Output (£mn)	138525	76654	1.81
Employment ('000s)	6602	4112	1.61
Average annual hours per worker	1630	1763	0.93
Gross capital stock (£mn)	347327	169322	2.05
Capital output ratio (£)	2.51	2.21	1.13
Capital employment ratio (£)	52613	41175	1.28
Capital hours ratio (£)	32.3	23.4	1.38
Labour productivity ratio			1.22
Total factor productivity ratio			1.13

Source: O'Mahony (1992)

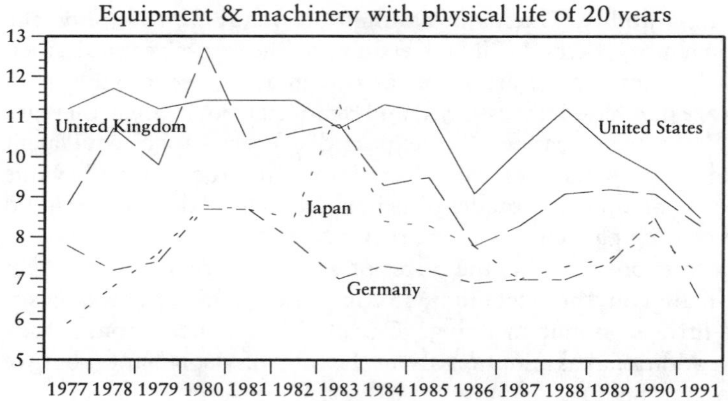

Equipment & machinery with physical life of 20 years

Chart 2.4 User cost of capital for two types of investment
Source: Fukao (1993)

13–38 per cent. (Using the two countries' own assumptions about asset lives would eliminate much of this discrepancy as the UK estimates result in a capital stock some 30 per cent higher. All these estimates are based on weakly founded assumptions but we find little evidence to suggest that these high UK figures are likely to be substantiated by a detailed survey (Mayes and Young, 1993).)

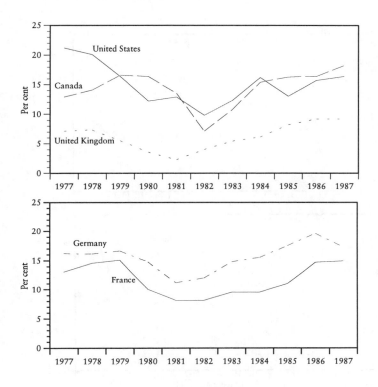

Chart 2.5 Net operating surplus as a proportion of the net capital stock: manufacturing

Source: OECD National Accounts, drawn from Eltis (1992)

The stock differential is matched by a difference in the savings ratios in the two countries. The German ratio of around 14 per cent (*National Institute Economic Review*, 1993) is nearly 3 points higher than that in the UK. While not all saving goes into domestic industrial investment and not all industrial investment is financed out of domestic saving the funds for investment have to come from somewhere. Not only is a much larger proportion of domestic investment financed from own resources in Germany (89.9 per cent compared with 58.2 per cent in the UK over the period 1982–8 (Mayer and Alexander, 1990) but the cost of capital appears to be lower (chart 2.4). The recent reductions in interest rates in the UK may have made some difference to this although the changes have been primarily in short-term rates.

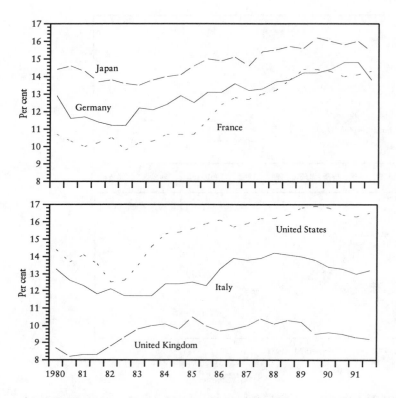

Chart 2.6 Net operating surplus as a proportion of the net capital stock: business sector

Source: OECD *Economic Outlook*, drawn from Eltis (1992)

The rate of return on capital in manufacturing has been particularly low in the UK (chart 2.5). It was the lowest of the major countries over the period 1977–88, although some improvement was visible by the end of the period. The range of outcomes is lower for the whole business sector but there the UK has shown an increasing divergence at the bottom of the range since the early 1980s (chart 2.6).

The consequence of higher investment rates in Germany is reflected in a higher capital stock across the whole economy (table 2.12).[6] What is striking is not the difference in manufacturing industry, which may in part be accounted for by the greater emphasis on 'heavy' industries in Germany, but the discrepancy for the rest of the economy, which suggests a much more developed infrastructure and capital resources for service

Table 2.12 *Gross tangible physical capital stocks, 1989 (1985 $)*

	Total economy			Manufacturing		
	Value	per worker-hour		Value	per worker-hour	
	billion $	$	UK=100	billion $	$	UK=100
UK	1367	30.6	100	267	30.7	100
Germany	2589	58.3	190	578	41.1	134

Source: O'Mahony (1993)
Note: Capital stocks estimated using the perpetual inventory method. Service lives are approximately forty years and fifteen years for structures and equipment, respectively, for the aggregate economy and thirty-one years and seventeen years for structures and equipment, respectively, in manufacturing. Sources for investment data: UK: unpublished data from the Central Statistical Office, London; Germany: 1960–89 from *Volkswirtschaftliche Gesamtrechnungen, Fachserie 18, Reihe 5, 15, Revidierie Ergebnisse, 1950 bis 1990*, Statistisches Bundesamt 1991 and prior to 1960 from Kirner (1968).

industries. This stronger base of physical capital could be a considerable asset in facilitating change.

It therefore appears that German companies may be better equipped for change in terms of physical capital than the general run of their British counterparts. We shall qualify this in two respects in the ensuing sections, first by arguing that it is not the difference in capital–output ratios that is particularly important but the differences in the quality of the labour input. Daly *et al.* (1985) argue that, in many of the firms compared, the age and technical sophistication of the capital equipment in UK plants is similar to that in Germany – indeed in the biscuit industry (Mason *et al.*, 1993) they suggest it may be younger – it is the lower training and qualifications of the UK workforce which tends to mean that the equipment is not so well utilised. Secondly, it is clear that there is considerable variation across the spectrum of UK firms. Those that are heavily involved in international trade tend to be better equipped and have a better trained labour force than the average. Hence, if it is these firms that are likely to provide the bulk of the response to the single market the picture may not be as black as it has been painted.

Insofar as the response requires new capital then the UK is likely to be rather less responsive than Germany. Investment in the UK responds a little more slowly to external shocks than does investment in Germany according to the relationships estimated for the National Institute's world model NiGEM. Burridge and Mayes (1993b) suggest very clearly from the OEF 91-sector econometric model that the construction and investment goods sectors are most likely to be favourably affected by the single market programme. Indeed, since this is a general response, countries like Germany, whose output is relatively concentrated on capital goods, are likely to be greater beneficiaries.

Thus far we have focussed on the private capital available to firms. But this only forms part of the picture as the firm can also draw on the services provided by public capital (Lynde and Richmond, 1993). Some of these services are paid for directly, others indirectly through taxation on the firm itself but much is often in effect provided through transfers from income earners or wealth holders elsewhere in the economy. The existence of these services, often relating to transport, communication and the supply of utilities, is one of the vital elements affecting the attractiveness of regions to inward investment as listed by Nam and Reuter (1991). However, these same arguments apply equally to domestic investment. In a region facing structural change, particularly one where existing industries are in decline (the Objective 2 regions in the parlance of the EC's structural policies), the network of public and private services is vital in the encouragement of new firms to start up or existing ones to change activities within the same region. Cultural and leisure facilities are important in attracting high quality employees so it is not just a matter of business services.

We have little other than circumstantial evidence to compare the provision of such services in the UK and Germany. The data on public sector investment and case studies on the behaviour of regional authorities (NIESR, 1991) suggest that the German Länder and the authorities in Wales, Scotland and Northern Ireland are well aware of these problems and are attempting to settle them. England on the other hand has no such strong system of regional government and consistent attempts to control public expenditure since the mid-1970s have led to considerable pressures on the public infrastructure (Mayes, 1990). It is therefore arguable that there is a considerable need for investment purely to refurbish existing structures. Unfortunately there have been no new published statistics on this part of the capital stock since 1987 and assumptions made then about refurbishment and depreciation preclude the observation of the extent of any such dilapidation. A simpler measure is purely that the taxable capacity of German regions is greater than that in the UK. Tax rates are higher and although some of the excess has gone into greater social provision there is clearly a much better opportunity for this form of capital as well.[7] The drawback comes from the need to provide massive assistance of this sort for the new Länder which is resulting in a considerable diversion of resources. Therefore just at the time that Germany could need to benefit from this social capital it has become more difficult to provide it.

Skills and knowledge capital

The second major aspect of resources which affects British and German companies is the human resource – labour. However, this is more than simply an assessment of numbers of working age as the potential ability of the labour force to achieve output depends upon its skills. Clearly skills are required in appropriate combination but an assessment of the stock of skills through existing qualifications and the capacity for training and re-training will provide an indication of the human capital capabilities available. There is, however, a second aspect to human capital through accumulated knowledge and the capacity to innovate. This latter is particularly important as it reflects dynamic ability – the ability to undertake new activities and develop new products and processes to meet the new challenges as regulations change and new markets and competitors emerge.

This technological ability is reflected in three main ways: first by the revealed ability of the two countries in innovation as indicated by patenting, for example; second by the effort put into innovation through research and development expenditures and, third, by the structure of organisation of the process of innovation. Mason *et al.* (1993) highlight two aspects of the relative advantage that Germany has in this regard – first through the network of Max Planck, Fraunhofer and other institutions involved in the process of technology transfer and second through the larger proportionate use of skilled scientific and engineering personnel in these functions rather than merely within existing firms.

Dosi *et al.* (1990) put their major emphasis on the role of innovation in the process of competitive evolution among firms. Although all the suggested measures of this activity are imperfect they all appear to indicate the same picture, namely a greater effort by German companies. The position over patents, shown in table 2.13, is that the number of patents granted in the US to German companies was twice that granted to UK companies in 1986 (compared with virtual parity thirty years earlier). (Patenting in the US as the largest market gives a good comparable indicator of valuable innovations in other countries.)

Patenting and R&D vary considerably across industries. Some are characterised by mature and only slowly developing technologies, whereas

Table 2.13 *Patents granted in the United States by country of origin as per cent of all foreign patenting 1958–86*

	1958	1965	1973	1979	1986
Canada	7.99	7.00	6.20	4.56	4.01
France	10.36	10.90	9.38	8.46	7.22
Germany	25.60	26.40	24.25	23.87	20.80
Japan	1.93	7.43	22.10	27.69	40.35
Switzerland	8.80	6.97	5.79	5.40	3.70
UK	23.45	20.62	12.56	10.07	7.37
Others	21.87	20.68	19.72	19.95	16.55

Source: Drawn from Dosi *et al.* (1990)

others show a continuing high rate of growth. Aggregration over industries is therefore misleading if one country has a much greater emphasis on innovation-intensive industries.

Only in specific cases, like that of pharmaceuticals, which we consider in detail in chapter 4, does the UK appear to have a clear lead. A similar picture exists for R&D expenditure. As chart 2.7 shows, R&D per head and patents per head conform quite closely to a straight line in logarithms.

Information on the existence of institutions for the transfer of technology is, however, much more sketchy. If we take the example of just one Land, Nord Rhein-Westfalen, admittedly one whose industrial structure is likely to reflect the highest levels of such activity, there are 155 such institutions employing 59,000 people in a region with a population of 17½ million.

Information on any area of human skills is worse than that for physical capital, not just because qualifications are difficult to compare internationally but because such skills and knowledge can depreciate very rapidly and their current value depends very much on the success with which they are kept up to date in the course of work. Such in-house training and learning-by-doing are not recorded in any systematic manner. Nevertheless, the particular case of the comparison of human skills in the UK and Germany has been a focus of research at NIESR (including the present authors – Hart and Shipman, 1991b).

The relative lack of vocational skills in the UK and the thorough vocational training and education system in Germany have been the subject of a series of studies at the NIESR, summarised in Prais *et al.* (1989). The German schooling system provides a broader curriculum, more pre-vocational instruction with commercial and industrial em-

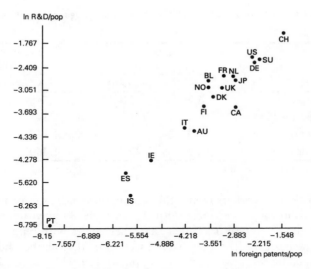

Key: CA = Canada, US = United States, JP = Japan, AU = Australia, BL = Belgium-Luxembourg, DK = Denmark, FI = Finland, FR = France, DE = Germany, IS = Iceland, IE = Ireland, IT = Italy, NL = The Netherlands, NO = Norway, PT = Portugal, ES = Spain, SU = Sweden, CH = Switzerland, UK = United Kingdom.

Chart 2.7 The relationship between foreign patent-intensity in the United States and national R&D intensity

Source: Dosi *et al.* (1990)

phasis and stronger links between German schools and vocational education institutions than in the UK. The German system has twin advantages. The first is that a much wider proportion of the labour force is trained (table 2.14).

The difference is particularly noticeable at the intermediate skill levels. A very similar proportion of the UK and German labour forces have degree level and related qualifications but as soon as we get to the general range of craft and other mainstream technical skills the two countries are completely different. Over half of German employees have such qualifications while only a quarter of UK employees do. Thus German employers have twice as large a pool of skilled labour to draw on. Conversely only 30 per cent of German employees have no qualifications while double that number have none in the UK. The typical UK worker is unqualified while his typical German counterpart does have qualifications. One advantage for the German employer is that there is no need

Table 2.14 *Qualification proportions and relative wage rates of the manufacturing workforce, 1987*

	Qualification proportions		Wage rates relative to unskilled	
	UK	Germany	UK	Germany
Higher level	6.7	6.0	1.748	2.218
Upper intermediate	4.4	8.2	1.345	1.710
Lower intermediate	26.3	56.4	1.165	1.176
No qualifications	62.6	29.4	1.000	1.000

Source: O'Mahony (1992)

to poach skilled workers from other companies and, as a result, companies can train their workforce with transferable skills without any great fear that their competitors rather than themselves will reap the benefit in subsequent years. The UK system by contrast discourages both universal and specific training. Hart and Shipman (1991b) found that labour turnover rates are higher in the UK than in Germany.

The second advantage of the German system lies in the nature of the training itself. By having a much higher proportion of formal skills, German trainees typically spend two days a week out of the factory acquiring these more general skills, and they are able to obtain qualifications which fit them to more responsibility. These skills involve the handling of mathematics, the ability to plan and to take decisions. In this way the typical German worker can be more flexible, maintaining as well as running machines, being able to make improving adjustments, for example. This flexibility is a key component of companies' ability to respond rapidly to pressures for change. Although much emphasis has been placed on labour market flexibility in the UK, much of this relates to shifts between firms. The ability to change within the firm is also important, particularly because much of the specific knowledge relating to the firm is still relevant despite the change of job or product. Hence the deadweight loss from the change is lower than when the employee has to switch firms.

To some extent, the quality of labour and the quality of capital go hand in hand as more sophisticated machines require more sophisticated labour to handle them. However, the more automated the process, the less the need for traditional craft skills and indeed the greater the ability to separate out the highly skilled programming tasks from the lower skilled operating requirements.

Prais and Wagner (1988) suggest that a simple indication of the worth of this extra training can be estimated from the wage differentials between

the various skill levels. Thus (table 2.14) the lower group of intermediate skills are worth around 17 per cent compared with no qualifications in both countries. The higher skills are, however, more highly
valued in Germany. Multiplying this through for the labour force as a
whole implies that qualifications add about 11 per cent to the value of
UK labour, while in Germany they add 23 per cent. This, of course, implies that the standards of basic education are also similar – a finding
challenged by Prais (1991), who argues that German education is also
clearly better. Again this is not so much a matter of the standards of the
best, which are comparable, but that much higher proportions of German schoolchildren attain high standards.

Since we are looking for the ability to change in the face of the single
market measures, these superior German abilities imply that Germany
is much better positioned. The difference in the quality of capital may
only be 12 per cent, but such marginal differences may be all that is
required for success in a competitive environment rather than failure.
Where the difference occurs is also of great importance. To quite a large
extent modern industries are knowledge-intensive rather than skill-
intensive in the traditional sense. This knowledge intensity relates not
just to the operation of the production process but to its organisation, to
the whole ability to innovate, design, develop and market new products. Stevenson (1980) argues that the rate of change depreciates the
stock of knowledge by about 7 per cent each year. Therefore, to offset
this, a very high rate of knowledge investment is required. The modern
firm needs to be able to handle massive amounts of information at relatively low levels of responsibility if it is not to be overwhelmed by the
process. This reflects the trend towards networking and towards more
horizontal rather than the traditional pyramid structures.

We have argued earlier about the importance of externalities in three
areas relating to physical capital, the pay-off from infrastructure, the importance of the network of local business services and economies of scope
in production and distribution. Similar arguments can be put forward
for human capital (Lucas, 1988), where the gain for the production
process comes not just from the skills of the individual but from the fact
that the firm can draw on the whole body of knowledge. This would
imply a more than proportionate pay-off from the German knowledge
advantage over the UK.

Productivity

The consequences of these differences in the extent and quality of

Table 2.15 *Productivity ratios, Germany/UK, 1987 (UK=100)*

	Per worker	Per worker-hour
Metal manufacture	96.1	110.8
Non-metallic mineral products	103.1	111.2
Chemicals	88.5	94.7
Metal products	118.4	131.4
Mechanical engineering	121.5	135.2
Electrical engineering	90.4	102.3
Vehicles	118.9	141.1
Instrument engineering	141.6	149.0
Food, drink & tobacco	114.1	106.8
Textiles	104.4	95.8
Clothing, footwear & leather	113.0	116.2
Timber & furniture	147.6	157.2
Paper & board	187.4	185.1
Rubber, plastics & other mfg.	114.1	120.0
Total manufacturing	112.7	121.8

Source: O'Mahony (1992)

physical and human capital are partly reflected in estimated productivity.

It is often suggested that UK industry is substantially less productive than its German counterparts (Hitchens *et al.*, 1990; Hooper and Larin, 1989; van Ark, 1990). Indeed with the possible exception of chemicals and textiles all sectors of German manufacturing do have higher output per worker hour (table 2.15). It is easy to exaggerate these differences but in 1987 output per worker hour in Germany was some 22 per cent higher than in the UK (O'Mahony, 1992). On a per worker basis the discrepancy is rather smaller, 13 per cent, and both fell further until the onset of the recession in the UK. These figures are based on a comparison of unit values in matched industries. If the exchange rate is used as a comparator (table 2.16) the discrepancy would appear to be over 45 per cent (figures for 1993 will show an even bigger discrepancy now that the exchange rate has fallen to around 2.50 DM/£). However, the exchange rate is influenced by many other factors as well as the price of manufactures so it is not the most suitable basis for comparing productivity. (Similarly, using purchasing power parities, which reflect consumption patterns, would give smaller ratios but these are also a less relevant basis for comparison of the output of manufacturing industry.)[8]

Table 2.16 *Comparative labour productivity in German and UK manu-facturing, 1987*

	Conversion factor (DM/£)	Output per worker (UK=100)	Output per hour (UK=100)
UVR	3.50	112.7	121.8
Exchange rate	2.94	134.0	144.9
Proxy PPP(a)	3.63	108.4	117.1

Source: O'Mahony (1992)
(a)Proxy PPP measured by weighting the 1985 PPPs for manufactured products by their shares in expenditure on manufactures in both countries.

Unit value ratios may underestimate the extent to which German productivity is higher than that in the UK if the nature of the product is different in the two countries. It is argued in National Institute studies of kitchen furniture (Steedman and Wagner, 1987), women's clothing (Steedman and Wagner, 1989) and biscuits (Mason *et al.* 1993) that the German industry focusses on higher quality, higher value-added products. The lower quality, mass production lines may permit higher productivity because less skilled intervention is required in the production process. In the case of biscuits for example, Mason *et al.* are able to show from their sample of plants across the UK, Germany, the Netherlands and France, that if plants are placed in one of three categories, according to whether they produce predominantly basic, medium or high quality biscuits, output per hour increases significantly (at the 5 per cent level) for each lower quality class. Unadjusted differences in productivity, which show a gap of 20 per cent in favour of the UK, become 40 per cent in favour of Germany when adjusted for quality. British plants also tend to be larger than their German counterparts. The estimates we have quoted above for the effect of differences in quality on productivity allow for the effect of economies of scale, which Mason *et al.* suggest are considerable, with a doubling of output leading on average to a 16 per cent increase in productivity.

We must not overgeneralise from this example, since on average German manufacturing plants are larger than those in the UK in terms of employment. Moreover, there is a tendency for German plants to remain effectively private companies, often still largely family owned, which tends to alter the style of management as well as the nature of the product and the production processes employed.

We have argued strongly that it is inappropriate to view productivity differentials and other structural discrepancies in purely static terms. The single market is imposed on an existing process of change. O'Mahony points out that over the twenty years up to 1987 there had been a clear trend to reduce productivity differences between the UK and Germany where the discrepancies are highest. The correlation between the ratio of German to UK productivity in 1968 and the rate of improvement in those ratios from the point of view of the UK in the period up to 1987 is 0.58. However, the way that improvement has come about is not so much that existing firms have improved their productivity markedly but that the industries have contracted sharply. Just taking the period 1979 to 1982 when the restructuring was fastest, employment decline had a correlation of 0.63 with the size of the improvement in the productivity ratio between 1968 and 1987.

The worry for the UK is that the structural change does not appear to have moved towards the higher productivity growth industries. O'Mahony concludes 'in the absence of structural change the ratio of German to UK output per head would have been about three percentage points *lower* in 1987 [compared with 1968]' (p.50, emphasis added). Both the UK and Germany have been increasing their production in sectors with above average productivity levels but the effect has been slightly stronger in Germany.

Inefficiency

Up to this point we have considered first of all the nature of the inputs to the productive process in the two countries. Their volume and quality go far to explaining the better current and potential performance of the German economy. O'Mahony (1992) suggests that 80 per cent of that differential is explained by the inputs of labour and capital alone. We have suggested that more of this may be explicable by differences in the provision of public and private infrastructure. Although much of the analysis has been undertaken at the aggregate level we have also noted that the structure of UK manufacturing industry leaves it at a further disadvantage. If anything the UK has been moving towards lower growth potential industries. However, it is not clear that these industries will also be those most favourably affected by the single market programme. Analysis in *European Economy* suggests, however, that there is a greater concentration in Germany on industries where the effect is likely to be favourable (chart 2.8 compared with table 2.17).

However, it is our hypothesis that the UK may be subject to further disadvantage. The framework that we have used thus far is akin to the

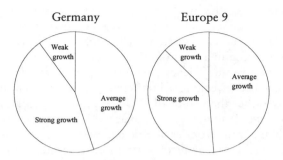

Chart 2.8 Position of the sensitive industries – allocation of employees by industries with different trends in European demand
Source: *European Economy*, Special Edition (1990)

Table 2.17 *Relative importance of sensitive sectors in the United Kingdom*

Group	Share in value added in mfg % (1987)	Share in mfg employ- ment % (1988)	Ratio of intra-EC to extra-EC imports (1987)	Intra-EC import penetration ratio % (1987)
High-tech public procurement markets	6.9	6.8	0.57	27.9
Traditional public procurement markets & regulated markets	8.7	3.6	2.25	5.5
Sectors facing competition from NICs	4.3	4.2	1.31	14.9
Sectors with moderate NTBs	32.6	35.5	1.31	29.2
Total of sensitive sectors	52.5	50.0	1.12	25.3
Total manufacturing	100.0	100.0	0.95	19.1

Source: *European Economy*, Special Edition (1990)

growth accounting approach. In effect it makes simple assumptions about the implicit form of the production function which explains output using the inputs of capital and labour. In practice differences can occur not just because of the quantity and quality of the inputs but because the form of the implicit production function (or rather sum of the individual industry functions) is different. The simplest difference would be due to technology or to the product mix. In this section we consider the possibility that actual production may be inefficient compared with that possible production function. That inefficiency may take the form of suboptimal combinations of the factors of production (normally labelled 'allocative inefficiency') or smaller than feasible outputs from the resources used (technical inefficiency), which should be treated dynamically rather than statically (Mayes et al. 1993). As was shown many years ago (Salter, 1966), apparent inefficiency can coexist with firms which are at the frontier of efficient performance. (We also explore inefficiency further in the next section in the context of what has been described as X-inefficiency, see Leibenstein, 1966, for example.)

We can show the usefulness of exploring this variation in productivity quite simply. In chart 2.9 the surface $ABCD$ represents the frontier of what can be produced with various combinations of capital, K, and labour, L. Firms normally operate inside that frontier, illustrated by the points x, using more capital and/or labour than is technically necessary to produce any given output, Y. We can compute average labour productivity $\Sigma(Y/L)/N$ where N is the number of plants in the industry but as the mean value of L/Y shows, the vertical line passing through 0, a difference between average productivity in the UK and Germany is only an imperfect guide to the position of the two production frontiers because it also includes inefficiency relative to the frontier. If the two countries already have similar frontiers then the one with the greater inefficiency of production has the opportunity to improve, as competitive pressures become harsher, without needing to embark on a major programme of investment to advance the frontier itself. Posed the other way round, the larger the dispersion of productivity in one country compared with the other then the larger the potential number of plants at risk when the two are brought together in a single market.

Rather than follow the full production function approach here, which would require us to have the data on individual plants to estimate the parameters of the functions, we look simply at the distribution of productivity in the two economies. Recently the results of a six nation (UK, US, Canada, Japan, Australia and South Korea) comparison of inefficiency using stochastic frontier production functions have been published in Caves et al. (1992) but it has not as yet been possible to include Germany in this analysis.[9]

However, the most convincing argument for our simple approach here is that the more complex production function approach met with only modest success for the UK (Mayes et al., 1993). We are, therefore, currently conducting a much more detailed analysis of the variation of

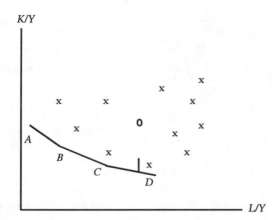

Chart 2.9 Farrell production frontier
Source: Hart and Shipman (1991a)

productivity across nearly 20,000 plants in the UK over the years 1980–90 looking at both approaches and their relative merits.[10] However, these results are not yet available to assist the analysis in the present book.

The chances are that the more skewed the distribution of plants by productivity and the longer the 'tail' of lower productivity, then the more inefficient will be the industry and the more difficult it will be for it to compete when the barriers to the single market are reduced. The different skewness could arise if the larger British and German firms in comparable industries had similar productivities while the small and medium sized British firms had lower productivities than their German counterparts. Evidence of the importance and strength of small and medium sized firms in Germany (Mittelstand) has been provided by Simon (1992) who investigated thirty-nine of these 'hidden champions'. Simon found that they 'have world market shares in the range of 70–90 per cent of their products and when combined they account for the bulk of Germany's considerable trade surplus'.

Unfortunately there are no published measures of skewness for the UK and Germany, although the raw data on which such calculations could be performed have been collected by the statistical authorities.[11]

Therefore, although we are currently undertaking an exercise with the CSO to estimate the dispersion of value-added per head in UK industry over the years 1980–90, we had to be content with a more indirect approach in order to obtain a matching comparison of British and German industry.[12] Data are available for Britain and Germany on

Table 2.18 *Metal-working machine tools. Distribution of German and UK businesses by employment 1987*

Employment (size class)	No. of businesses	Employment ('000s)	Value added	Value added/ employment
United Kingdom			*(£mn)*	*(£)*
1-9	2821	8.3		
10-19	509	7.4		
20-49	434	13.0	625.2	17364
50-99	107	7.4		
100-199	44	6.2	98.4	15930
200-299	19	4.6	73.3	15878
300-399	10	3.5	84.0	23945
400-749	7	3.4	51.5	15092
750 plus	4	3.4	51.8	15103
Total	3955	57.1	984.2	17221
Germany			*(DMmn)*	*(DMmn)*
20-49	371	12.7	970.8	76479
50-99	229	15.8	1325.1	83740
100-199	150	21.2	1727.7	81399
200-999	146	62.5	5718.7	91479
1000 plus	21	33.3	3137.8	94255
Total	917	145.5	12880.0	88495

Source: Hart and Shipman (1991a)

value-added and employment by employment size class, illustrated here for machine tools (table 2.18).

The figures in column 4 give estimates of average value-added per head weighted by employment. This measure is the most appropriate if we are interested in the number of jobs 'at risk' from the single market programme. Here our discussion has been rather more in terms of the number of firms, in which we want an unweighted average which we can obtain if we assume that net output per head and the number of employees are uncorrelated within each size class (see Hart and Shipman, 1992). We were able to compute both on a comparable basis for Britain and Germany for twenty-three industries shown in table 2.19. The ratios shown in the first two columns indicate whether German productivity exceeds that in Britain if they are normalised by an appropriate exchange rate. We show two in the table: that derived by O'Mahony (1992) on the basis of unit

Table 2.19 *Ratio of German to British nominal labour productivity (weighted and unweighted) in selected industries, 1987*

Industry	W(G)/W(B)	U(G)/U(B)	Unit value exchange rate
	(DM per £)		
221 Iron & steel	2.32*	2.87*	} 3.19
223 Steel rolling etc.	4.47	4.29	
247 Glass	3.92	4.26	2.87
256 Agricultural chemicals	2.85*	3.37**	} 3.54
257 Pharmaceuticals	3.58	5.00	
312 Steel forging etc.	4.97	5.08	3.19
321 Agricultural machines	3.96	4.33	
322 Machine tools	5.15	4.74	
323 Textile machines	5.26	4.99	
324 Food machines	3.25**	3.37	} 3.35
326 Transmission equipment	4.49	4.64	
327 Printing etc. machines	4.69	4.21	
328 Misc. machines	4.38	4.44	
341 Wire & cable	3.89**	3.36**	} 4.67
344 Telecoms equipment	4.39**	4.05**	
346 Domestic electrical appls	4.82	4.33	4.31
352 Motor vehicle bodies	4.53	4.55	} 3.82
353 Motor vehicle parts	5.01	5.12	
412 Meat products	3.38**	3.08**	4.15
453 Clothing, etc.	6.04	5.38	4.17
461 Wood processing	4.39	4.74	1.55
462 Semi-finished wood	2.56*	1.31*	2.65
481 Rubber products	4.06	4.15	3.80

* British productivity exceeds German productivity at spot and unit-value exchange rates.
** British productivity exceeds German productivity at unit-value rate only.
(a) Average daily spot rate for DM per £ 1987: 2.95.

values for the two industries and the average spot rate for the year 2.95DM/£. Up till September 1992 that was also the central rate in the ERM grid.

Only in three cases (iron and steel, agricultural chemicals and semi-finished wood) did average British productivity exceed that for Germany according to both exchange rates. German ratios were generally higher, with the highest ratios being for clothing etc. The rankings according to the weighted (W) and unweighted (U) measures are similar. Both countries have eighteen instances of $W > U$ and only five of $W < U$. Of these seventeen are for the same industries in the two countries, fifteen being in the $W > U$ category. If W is greater than U then productivity is higher in the larger businesses.

We can now obtain an indicator of the relative inefficiency of the plants in the two countries by looking at the dispersion of productivity in each industry. Because of the weighted form in which the data are published we cannot estimate s, the standard deviation, separately, only the product rs (Hart and Shipman, 1992) where r is the correlation between productivity and size of employment. The fifteen industries shown in table 2.20 have positive r for both Britain and Germany; (rs/U) is shown because it removes the problems of differences in units of measurement between Britain and Germany. In eight cases the BSO were also able to compute r for these industries, shown in column 2. In seven out of the eight cases r is close to unity so it would not be unreasonable to use rs/U as a measure of the coefficient of variation of productivity.[13] We cannot of course say what the result would be for the other industries. However, if we do make the assumption that this comparison is representative there seems to be a fairly even split between cases where British industry is more dispersed than its German counterpart and *vice versa*. This evidence is similar to that found in the comparisons of inefficiency in Caves *et al.* (1992) and Mayes *et al.* (1993), where even though average productivity may have varied markedly between the US and Japan or the UK and Australia, average dispersion was much more similar and did not indicate a relation between the productivity differential and inefficiency.[14]

We therefore expect that the relative vulnerability of industries to the single market programme will vary considerably. The extreme case of pharmaceuticals probably ought to be discarded because only three size classes were available to make the German estimates (see Hart and Shipman, 1992). Among the remainder, steel forging, food machinery, miscellaneous machines and motor vehicle bodies and parts seem to conform to the hypothesis that the best firms may be at the frontier and that the lower average productivity observed in the UK is due to a longer tail of less efficient firms (as in these cases UK dispersion is greater but average productivity lower). Note also that, because of the positive correlation between size and productivity, it is the larger firms that tend to be more efficient, although this may merely represent economies of scale.

Table 2.20 *Distribution of firms by labour productivity, Q/L, within matched British and German industries with W > U, 1987*

	Britain		Germany	Britain/
	rs/U	*r*	*rs/U*	Germany
223 Steel rolling etc.	0.016	-	0.023	0.67
247 Glass	0.139	0.944	0.150	0.93
257 Pharmaceuticals	0.206	0.940	0.004	51.40
312 Steel forging etc.	0.048	-	0.038	1.27
324 Food machines	0.099	0.722	0.064	1.55
327 Printing machines etc.	0.015	0.946	0.088	0.17
328 Misc. machines	0.046	-	0.038	1.21
344 Telecoms equipment	0.027	0.949	0.065	0.42
346 Domestic electrical appliances	0.015	0.959	0.050	0.30
352 Motor vehicle bodies	0.073	-	0.069	1.06
353 Motor vehicle parts	0.021	0.931	0.010	2.08
453 Clothing etc.	0.020	0.929	0.068	0.29
461 Wood processing	0.071	-	0.004	17.29
462 Semi-finished wood	0.315	-	0.054	5.83
481 Rubber products	0.061	-	0.081	0.75

Source: Hart and Shipman (1992)

Semi-finished wood products had both a higher average and a higher dispersion but the remaining seven industries had both a lower mean and a lower dispersion. This must make us *prima facie* less confident about their ability to compete with German firms in the single market as these industries lack firms near the frontier. Competitiveness therefore would need to be improved right across the whole industry in these cases.

It is difficult to find other measures which will support or refute these conclusions. In Hart and Shipman (1991a) we explored the possibility that profitability might provide a key. In the event of pressure on an industry it tends to be the low profitability firms which have the greatest difficulty in responding and indeed tend to go out of business first. In most industries in our sample (table 2.21) large firms have below average profitability. (Note that this is a very broad definition of profitability computed by subtracting the wage and salary element from value-added.) Of course, if the small firms are niche players and the large firms are in a much more cut-throat mass market these figures are perfectly consistent with a viable industry. However, there must be some worry where

Table 2.21 *Profitability of large businesses relative to average profitability,* 1987

Industry	Britain	Germany
221 Iron & steel	1.00	0.63
223 Steel rolling etc.	0.82	0.90
247 Glass	1.05	1.02
256 Specialised chemicals	0.96	0.96
257 Pharmaceuticals	0.80	0.96
312 Steel forging etc.	1.02	1.00
321 Agricultural machines	1.04	0.83
322 Machine tools	0.96	0.97
323 Textile machines	0.42	0.97
324 Food machines	0.87	1.00
326 Transmission equipment	0.58	0.87
327 Printing etc. machines	1.06	1.05
328 Miscellaneous machines	1.19	0.97
341 Wire & cable	0.87	0.87
344 Telecoms equipment	0.93	0.97
346 Domestic electrical appls	0.96	0.97
352 Motor vehicle bodies	0.99	0.97
353 Motor vehicle parts	0.83	0.96
412 Meat & by-products	0.95	0.93
453 Clothing etc.	0.84	1.05
461 Wood processing etc.	1.12	1.02
462 Semi-finished wood	0.69	0.85
481 Rubber products	1.05	1.00

Source: Hart and Shipman (1991a)

large firms have below average profitability and productivity in industries where average productivity is also lower than in Germany. This covers steel rolling, drawing and cold forming, machine tools, textile machinery, transmission equipment, motor vehicle parts and clothing, hats and gloves.

To complete the picture we cross-classified these indicators of vulnerability with the forty manufacturing industries regarded as 'sensitive' by the Commission in Buigues *et al.* (1990) (table 2.22). Here, strength, measured on a scale of −4 to +4 with an average of 0, relies on trade performance and production specialisation. German performance

Table 2.22 *Competitive position of sample industries regarded as 'sensitive' to the European single market*

Industry	Score	
	Britain	Germany
247 Glass	-4	-1
256 Specialised chemicals (a)	4	N/A
257 Pharmaceuticals	4	-2
321 Agricultural machines	0	3
322 Machine tools	-3	4
323 Textile machines	-4	4
324 Food machines	-3	4
326 Transmission equipment	1	4
327 Printing etc. machines	-2	4
328 Miscellaneous machines (a)	3	N/A
341 Wires & cables (a)	0	N/A
344 Telecoms equipment	4	2
346 Domestic electrical appls	-4	2
453 Clothing etc.	-3	-4
481 Rubber products	-1	-2

Source: Hart and Shipman (1991a)
(a) Industry classed as 'sensitive' in UK only.

is superior to the British in eight out of the fifteen industries (in three there is no match so only four show British superiority). Productivity is also higher than in Britain for these eight industries as it is in the four which show British superior performance. This could have a number of explanations. The simplest might be that smaller firms in the industries have been effectively protected. In any event the inferiority of British labour productivity in thirteen out of fifteen of the sensitive industries must be a cause for concern. We have, therefore, deliberately chosen two industries at different points in this spectrum, machine tools and pharmaceuticals, for more detailed study to explore how far this disadvantage may actually extend (chapters 6 and 4).

Ownership and organisation

Although much of the variation in productivity and indeed in inefficiency can be explained by conventional measures relating to the quality and quantity of inputs, the structure and openness of the industry, the degree of product differentiation and the separability of markets, a substantial residual remains – often referred to as X-efficiency following the work of Leibenstein (1966). This is usually interpreted as being related to factors involved in the organisation of the firm, inefficiency not inherent in the factors of production. However, this is complicated when we are considering more than one country as it represents not just differences between firms but also differences in intangible factors which apply at a national level. These are not just static factors but relate to the organisation of the firm and indeed the industry in the longer run.

Corporate governance

A large portion of this concern relates to how companies are run – to corporate governance. Some of this can be ascribed to the external framework, control over restrictive practices, control over exercise of dominant position and control over forms of trading through regulations on terms and conditions, product specifications, prices, and so on. Much of the rest of it relates to the management of the company itself. Although elementary textbooks talk about the pressure of competition, the practice is that not all companies are aggressively pursuing every competitive opportunity and are able to sustain this form of behaviour. In PEP (1965) these different groups were characterised as 'thrusters' and 'sleepers'. It was argued that if an economy is characterised rather more by thrusters then it will tend to grow faster. This thrusting behaviour involves not just a higher rate of return but a higher risk and this is the main reason why firms avoid it.

It is widely argued that there is a second reason why UK firms opt for a lower combination of risk and return, namely, 'short-termism'. UK firms, it is suggested, always face the threat that they might be taken over if their stock market performance appears weak.

The threat of takeover

The hostile takeover bid is in this view part of what can be described as part of the 'market for corporate control' in which different management teams compete for the right to manage a company by offering more attractive terms to the shareholders. The threat of a takeover has replaced the voting of shareholders at annual general meetings as the major method of supervising the incumbent management of a company (Fairburn and Kay, 1989)[15] and thereby trying to ensure its profitable development.

By contrast German managers are protected against takeovers by a legal and institutional bulwark and are able to concentrate on internal growth through fixed capital formation. They are also able to take a longer view and therefore spend more on investment, training, and research than their British counterparts.[16] This ability to replace inefficient management can be viewed as an advantage of the UK (Anglo-Saxon) system.

The shareholders can exert pressure on management – not only through the annual meeting when directors are technically appointed but also through their representatives on the board – the equivalent of 'voice' in public choice theory, or they can vote with their feet by selling their shares on the open market ('exit'). Dissatisfied shareholders can seek a buyer. One who thinks it could put in a better management team, and get a higher rate of return on the assets, may bid for the shares.

The drawback is that this a rather blunt instrument for achieving change. Most shareholders are small and can exercise very little concerted power. Those with the power are dominated by insurance companies and pension funds who have an interest in the company as an investment rather than as a beneficiary from its success as a producer. The German system is rather different. A much smaller proportion of companies is publicly traded and even so the real opportunity for purchase of the company as a whole is more limited than it might appear as major shareholders are usually reluctant to sell because they have a longer-term stake in the company. German companies tend to be privately held, sometimes with banks playing a much stronger role in their running. A German company which gets into difficulties stands a good chance of being rescued by its shareholders rather than being taken over.[17]

However, much of the explanation for this lies in the way in which the company is managed. This may stem from the two-tier structure of the board, where the stakeholders in the company, including the workforce, have a guaranteed position. It may also stem from the relationship between the main shareholders and the management. As a result German companies are far less dependent on external funds in trying to develop. It therefore appears to be easier to generate the resources for development and innovation. This is not, however, thought to be to the same extent as in Japan, where companies are said to take an even longer view and be prepared to aim more for growth and market share rather than for short-term profitability. Nevertheless there is some similarity in the way in which there is a flexible network of companies built up which will act together to bid for contracts and exploit economies of scope.

The belief that British companies are biased towards obtaining short-term results may be widespread, but that does not mean that it is

Table 2.23 *Numbers of and expenditure on acquisitions and mergers of industrial and commercial companies within the UK, 1967–90*

Annual averages	Number	Expenditure £mn	Expenditure as % of gross fixed capital formation
1969-73	988	1388	38.6
1974-81	459	947	7.7
1982-5	488	4278	20.1
1986-9	1301	20500	48.8
1986	842	15370	50.7
1987	1527	16539	44.8
1988	1499	22836	49.1
1989	1336	27253	50.6

Source: Hughes (1991)

correct. Littlechild (1989, pp. 310–11) thinks that it is a myth and cites evidence that in the United States acquired companies do little research and development. He also notes that in Britain merging companies have higher post-merger growth rates than do non-merging companies. But in the same volume George (1989, p. 286) quotes examples of British companies subjected to takeover bids when their share prices were depressed because they were in the middle of expensive reorganisation programmes to improve their long-term competitiveness.

Cosh, Hughes and Singh (1990) note that the average profitability of merging firms does not improve after merger, which counters the growth argument of Littlechild (1989). They also report on their interviews with seventeen financial institutions (four major insurance companies, four large self-managed pension funds, the investment arms of four merchant banks and three clearing banks, a stockbroking firm and a major unit trust) which revealed that all were becoming more short-term oriented. Another survey of the finance directors of 215 major companies by 3i plc (1992) showed that most of the respondents thought that their companies were biased towards short-term results at the expense of investment and long-term performance.

Contributions to this debate made by Ball (1991) and Williams (1991) suggest that even if there is no conclusive evidence that City financial institutions are biased against companies with long-term research programmes, industrialists think that they are and opt for short-term results to protect their share prices. This belief may be wrong, but it is very

Table 2.24 *Annual percentage external and internal growth rates of companies, UK, 1960–76*

		All industries	Manu-facturing	Chemicals	Retailing
1960-5	External	3.41	3.26	2.7	5.3
	Internal	4.51	4.17	4.1	5.8
1966-71	External	4.91	4.66	3.9	2.8
	Internal	3.95	3.54	4.5	4.2
1972-6	External	3.82	3.37	3.1	3.4
	Internal	5.27	4.51	5.2	7.5

Source: Kumar (1984), table 4.1, p.53

powerful nevertheless. After all, much of the incumbent directors' expertise is specific to their companies so their loss of earnings on being ousted is likely to be very large. Statistics of hostile bids underestimate the perceived risk of hostile takeover because British companies concentrate on short-term optimisation in order to avoid potential takeover raiders.

There are two consequences of this difference in behaviour in the context of the single market. The first is that UK companies may find it more difficult to undertake the scale of investment and concerted period of change necessary to respond fully. The second is that it is highly likely that UK companies will continue to use takeovers and mergers – external growth – much more frequently as a route to expansion, rather than internal growth, compared with their German counterparts. The initial signs of this are already occurring (table 2.23) with mergers and acquisitions in 1986–9 running at a much higher level than in the 1970s and early 1980s (Hughes, 1991). Nevertheless, internal growth has tended to be more important than external, even in the UK (table 2.24).[18]

Mergers and acquisitions in Britain and Germany

In recent years acquisitions by overseas companies have also risen in the UK, thus adding to the takeover risk perceived by British management. Between 1988 and 1989 the number of acquisitions in Britain by other European Community countries increased from thirty-one to sixty-one (table 2.25) and the value of such acquisitions increased from £1.16

Table 2.25 *Cross-border acquisitions and mergers in Britain by overseas companies, £bn*

Country of acquirer	1988		1989		1991		1992	
	No.	Value	No.	Value	No.	Value	No.	Value
France	12	0.72	31	2.30	21	0.32	25	0.32
Germany	5	0.07	10	1.21	15	0.35	19	0.50
Netherlands	2	0.29	4	0.04	7	0.52	11	0.16
Other EC	12	0.08	16	0.43	18	0.56	35	0.14
Total EC	*31*	*1.16*	*61*	*3.98*	*61*	*1.75*	*90*	*1.12*
North America	27	0.90	44	4.86	44	3.13	66	1.46
Switzerland	5	2.70	8	0.16	2	0.48	7	0.02
Rest of world	31	0.94	59	2.28	40	1.31	38	0.87
Total	*94*	*5.70*	*172*	*11.28*	*147*	*6.67*	*201*	*3.47*

Source: 1987–9: DTI (1990), *Companies in 1989–90*; 1991–92: CSO Bulletin Issue 21/93, March 1993

Table 2.26 *Cross-border acquisitions and mergers by British companies, £bn*

Country of acquirer	1988		1989		1991		1992	
	No.	Value	No.	Value	No.	Value	No.	Value
France	41	0.56	69	0.37	50	0.24	49	0.84
Germany	34	0.27	53	0.50	44	0.60	39	0.27
Netherlands	40	0.48	53	0.67	42	1.65	39	0.45
Other EC	76	0.45	95	1.02	72	1.35	90	0.86
Total EC	*191*	*1.76*	*270*	*2.56*	*208*	*3.84*	*217*	*2.42*
North America	311	14.21	296	19.81	160	4.39	146	2.26
Rest of world	104	1.34	109	1.41	182	1.46	196	1.66
Total	*606*	*17.31*	*675*	*23.78*	*550*	*9.69*	*559*	*6.34*

Source: CSO Bulletin Issue 21/93, March 1993

billion to £3.98 billion. However, this is not just a European phenomenon. In 1989 acquisitions by North American companies were even more important at £4.86 billion. The total value of acquisitions in Britain by overseas companies in 1989 was £11.28 billion, which may be compared with the 1989 domestic expenditure on acquisitions of £22.25 billion in table 2.23. Although the rate of acquisition fell between 1989 and 1992, this external threat persists.[19]

Cross-border acquisition activity is not only one-way: British companies acquire and merge with companies overseas. Tables 2.26 and 2.27

Table 2.27 *Mergers involving foreign parties notified to the federal cartel offices in Germany, 1973–89*

Year	No. of mergers
1973	34
1974	294
1975	445
1976	453
1977	554
1978	558
1979	602
1980	635
1981	618
1982	603
1983	506
1984	575
1985	709
1986	802
1987	887
1988	1159
1989	1415

show that in 1988–92 the *number* of German companies acquired by British firms exceeded the number of British companies acquired by German firms. But in 1989 the *value* of the German acquisitions was higher at £1.21 billion in table 2.26 compared with the £0.5 billion in table 2.25 and in 1992 the value of German acquisitions was also higher than the value of British acquisitions.

The most striking figure in table 2.26 is the large number and value of acquisitions of North American companies made by British firms. There are many economic and cultural reasons for this, but readily accessible information for valuation is one important explanation. If it is easier for company A to value company B than to value company C, then A is more likely to bid for B than for C. More information is available on British and American companies than on German companies, partly as a result of the requirements of the British and American stock markets, and hence a British company is more likely to try to acquire an American company than a German one where market prospects are thought similar. It is true that a common language reinforces this tendency but this must not be given too much emphasis; even a poor linguist can quickly understand the figures of a foreign country, especially when money is involved. Fundamental informational deficiencies, such as the lack of published consolidated accounts (that is, of the parent plus all subsidiary companies) are more important. The likelihood of a British company being taken over is also helped by an efficient British stock market on which the required finance can be raised readily enough if the takeover is deemed profitable. While it is not possible to compute similar figures for Germany, it is possible to show (table 2.27) that mergers and acquisitions have increased markedly following a fairly stable period between 1977 and 1984, nearly trebling the 1983 figures in 1989.

As our focus in this section is on the importance of institutional and organisational differences in the two countries, it is worth developing this difference in company structure and its consequences in rather more detail.

Corporate governance in Germany

In the case of Germany, we must distinguish between the *Aktiengesellschaft* (AG), or stock corporation, and the *Gesellschaft mit beschränkter Haftung* (GmbH), or limited liability company. The AG is larger than the GmbH and more closely corresponds to the British public company. But there are only 545 AGs with a stock exchange quotation (plus ninety-four in the unlisted securities market) and only about thirty large AGs do not have majorities of voting shares controlled by a parent company, families or other institutions (particularly banks) closely linked to incumbent management. The scope for a hostile takeover is extremely limited.

Each AG appoints two boards of directors: a managing board (*Vorstand*) and a supervisory board (*Aufsichtsrat*). The members of the *Aufsichtsrat* are elected by the employees and the shareholders of the AG, with the chairman being elected by the shareholders. The *Aufsichtsrat* has the power to appoint and dismiss members of the *Vorstand* and also fixes their salaries. It can monitor the general performance of the AG and can obtain any information from the *Vorstand*, including future business policies, which it desires.

A GmbH does not normally issue shares and must have an *Aufsichtsrat* in addition to a *Vorstand* only if its employment regularly exceeds 500. Clearly it cannot be taken over by a hostile predator because there is no market access to its shares. Whether an AG has such immunity is still controversial, though most British observers think that the strong representation of the banks on the supervisory boards acts as a barrier to hostile takeovers.[20]

A takeover raider would be deterred by the fact that he could not easily remove the members of the *Aufsichtsrat*, especially those elected by the employees, and thus could not control the *Vorstand* even if he acquired a simple majority of the shares. This is because the removal of those members elected by the shareholders has traditionally required a 75 per cent majority. Members of an *Aufsichtsrat* can have staggered periods of office of five years and so the raider could not plan to make his hostile bid at a time when they were all due for re-election. The attitudes of German banks, especially if they are shareholders and have representatives on the *Aufsichtsrat*, would also tend to be opposed to a takeover raider. The two-tiered board system and the influence of the German banks reinforce the barriers to takeover.

In recent years this barrier has been reduced because many AGs have changed their bye-laws to allow a simple majority, rather than a 75 per cent majority, to determine the vote on a merger. Thus in these AGs a 25 per cent holding by a bank or anyone else can no longer block a merger. Again the common bye-law that no shareholder may cast more than 5 per cent of the votes, irrespective of the size of his shareholding, can be suspended by the shareholders if they wish to encourage a bid. Otto (1991) uses these arguments to support his thesis that the reason why there are hardly any hostile takeovers in Germany is because potential acquirers believe that they are very difficult, if not impossible, and this myth is self-perpetuating. But the evidence of Immenga (1993), together with that of North and Mollett (1989) cited in Hart (1992a), outweighs the arguments of Otto. The system of corporate governance in Germany deters hostile takeovers and this is reinforced by complex cross-shareholdings, by the voting power (including proxy votes) of the German banks, by the absence of accessible data on target companies and by the general business culture in Germany. The interests of the AG are not automatically equated with the short-term interests of its shareholders: the long-term interests of the AG through its research and development programme and the long-term interests of its employees through its training programmes are not neglected as they are in Britain.

The indirect influence of banks is also important and arises from the proxy votes of shareholders. Share dealings normally take place through the banks, with most undertaken through the big three, Deutsche, Dresdner and Commerz. It is natural for shareholders to assign proxy votes to their banks, through which they purchased their shares and which can be relied upon to act responsibly. These proxy votes are assigned to the banks for a limited time (*Depotstimmrecht*) but they may be exchanged between banks as loaned votes (*Stimmenleihe*) without referring to the shareholders should a bank wish to increase its voting power in a particular meeting of an *Aufsichtsrat*. To give an indication of the degree of control exercised by German banks, Shonfield (1965) states that in 1960 they controlled 70 per cent of a sample of companies which constituted 75 per cent of the nominal values of all shares quoted on the stock market. Moreover, the banks invariably provided the chairmen or vice-chairmen of the supervisory boards.

Subsequent research by Bannock (1981) qualified these results. He showed that the direct shareholdings of German banks ranged between 7.3 and 7.9 per cent of quoted shares over the years 1971–8. But when their proxy votes were added to their own votes as shareholders, German banks still commanded 60 per cent of the voting rights in 1977. Even so, there was no instance where one bank by itself was able to control more than 50 per cent of the votes in any of the largest seventy-four companies and these giants accounted for 84 per cent of the total stock market equity capitalisation.

Nevertheless, it is fair to say that in Germany the internal growth of companies is fostered by the banks. A German businessman expects his bank to have an intimate knowledge of his business, which it does in fact have as a result of its extensive technical (including engineering) expertise.[21] The network of bank representation on the *Aufsichtsräte* of AGs facilitates the transfer of technical information and is particularly helpful in influencing the timing of investment. Expensive mistakes from unnecessary duplication or from inappropriate investment can be reduced.

Cable (1985) stresses the importance of this flow of information in producing efficiency. In Britain there are information asymmetries and imperfections which arise between borrowers and lenders and which can result in credit rationing and onerous lending terms. In Germany the banks' representation on the *Aufsichtsräte* reduces these asymmetries and imperfections. It might also reduce the transactions costs of changing or constraining managerial decision-making in accordance with shareholders' wishes. Cable's empirical research supports the thesis that the close involvement of a company with a bank tends to increase its profitability.

North and Mollett (1989) are partners in Coopers and Lybrand and reported on a study carried out by their firm into barriers to take-over in the European Community. Up to the time of their article, they claim there had never been a successful major contested takeover in Germany.[22] They attribute this to the two-tiered board which delays change, to the proxy votes held by the banks, to the influence of the big three banks, and to the fact that a company may restrict the voting power of any shareholding (irrespective of size) to 5 per cent.

They also cite important differences in business culture. In the European countries outside Britain the possibility of predators seizing control of companies without regard to companies' interests is considered unethical. There is also an even greater emphasis on the confidentiality of business information than in Britain. A potential British acquirer of a German company is likely to be refused access to its employees or premises until a binding contract is signed, which can make pre-purchase investigations very difficult.

Again, as Immenga (1993) reminds us, there is no German equivalent to the centralised British company registration office. In Germany there are company registration offices for each locality in which the head office is situated. Furthermore, the widespread use of bearer shares also makes it difficult to establish the ownership of companies. While it is true that EC directives have made German companies prepare financial statements broadly in line with those compiled by British companies, the fact remains that a substantial number of German companies do not comply with the filing requirements. The local Commercial Registers in Germany do not have sufficient powers to enforce compliance.

Implications for internal and external growth by British and German companies

The general thrust of all these studies is that in Germany the internal growth of companies is much more important than their external growth and that this will continue to be the case after 1992. The barriers to takeovers in Germany will remain strong as a result of their different company law, of their different banking tradition, and of their different business culture. Shonfield (1965) claims that while German businessmen welcome private enterprise, they have never accepted the idea that Adam Smith's hidden hand should be relied upon to determine the growth of their firms. They have a tradition – dating back to Imperial Germany – of an organised private enterprise rather than a free-for-all fight in the market place.

The question arises, 'Is this tradition still maintained?' The studies outlined above suggest that it is. But there are important qualifications to this conclusion, to which we now turn.

Mayer and Alexander (1990) compared the financing of the largest 115 corporations (excluding banks and other financial institutions) quoted on the stock markets of Britain and Germany. Over the period 1982–8 the German firms raised 89.6 per cent of their gross finance from retentions, compared with the 58.2 per cent raised by the British firms. British firms paid out more of their profits in dividends (28.1 per cent in 1987 compared with the German 6.5 per cent). Because of their higher pay-out ratios,[23] the large British corporations have to raise more external finance to fund any given level of investment. They are able to do this by raising more new equity finance on the stock market than do the German firms. But they also spend more of it on takeovers. It does not appear that the largest British firms suffer from any financial disadvantage through not having a German-type banking system; they have ready access to a large and efficient stock market.

Edwards and Fischer (1991) show that for the non-financial enterprise sector as a whole the sources of funds in Britain and Germany were similar and both were quite different from Japan. Over the period 1970–85, German non-financial enterprises raised 12.5 per cent (net) and 21.5 per cent (gross) of their investment finance from banks and insurance companies. The corresponding figures for British non-financial enterprises were 12.7 per cent and 22.4 per cent. There is no evidence that bank loans are a more important source of finance for German non-financial enterprises than for the British. In any case, the major source in both countries is retentions.

The figures also show that for AGs in manufacturing over this period bank borrowing was a very small (less than 2 per cent) source of finance for investment. Retentions were by far the most important sources.[24] Bank loans were more important for the smaller German firms without *Aufsichtsräte*. This does not appear to support the thesis that bank representation on the supervisory boards reduces asymmetric information and encourages more bank lending.

According to these authors the direct AG shareholdings of German banks are small (of the order of 10.3 per cent in 1984 and 11.6 per cent in 1988) and certainly insufficient to control the voting at shareholders' meetings. But they confirm the importance of the banks' use of proxy votes, especially by the big three. But the big three banks do not dominate the loan market and AGs may borrow from many banks besides the big three. Hence the extent of the influence of the big three banks must not be exaggerated. Of course other routes of finance such as leasing may also draw on funds from the big three banks even though the lessor may be largely independent.

They cite the work of Gerum (1987) who found that in 86 per cent of the 281 AGs they studied the supervisory board met only twice a year, the legal minimum. This does not appear to be frequent enough to monitor the management board very closely. They also examined the articles of incorporation of these AGs and found that in 37 per cent of cases these articles did not stipulate that any management board decision required supervisory board consent. In these AGs, the two-tiered board system does not appear to provide an insurmountable barrier to take-over.

It is easy to exaggerate the role of larger firms, although we have noted the significant role played in Germany by the Mittelstand, smaller firms (Simon, 1992), particularly in exports. However, venture capital plays a much greater role in the UK than elsewhere in Europe, including Germany. In 1992, 30 per cent of the EC total was raised in the UK (Ecu 1¼bn) compared with 20 per cent in Germany. This reflects, on the one hand, the ease with which German companies can get finance from other sources and, on the other, the relative reluctance of German companies to form alliances (Audretsch, 1993). In the case of technological advance this is reflected with greater tendency to use government supported research and technology transfer institutes like Max Planck or Fraunhofer.

There are barriers to hostile takeovers even in Britain. Small companies in which shareholdings are still concentrated in the ownership of the founding families are obviously protected against hostile takeovers. Very large companies in the past have had a very low probability of being taken over, although the takeovers of Rowntree, the Imperial Group, Distillers, and Britoil show that large size does not always provide a takeover barrier (Cosh, Hughes and Singh 1990). Even the medium-sized quoted companies, which have been most vulnerable in the past, can introduce constraints on takeover in the form of 'poison pills' or 'golden parachutes' such as triggering the sale of key parts of the company or payment of expensive severance packages to prominent executives if the acquisition is successful. The result is that the chance of a hostile bid for a company listed on the stock market was 32/116 or 27.6 per cent in 1985 and 52/211 or 24.6 per cent in 1986, according to Franks and Mayer (1990b). Moreover, only sixteen of the thirty-two hostile bids in 1985, and twenty-one of the fifty-two hostile bids in 1986 were successful. Thus the managements of the companies targeted by predators can certainly defend themselves.[25]

Such defence is expensive in terms of management time and also in consultancy fees. The expenses of the raiders are just as large so that the total transactions costs of hostile takeovers, which have to be offset against any gains in managerial efficiency in the market for corporate control, are important. Hughes (1989) cites the case of one unsuccessful bid in 1986 which is thought to have cost the raider £54 million in advisers' and other bid fees. Franks and Harris (1989) quote Kay's earlier estimate of £500 million in annual fees to third parties in the merger process and suggest that in 1985 the transactions costs of mergers, excluding the management costs of the companies involved, were some 7 per cent of the total value of acquisitions. The net managerial gains may or may not be positive; they are very difficult to estimate because they depend on what would have happened in the absence of the takeover activity. We know that hostile takeovers rarely occur in Germany and that the average economic performance of German firms is superior to that of British firms.[26] But it could be argued that the productivity gap between Germany and Britain would be even larger if the less efficient of the British managers were not kept on their toes by the threat of takeover.

The role of the bank can be particularly important in the case of a company in difficulty. To quote Prais (1981, p. 43), 'the German bank, with its staff of industrial advisers, normally takes an active role in reviving the company by appointing new boards of directors, providing managerial advice and refinancing. In some cases the shares are sold again as soon as the company is in good shape, in others the shares are retained; the banks thus act as both industrial investors and industrial financiers. Whatever else may happen, an event such as the failure of the British Rolls-Royce company is regarded as inconceivable in Germany.' Thus German banks not only have the industrial expertise required to revive a company, they are prepared to use it and to provide the necessary finance.

On balance, the evidence summarised in Fairburn and Kay (1989) supports the view that takeover activity in Britain may have been too large. The likely benefits of takeovers tend to be overestimated by the acquirers.[27] Even with a market for corporate control, the economic performance of British companies has been inferior to that of German companies. The implication is that the system of corporate control in Germany will therefore provide competitive advantage for German companies over British companies in the single European market.

Other aspects of firm structure and performance

We have placed extensive emphasis on the organisational differences between British and German firms because this is crucial to assessing the means of response to the single market available for existing companies. However, it is but one illustration of the much wider contribution that institutional differences and accepted ways of reacting make to generating differing responses in the two countries.

Great emphasis is laid in the modern American literature on the culture of the company and on the involvement and motivation of the workforce. This is certainly thought to be an explanation of Japanese success (Mayes and Ogiwara, 1992). The process of consultation which is required for German companies may assist this. Certainly, successful experience with Japanese transplants in the UK shows that weak performance in the UK does not stem especially from the workforce, despite the problems with vocational training that we have outlined. Some have argued (Prais, 1981 and Oulton, 1987) that trade union practices have appeared to restrain progress in some larger firms in the UK, particularly in the more traditional industries. However, the problem does appear to lie firmly with management and the framework in which it operates.

This emphasis on framework is particularly important in the current context as the single market is likely to break down some traditional national frameworks as a result of the expected 'competition among rules'. Corporate governance is only part of the German framework aided by a more heavily regulated economy and a system of wage bargaining which is more consensual, allowing both more rapid response to adverse external shocks and lower unemployment levels than most of the rest of Europe in achieving low inflation. It has been argued (Hager *et al.*, 1993) that the higher level of regulation, whether on environmental or social protection, acts as an incentive to German firms to achieve greater efficiency and competitiveness. However, in part the success of the German system has come because it is different from that of its competitors (Mayes *et al.*, 1993). If all EC countries had followed the same strategies then the heavily regulated system would have led to a much more deflationary outcome.

We had hoped to study enough companies in detail in this project to be able draw some conclusions about the nature of differences in X-efficiency in the two countries and to offer explanations of them but demands on resources from the unification of Germany meant that we have restricted ourselves to generalisations in specific sectors, particularly retailing and insurance.

Unification

We therefore conclude this chapter by turning to the specific issue of German unification. Unification was not foreseen at the time of the creation of the single market programme. It has dominated German economic behaviour in the ensuing years, transforming the location of investment, altering the structure of the public budget, upsetting the balance of trade and payments and introducing considerable social instability into what had been a smoothly operating system. It has provided an opportunity for German firms to expand their activity internally after several had reached limits to expansion because of the anti-monopoly legislation. The extent of the problems has meant that there has been some relaxation of the controls. A particular opportunity comes from the large number of former East German public enterprises that the Treuhandanstalt has been seeking to sell.

However, the impact has been relatively contained in that the new Länder represent a market of only eighteen million in a European Economic Area twenty times that size. Our detailed investigations have suggested that most (West) German firms of any size have thought about the opportunities in the new Länder. Many have acted upon them but the scope has proved rather less than expected in many cases and the time-frame needed to reap the returns desired rather longer in many instances than was originally planned. Larger companies which can afford the wait and can raise the necessary finance for the investment have been prepared to act. So have smaller ones, with specific abilities to profit from opportunities available. But problems over ownership, difficulties with infrastructure and the substantial irrelevance of much of the industrial capital stock have made many companies step back.

Thus, although unification may have meant that the attention of many German companies has been diverted, this will only have slowed their response to the single market, not halted it. However, the effect will be protracted if costs are greater than anticipated and payback periods longer.

Ironically the effect on the single market has mainly come at the macroeconomic level. German unification, initially a stimulus to the integration of the European Community, has become a major contributor to its slowing down and loss of direction. The higher rates of interest required to finance the substantial budget deficit which has developed have helped slow the rate of growth of Europe as a whole through the restrictive mechanism of the ERM, which has meant that other European countries have had to follow suit. In September 1992 that pressure became impossible and involuntary devaluations of several currencies, principally the lira and sterling, have destabilised the system. At the time of writing, the system has still not recovered and the permitted fluctuation bands were extended to 15 per cent in August 1993 in the face of overwhelming market pressure. This has destroyed much of the credibility of the path to monetary union. Even though the Maastricht Treaty has been ratified, the path of integration which it foresaw is now unlikely.

The Bundesbank has been widely criticised for undermining the European Monetary System and its President has made it clear that he does not expect to see a single European currency this century (*Financial Times*, 29 January, 1993) In many respects these criticisms are unjustified as the Bundesbank has merely been performing its statutory role and does not have a duty to support the European system if that does not assist monetary control and price stability in Germany. The fault, if that is the right word, lies more widely with the EC countries as a whole not following the obvious course of realigning the DM upwards in order to prevent the problems stemming from unification spilling over so far into the rest of Europe. Even a month before the September 1992 collapse, the opportunity to realign the system was available at the finance ministers' meeting in Bath. Wider political concerns meant that they did not take it.

Thus while the direct impact of German unification on the response of German and UK firms to the single market may be relatively limited, particularly in the industries we have chosen to study in detail because they are not strongly affected by public infrastructure investment, the impact on the development of the single market as a whole is considerable and may ultimately alter its character. The single market was intended to stimulate European growth. Although it was expected to result in short-run costs, particularly in terms of unemployment, before the long-run benefits were felt, it was expected that the initial momentum would see it through. Now the process is much more doubtful and some of the objectives no longer seem believable for those parts of the Community which have to undertake the harshest change. A turning-back seems unlikely but, assisted by the widening of the EC to include Austria, Finland, Sweden and possibly Norway, a change in emphasis and direction is clearly possible. It is already appreciated by the Commission that a further phase of activity is necessary if the single market is to approach the reality which was intended. Initial suggestions have been set out in the Sutherland (1993) report. The ideas of subsidiarity and the variety of pace of change permitted by the Maastricht Treaty may presage a more uneven development of the Community and one which is likely to emphasise Germany's position in the centre of the single market and the UK's towards one side.

3 The retailing industry

The organisation of the distribution of goods and services can be expected to be one of the areas of activity most affected by the removal of effective borders which bear no good relation to the efficient organisation of economic activity given the location of the population, its skills, tastes and income distribution, subject to transport costs. Many of the borders within the European Community are arbitrary in geographical terms and represent the result of wars, some of which took place centuries ago. The effective border between England and Scotland has moved only slightly from that demarcated by Hadrian's Wall at the end of the first century AD. Had the Romans been successful in conquering the whole of Britain, history might have been rather different. Even the main boundaries of the system of local administration were set out around a thousand years ago.

Other boundaries were set much more recently, that of part of the German Federal Republic only being established on 3 October 1990. Very old established borders are often distinguished by differences in language and as a result of long periods of separation very different tastes and cultures have developed. Boundaries differ very much in character. Although mountains still provide quite effective borders, rivers are no longer the obstacle they were. Other borders have nothing to distinguish themselves from the surrounding countryside, such as that between the two parts of Ireland.

The opportunities for change are thus very much affected by the nature of the border. Even with the opening of the Channel tunnel, there will still be an important step difference between supplying two towns 25–30 miles apart on one side or other of the Channel and supplying the nearest English or French towns. Even with a very efficient service the effective distance will be more than trebled in terms of time and there will be the additional transport costs of paying for the ferry or train over that of a land link. While those costs may be small for the individual traveller they will be considerable for a vehicle, pushing the effective distance over at least 100 miles. Even the border between the two parts of Ireland will continue to be more substantial as those crossing it will be subject to intensive search for reasons of security.

The nature of the change in the distribution system between the UK and Germany stemming from 1992 will thus be considerable. UK borders are, in the main, very long-standing and will remain high cost obstacles. Many of Germany's borders on the other hand could be effectively eliminated from the point of view of retailing. For some consumers the nearest outlets may actually lie across a border. Similarly regional distribution networks between retail outlets can themselves run across the borders almost as readily as within the member state boundaries. In some cases, such as that between Germany and Austria, even language does not change.

However, the changes involved in completing the internal market which affect retailing are not as simple as the mere removal of frontier controls. Expenditure taxation, for example, will have a major impact as differences can be exploited by consumers. Such differences will be eroded by market forces but, as mature markets like the United States show, not necessarily eliminated. Differences in tax rates, opening hours and other regulations can persist with only some relatively minor impact near the borders. Large stores exist, for example, on the New Hampshire–Massachusetts border because of the higher sales tax rates in Massachusetts. There is, however, an important distinction between whether such differences can persist and the impact that occurs when borders are opened up.

Before 1 January 1993, the scope for cross-border retailing activity was strictly limited. Luxembourg's lower excise duty on petrol meant that there was growth in petrol stations just inside Luxembourg and closure of them nearby in Belgium. The Belgian enclaves in the Netherlands attract Dutch shoppers and shopping trips across the Channel from Britain have been organised as a full duty free allowance results in a cost saving greater than a discounted fare. Opening up borders could have a much more substantial effect on those trading either side of the border. If retail outlets are primarily locally owned and it is difficult for an individual store owner to compensate for closure on one side of the border by opening on the other, there will be clear gainers and losers. However, for larger entities retailing is like many other consumer services, it can leap across boundaries as well as step across them, by purchase of outlets in other countries or by direct investment in new outlets. Indeed in retailing there are some specific routes for cross-border activity such as mail-order, franchising and shops-within-shops: 'concessions'.

In the rest of this chapter therefore we begin by discussing the aspects of the single market programme that are likely to have an impact on retailing. We then consider the structure of retailing in the two countries to see how they might be differentially affected and then in the third section we explore how the industries are responding and the ways in which this seems likely to continue.

The stimulus from the single market

Not all the changes involved in the single market programme have immediate effect, either because they have not yet been agreed or because their implementation is yet to take effect, while others will take a long time to have their full effect because of the size of the adjustment costs involved. Relocation, establishing new brands and developing new products all take considerable time and expense. It is thus important to bear in mind the time dimension as well as the range of changes that will have an impact.

The measures which will have the main effects can be classified under eight main headings:

- removal of border restrictions
- reduction in transport costs
- harmonisation of technical specifications
- harmonisation of indirect tax rates
- ease of establishment in other member states
- improved operation of financial markets across borders
- easier cross-border labour movement
- associated programmes (social action programme, economic and monetary union, agricultural policy reform, changes in external protection, information technology initiatives and the structural funds).

Movement across the common borders of most of the continental members of the EC has been eased further by the Schengen agreement among their governments, to which Germany is a signatory and the UK is not.

Removal of border restrictions

The removal of border restrictions assists both purchasers and suppliers. In the foregoing remarks we concentrated largely on the gains from the purchaser being able to cross borders without hindrance to buy goods and services for personal consumption. They pay the same tax-inclusive prices in the shops as domestic customers but normally have to use that country's currency unless the particular store is prepared to quote prices in the other currency, thereby effectively offering its own exchange rate. It will still be possible to make adjustments for specific larger items, where the home tax rate is lower. In the same way parallel importing will be permitted so that UK purchasers can buy for resale in the UK and make the appropriate adjustment to avoid either double taxation or paying the higher rate. However, the origin of bulk or large purchases is less likely to be retail but wholesale or direct from the manufacturer.

Retailers themselves can take advantage of these easier cross-frontier movements, both by sourcing their supplies in a more rational manner and by relocating their outlets. This will enable them to exploit economies of scale. A retailer with outlets in more than one country can buy products from a single source in one country and distribute them among all its stores, with less need to run each country on a national basis. Similarly purchasing cooperatives both within countries and across borders will be able to reap the gains from larger-scale buying.

Cross-border shopping was not banned before, merely the permitted quantities before any appropriate taxes had to be paid were smaller. Frontier delays for consumers in most cases were not so much a matter of financial cost as opportunity cost. Since in many cases some utility was gained from making the trip itself, the net effect may not always have been negative. The novelty element will of course diminish as the frequency of cross-border shopping increases and as price differentials are eroded. For retailers themselves the delays at the frontier do represent a cost. In part this is represented by the wage cost of the drivers and in part by the need to use a greater number of trucks and have a larger amount of goods in transit at any one time. In the case of food retailing it alters both the range over which perishable goods can be transported and the means of carriage used. Fruit shipped over short distances can be packed in cartons at or near where it is grown and driven in the back of a conventional lorry to retail outlets, either cutting out the wholesaler or, in the case of a retailer with multiple outlets, breaking down the load at local depots. Over longer distances some element of cooling may be necessary or special containers provided. In the case of meat, fish and dairy products then the choice is likely to be between chilling and freezing. Chilling, freezing and special containers all put up the cost.

Differences in the structure of retailing affect the incidence of the gains from the removal of border restrictions. In the UK up to half of the movement of goods has been contracted out to third party specialists, who claim that new handling technologies, better stock planning and scheduling have greatly decreased costs (and raised margins). In Germany, however, less than a quarter of distribution is third party, retailers themselves moving and storing goods as well as selling them.

Retailers who have contracted out are insulated from the border delays and carriage restrictions although the consequences of these will be included in the contractors' prices. However, if the cost gains from third party contracting are as large as claimed, there is a greater opportunity for cost reduction in Germany which could help expand margins or harshen the competitive threat.

Reduction in transport costs

The cross-border transport industry in Europe has also been subject to extra costs, not just because of delays at the frontier but because of restrictions on transit and picking up loads for return trips (cabotage). Most emphasis has been placed on shipment by road but there are also restrictions on transport by air and by rail which have increased costs. Considerable progress is being made on road transport, although changes in both air and rail are more difficult to achieve, in the former case because of public or monopoly control of airport facilities and in the latter because of state control of the means of transport as well (wagon leasing excepted). The restraints on road transport have been more important in Germany than in the UK as the UK has had no system of licensing, which affects numbers of transits or numbers of vehicles, although lorries do have to pay a substantial licence fee, which increases with size of vehicle. Similarly the UK has had no restrictions on back loads. However, since goods coming to the UK have been subject to such restrictions this will have an impact on UK retailers' input costs.

Harmonisation of technical specifications

Technical specifications have grown up on a national basis. Although usually motivated by the protection of domestic consumers or employees for reasons of health or safety, the measures often form effective barriers against products from other countries which are subject to different rules.

Particularly in the case of foodstuffs there have been complex differences among the ways in which the member states regulate retail sales. These include:

- safety standards, with different national testing and certification requirements
- proscribed materials, on grounds of human or environmental safety
- prescribed ingredients for particular products, for example, ingredients in certain types of food
- labelling requirements such as different classification systems for clothes, statement of ingredients of food products, language of instructions, and so on.
- packaging requirements, motivated by safety (for example, leakproof containers) or environmental concern (for example, recyclability)
- non-standard complementary products, for example, electrical sockets, plugs and voltages.

The single market is tackling many of these and many have been tackled already by previous legislation. Two main facets are involved, one is to harmonise minimum requirements across the EC. The other is the principle of 'mutual recognition' of provisions permitting products deemed to meet the requirements in one member state to enter the others without requiring further testing or requirements. Others, like electrical sockets, are not on the agenda because of the very high cost of changing all existing sockets. A particular advantage of the EC as opposed to the US approach is that these new common requirements apply even if the state of production and consumption is the same. In the US some federal requirements only come into force if the product crosses the state line, thus permitting greater local flexibility. Of course this may not be seen as an advantage if traditional local products are outlawed or production costs are increased.

Some fundamental differences which currently segment markets will not, however, be eliminated directly by 1992. Language differences will continue to complicate labelling, location of population will only change gradually as will infrastructure. Trademark and brandname registration is to have a central office and register but delay and difficulty are expected to persist especially where the name is not a proper noun. Pan-European brands have been slow to emerge. Differences in tastes and customer preferences are likely to continue, especially where reinforced by climatic differences, although some internationalisation of behaviour seems set to develop as exemplified by jeans, trainers and T-shirts. Localised production even by multinational companies seems set to continue. The differences between the UK and Germany are surprisingly large even in some traditional products (see table 3.1).

There are also some concerns that the harmonisation process may not go as far as expected. Increased environmental concerns may add re-

Table 3.1 *Annual consumption of selected food items, Britain and Germany*

Product	Year	Unit	UK	W Germany
Milk	1984-5	kg/head	125	70.5
Fish	1985	kg/head	17.7	9.3
Pig meat	1988	kg/head	24.9	62.1
Fresh fruit	1988	kg/head	37.8	81.4
Biscuits	1987	'000 tonnes	746.9	377.2
Coffee	1989	bags	2177	8642
Tea	1988	tonnes	162699	13600

Source: Corporate Intelligence Group (1990)

straints on road transport, particularly if common agreements on carbon taxation and other restraints are difficult to achieve. Programmes to encourage recycling and proscribe non-renewable materials in packaging may constitute non-renewable resources, even if agreed at a Community level. Packaging may need to be of a form which fits in with that common in the destination market if it is not to be shipped all the way back to the originating destination. Someone will have to bear these costs and hence this will help to keep markets segmented along national lines. Standardisation and restriction in the use of names may actually reduce competition, thereby increasing market segmentation beyond that which currently exists.

Harmonisation of indirect tax rates

The eventual aim of the Community is to change VAT from the 'destination' principle to the 'origin' principle. Currently if a product is to be exported it is zero-rated in the country of export but taxed at the full rate in the country of purchase. This means that VAT on inputs has to be reclaimed by the exporter, complicating the system. An origin principle would mean that any trader merely had to show what VAT had been paid on a product within the EC and that difficulties over destination would only apply to goods originating outside the EEA or being exported outside it. Thus internal frontiers would not be relevant. However, unless VAT rates are similar across the member states this will result in a considerable inequity. For example, a country with low VAT rates importing goods which had already been taxed in a high VAT country would hardly collect any revenue on the final sale. Evening this up would require an extensive clearing house.

For businesses, the Single Administrative Document (SAD), which provided all the necessary details for tax, customs, shipment and statistics, has been replaced with an even more complex document, the purpose of which is to provide the information necessary to operate a computerised VAT information exchange (VRIES), intended to speed up VAT returns. The danger, however, is that new administrative costs incurred by the requirements of the VRIES document will outweigh the intended benefits.

Thus far agreement has been obtained over some of the range of goods to be taxed and over minimum rates to be charged on the general range of goods (this involves almost no change by any member state). But the full path to the change in system is not yet clear. Excise duties provide a similar barrier although the range of goods they apply to (some petroleum products, alcohol, tobacco and perfumes) is relatively limited. Here harmonisation would ease problems considerably and suggestions of harmonisation into zones have been made. The process is still to be completed. Agreement has been reached on VAT rates and excise duties for an initial period of four years. Under the terms of this agreement, a minimum VAT rate of 5 per cent came into force on 1 January 1993. In addition, zero-rated products will have their status maintained until the 1997 review date, when the impact of the package will be reassessed.

Ease of establishment in other member states

Retailing is a networked activity. Even single outlets are the end of a long network of suppliers. Hence changes in the system have to be consonant with the rest of the system. Adding individual outlets which are widely separated makes sense if the main markets are highly concentrated, like financial centres, or require the major catchment areas only present in large cities, or particular industries or locations (marine services are normally only provided close to the water's edge) or centres where there are ethnic populations, such as foods prepared according to Jewish or Moslem religious law. For that reason many retail networks expand outwards on a regional basis, although they may develop nodes in substantially new locations to build up a new framework. There is thus a considerable incentive for a large retailer wishing to enter new markets to do so by purchasing an existing network.

Purchasing individual sites or developing new ones requires a great deal of local knowledge and has substantial administrative cost. Key locations may not be publicly advertised and incumbents have an incentive to try to keep the information available to new entrants to a minimum. For completely new sites or major refurbishments, planning and other permissions will normally be required from local administrations. These can be very tedious to obtain and offer ample opportunity for covert protection as many of the rules are not particularly transparent. Treadgold (1990a) sets out some of the barriers which exist and are not directly affected by the 1992 legislation. Right of establishment under the terms of the single market legislation does not necessarily make access easy.

In the same way, those following the route of acquisition may find it difficult to get valuations of potential targets or to get sufficient information about the possible synergies with the company, such as computer and EPOS (electronic point-of-sale) systems (Hart, 1992a). EPOS systems record and process data on transactions in order to place automatic requests for new stock from warehouses and from suppliers as well as providing a continuing financial update on the profitability and turnover in particular product lines. Even with sufficient information to value a company and to identify sufficient shareholders willing to sell this does not mean that the purchaser can necessarily obtain managerial control, either because of restraints on the composition of the board or voting arrangements that do not have a straightforward relationship with share ownership. This results in a considerable difference between the UK and Germany which is not going to be resolved by the single market measures (see chapter 2).

In Germany, half of all companies are medium-sized (below 500 employees) and have private limited company (GmbH) status, requiring reporting of company information only to the workforce. Even public companies (AGs) are able to limit the voting rights attached to shares and the power of majority shareholders to appoint directors or determine company policy. Barriers often cited include two-tier boards, limitation of owners' rights to appoint managers, limits on the voting rights attached to shares, banks' exercise of proxy votes on the current management's behalf, and the power of national monopoly/cartel offices to delay the hostile bid (Treadgold, 1990a).

A simplified procedure for referral of large bids (with combined assets of more than Ecu 2 billion coming automatically under Commission jurisdiction) and standardisation of the rules for acquisition approval may make it easier for companies to mount successful bids. However, the working of the new system has yet to be clarified; it may introduce greater severity – and longer delays – than exist at present. The recent 'boom' in mergers, which continued in Europe after it had fallen away in North America, reflects some pre-emptive acquisitions in anticipation of new Community rules which will be tougher than existing national regimes.

Britain has one of the most highly developed secondary share markets in the Community, with many expanding companies finding it necessary to issue shares to the general public to supplement internally generated and bank-borrowed funds. This may reflect the restrictive lending policies of commercial banks (see below). Those institutions (pension funds, insurance companies, unit and investment trusts) which hold most UK company shares have been accused of constraining them to maximise short-term profits, inviting the acquisition of those that act more strategically by undervaluing their assets, and being willing to sell whenever a favourable price is offered. This 'short-termism' accusation is contested by analysts who regard takeovers as an efficient device to eliminate managerial inefficiency, and high dividend payments as a signal of competence (Bhattacharyya, 1979). In practice, however, the relative openness of the London stock market does appear to make it easier for other EC companies to acquire in Britain than for British companies to acquire elsewhere in Europe.

There is no legislative route by which the Community can (or would wish to) reduce the ability of firms in other EC countries to raise adequate finance from retained profits, bank-loans, private shareholdings, and shares placed with financial institutions who are unwilling to sell. The only mechanism for standardisation of corporate financing systems is through a form of evolutionary elimination or adaptation, in which firms financed by less efficient methods are out-competed by, or imitate, those financed by more efficient methods. Supporters of the efficient markets hypothesis argue that the UK's strong secondary share market imposes a spur to efficiency on its larger companies, which is absent in the more sheltered regimes of other countries. While the evidence is mixed, the largest companies in other EC countries have tended to become publicly quoted (first on their own stock market, then on those of other countries). Whether this will lead to a convergence of ownership-market practices and constraints, making it easier for British firms to acquire abroad, remains to be seen. But any change will take considerably longer than the legislative component of '1992'.

Improved operation of financial markets across borders

The free flow of financial services across borders in the EC should aid foreign direct investment in retailing quite considerably, although continuing capital controls in some of the southern member states following the problems of the ERM in September 1992 may delay this. Financial services themselves form part of the network of services provided by retailers. These may include charge cards, hire purchase, loans, stock market services, foreign exchange and even banking. The form of opening of the market for financial services has a strong influence on how that is to be done. To obtain a 'passport' to offer retail financial services in other member states, the parent organisation has to be a registered bank subject to the full supervision of its activities in the home market. Otherwise the retailer will itself have to become registered in whatever way is currently necessary in the other state, thereby not making any use of the single market provisions.

In some cases this form of market opening will be restrictive, as limited services can be provided locally without requiring the sorts of major controls necessary for banks. However, it is more common to provide these services either in the form of shops within shops, or for the parent to be a bank and to have a subsidiary involved in retail activities such as a travel agency or estate agency or for the services to be provided by a recognised bank as a joint venture.

Until we get to stage 3 of EMU, cross-border operation will still have all the ensuing costs of foreign exchange transactions and the attendant risks before exchange rates are fixed. This may present rather fewer new problems for retailers than for some other forms of companies. They are likely to have a high local content and to be part of a network where foreign exchange transactions are commonplace. Other constraints which affect most industries will also apply to retailing. Differences in corporate tax rates which are not being harmonised as part of the single market will affect a multinational firm's structure and its decisions over the repatriation of profits. Differences in the costs of finance, the extent of retained earnings, and the use of external funds between the UK and Germany may affect their ability to invest abroad (Mayer and Alexander, 1990; Laudy, 1991). In particular, the high level of investment in food retailing in the UK in recent years and the relatively depressed level of the economy may make it more difficult for UK firms to raise capital for foreign investment and may by the same token make them easier takeover targets. The single market is an incentive to that process rather than a facilitator of it.

Easier cross-border labour movement

In trying to set up cross-border and foreign operations the retailing industry, like others, will be aided by the ability to send managers abroad with relative ease. However, as a service industry, a high element of local knowledge is required and most staff will have to deal directly with the public, making local recruitment the norm, if only for language skills. However, the retail industry is a disproportionate employer of the young and of part-time workers. Demand during the day is highly variable, while shelf-filling is best done outside normal hours. Similarly the trend towards longer opening hours requires more staff rather than the same staff working even longer hours, with the exception of family run shops, which have often taken the lead with longer opening hours in the UK because they are not subject to trade union and other restraints on their hours. Because of the relatively low levels of skills required in several of these tasks, the unsocial hours and the relatively low rates of pay, these jobs may appeal to migrant workers from lower income parts of the Community and could help offset some of the difficulties caused by the ageing population. However it tends to be the higher skilled who migrate in the EC rather than the unskilled. By the same token retailers could benefit from that ageing process as more people will be available for part-time work, particularly if the increasing dependency ratio means that pension provision becomes a little less generous, at least as a ratio of normal earnings. There is, however, little sign of this as yet. Directives relating to part-time workers and to maximum working time under the social action programme may impinge on working methods in retailing, particularly in the UK, but all in all a noticeable effect from labour movement seems unlikely in this industry.

Associated programmes

SOCIAL ACTION PROGRAMME

As just mentioned, the retailing industry has a number of characteristics which mean that the UK industry in particular will be more affected by many of the proposed measures than most. About half the workforce is part-time, about half is female and both proportions are rising. Providing pro-rata benefits to full-time employees and providing improved maternity benefits, for example, would both increase costs. Although wage costs are only 20 per cent of retail sales in the UK, margins are so narrow that this is an important consideration. However, comparisons of retailing productivity between the UK and Germany (Smith and Hitchens, 1985, for example) suggest that German levels may be 20 per cent higher. Increased training may hence be able to offset these extra costs, which in the main will not be borne by the German industry.

Since there is little direct competition across the border such efficiency differences may not appear to matter but they could provide an opportunity for exploitation of underutilised resources in the case of a takeover. Issues of 'social dumping', which apply to activities which can be sited in different countries, thus have little application in the case of retailing except perhaps in mail order.

ECONOMIC AND MONETARY UNION

The benefits from EMU are found in general in the reduction of costs of capital, currency risk and transactions costs but the retail industry will benefit in particular by being able to deal with every consumer in the EC direct when the EC moves to a single currency. This would be a major force in opening markets and giving consumers the ability to treat all sources of goods and services on an equal basis. The consumer faces a considerable drawback in dealing with small transactions in other currencies. A single currency will ease the progress of cross-border mail order for smaller suppliers and help those who wish to undertake cross-border shopping. However, there is a disadvantage for those who have a large number of coin operated machines, whether for tickets or for goods, and who have most of their transactions with domestic consumers. The changing of prices and invoicing involved in the switch to the Ecu will not be a particularly onerous task now that all currencies are decimal systems. For example, the costs of expressing prices in both local currency and Ecu for a period both before and after the changeover date, in order to aid understanding and reduce the scope for inflation, are small (Burridge and Mayes, 1992).

AGRICULTURAL POLICY REFORM

One side consequence of the single market programme is that the funds available for agricultural price support are having to fall. Statutory monopsony suppliers such as marketing boards are also expected to lose their position. If, as a result, food retailers can drive prices down this will make a small contribution to increasing their own sales, as the demand for food is not particularly price elastic, but it will increase real incomes, permitting increases in demand for other retail sales. Since the fall in food prices has the greatest impact on those on low incomes much of the real income gain will be consumed rather than saved.

CHANGES IN EXTERNAL PROTECTION

There are specific gains, which will impact on retailers, to be obtained from the reductions in external protection in areas such as textiles, clothing and footwear, entailed by the abolition of national VERs or other quantitative constraints and their replacement by EC-wide restrictions. In any case the MFA may well be replaced by a much more limited international set of restrictions. This will not only assist retailers in offering lower prices to consumers but will tend to increase the range of choice available. The impact will differ between the UK and Germany because of the structure of their existing industries and their pattern of foreign sourcing (Steedman *et al.*, 1991). The UK has sourced more in the Far East, and Germany in Turkey. UK industry tends to concentrate on the more mass produced end of the market while German industry has moved towards the higher value-added end of the scale. UK producers could then be at greater risk but in many respects it is the retailers who are the architects of this change in purchasing and hence, except where there are vertical links back into production, will not be adversely affected by the change in source of supply.

The increasing choice available as a result of the reduction in barriers between member states will pose problems of stockholding costs for retailers who aim to be comprehensive but may result in a greater element of concentration as a consequence.

INFORMATION TECHNOLOGY INITIATIVES

The EC is still pursuing a number of positive policies to encourage European industry, particularly links across the member state boundaries. Technology policy is an example of this and IT policy in particular. Because of the importance of networking and the complex information requirements, retailing is likely to be a prime beneficiary from these policies. Relevant programmes includes TEDIS, which promotes electronic data interchange, especially through creating common standards, and SPRINT, particularly the elements relating to the take up of rapid response technology.

STRUCTURAL FUNDS

The use of the structural funds in Objective 1 and Objective 2 (declining industrial) regions includes through its encouragement of infrastructure a number of retail developments. This will tend to enhance the process of growth. It is a means of revitalising declining industrial areas. Where it works retailing will be contributing to encouraging the sources of indigenous growth from which it will itself benefit as incomes recover.

Taken together this is rather a hotchpotch of effects pushing retailing in a number of different directions. The structures of the German and

British industries give a good indication of how they might be expected to respond to this variety of pressures.

The structure of retailing in Germany and the UK

There is considerable similarity between the German and UK industries, (table 3.2). Turnover and turnover per capita are of the same orders of magnitude. However, in part this may be due to a somewhat wider definition of the sector in the UK (Weitzel, 1993). There are rather more firms in Germany and the number is growing slowly while there has been a small contraction in the UK (table 3.3). Average firm size is thus smaller in Germany.

As the retailing sector is very broad we have focussed our attention upon two parts of it, namely food and clothing and footwear. (Footwear firms were not interviewed in the UK part of the study.) Food retailing represents around a quarter of retailing as a whole. Clothing and footwear is somewhat smaller, 12 per cent in Germany and half that in the UK. The number of firms in food retailing has been falling fast in both countries but faster in the UK. However, while there has been a decline of around 15 per cent in the number of firms in the UK, its share of total retailing has risen. In Germany on the other hand the number of firms has risen but the share of the sector has fallen. The number of employees in food retailing set out in table 3.3 shows an important difference between the two economies. Nearly half of retail employment is in food retailing in the UK. Both clothing and food have nearly half of their employees working only part-time (a little more than in retailing as a whole) while in Germany only about a third of retailing employees worked part-time. Flexible opening hours and differences in regulation of the labour market are major explanations of this difference, as are the different rates of National Insurance (see Hart, 1988, on youth unemployment).

The UK industry is more concentrated than its German counterpart. Large multiples (more than ten stores) account for 53 per cent of employment, 60 per cent of turnover and 80 per cent of capital investment. This concentration is even greater in the case of food, where large multiples account for 81 per cent of employment (table 3.4). Indeed the top five firms account for 40 per cent of turnover in the food industry in the UK (table 3.5). Clothing is similarly concentrated.

The German data are derived somewhat differently. Department stores, hypermarkets and supermarkets between them only account for 30

Table 3.2 *Turnover in retailing and population, 1988*

Country	Population million	Turnover DM billion	Turnover per capita DM
Germany	61	538	8820
Great Britain	57	528(a)	9263

Source: Weitzel (1993), Dawson, John A., 'The Distribution Sector in the UK' (unpublished, 1992), Statistisches Bundesamt, Umsatzsteuerstatistiken
(a)= £169.2 billlion. Included are £56.7 billion for distribution, repair and servicing of motor vehicles and £7.6 billion for sales of petrol filling stations.

per cent of turnover (table 3.6). However, while the number of hyper-markets doubled between 1975 and 1989, the number of discount stores more than trebled (excluding Aldi) and are three times as numerous, although their turnover is only half that of the hypermarkets. However, Aldi on its own is bigger than all the other discount stores put together, with a turnover of DM21.5 billion compared with DM17.4 billion, so that jointly they account for a little more of the industry than the hypermarkets.

Insofar as we can express the UK data on the same basis (table 3.7), the number of hypermarkets is only 40 per cent of that in Germany, although they have shown a much faster rate of growth. It is an open question whether these differences reflect constraints on UK development and that as a result we can expect the number of hypermarkets and discount stores to grow towards the German levels.

The major players

The two largest multiples in food retailing in Germany, Rewe Zentral and Spar, accounted for two thirds of the stores run by the top five companies (table 3.8). However, this underestimates their impact on the market as they also act as buying groups for small owner-run retail firms. Around 4,600 independent traders were affiliated to Spar in 1989. However, the structure of the main groups is strikingly different. Rewe has similar shares of the market in terms of stores, sales area and turnover, all around 35–40 per cent. Spar on the other hand is dominated by small stores with below average turnover as its 31 per cent share of the number of stores represents only 16 per cent of sales area and only 12 per cent of turnover. Aldi shows different characteristics extracting a high turnover, 26 per cent, from only 12 per cent of the stores and 14 per cent of the sales area. Tengelmann, like Rewe, has similar shares of turnover, sales area and number of stores but, in its case, all around 16 per cent,

Table 3.3a *Structural changes in German retailing 1980–8*

Trade structure	Total retail trade		Food		Clothing, footwear	
	1980	1988	1980	1988	1980	1988
No. of firms	367505	396674	101841	85163	65120	69695
% change		7.9		-16.4		7.0
Percentage	100	100	27.7	21.5	17.7	17.6
Turnover (DM bn)	375.8	537.8	95.1	137.9	53.5	67.5
% change		43.1		44.9		26.2
Percentage	100	100	25.3	25.6	14.2	12.6
Employees (1000)	2431	2424	629	674	460	457
% change		-0.3		7.2		-1.7
Percentage	100	100	25.9	27.8	19.3	18.6

Source: Weitzel (1993),   Statistisches   Bundesamt: Handels-und
Gaststättenzählung. Einzelhandel Mebzahlen (Fachserie 6, Reihe 3.1).

Table 3.3b *Structural changes in British retailing 1980–8*

Trade structure	Total retail trade		Food		Clothing, footwear	
	1980	1988	1980	1988	1980	1988
No. of firms	323139	307460	90475	67755	35282	30170
% change		-4.9		-25.1		-14.5
Percentage	100	100	28.0	22.0	10.9	9.8
Turnover (£ bn)	84	169.2	(21.7)	47.7	4.9	10.3
% change		101.4				110.2
Percentage	100	100		28.2	5.8	6.1
Employees (1000)		2319		1078		293
% change						
Percentage	100	100		46.5		12.6

Source: Weitzel (1993), Institute for Retail Studies (University of Stirling) Distributive Trades Profile 1990. Dawson, John A., *The Distribution Sector in
the UK* (unpublished)

Table 3.4 *Retail employment, financial performance (by area), store size and productivity (by company size), UK, 1987*

	Employ- ment ('000)	Turn- over (£mn)	Gross margin (%)	Net invest- ment (£mn)	No. of stores	Ave. store employ- ment	Turn- over per employ- ee (£)
All retail	2319	104627	28.8	3581	345467	6.7	45100
Large multiple	1228	62925	28.6	2766	62706	19.6	51200
Food	806	37146	21.9	1676	98016	8.2	46100
Large multiple	499	27336	21.2	1484	12975	38.5	54800
Mixed	375	19060	34.7	548	11363	33.0	50800
Large multiple	302	14650	32.5	445	5272	57.3	48500
House- hold goods	307	17353	32.0	529	60406	5.1	56500
Large multiple	123	8611	31.2	334	9549	12.9	70000
Clothing etc	293	10255	41.4	305	58380	5.0	35000
Large multiple	159	5808	44.8	228	17122	9.3	36500
Drink etc	272	10538	17.8	149	59810	4.5	38700
Large multiple	73	3518	22.6	56	9771	7.5	48200
Other non-food	233	8983	33.2	229	52473	4.4	48600
Large multiple	47	1896	37.1	90	5321	8.8	40300

Source: Mayes and Shipman (1992), BSO (1990) table 2
Note: Gross margin = turnover – purchases + stock appreciation.

less than half the size. However, much of Rewe is more like Spar than the figures indicate as Rewe-Leibbrand oHG, a leading trading company with a turnover of DM16 billion in 1988, was taken over by Rewe in 1989.

Table 3.5. *Retailing industry concentration 1987*

	Sales (£mn)	CR_5	CR_{10}
All retail	105497	19.1	29.2
Food	31005	38.8	50.6
Household	22567	20.7	30.7
Clothing etc.	17808	35.9	49.2
Other non-food	17539	22.7	33.0
Drink etc.	14691	21.9	32.5
Mail order	4875	67.5	78.5

Source: Mayes and Shipman (1992), BSO (1990), table 13
Note: Commodity-group sales figures in the first column sum to more than the 'total retail trade' figure, perhaps because some 'mixed' businesses are double-counted, and because retail sales by non-retail businesses are included.
$CR_{5(10)}$ shows the percentage of sales by the largest 5(10) firms to the sector total.

Table 3.6 *Turnover in German retailing, 1989, by operating type*

Operating type	Turnover DM bn	Percentage
Department stores	29.3	5.7
Hypermarkets	30.0	5.8
Supermarkets	90.5	17.5
Other food stores	60.4	11.7
Other retail (non-food)	307.0	59.4
Total	517.2	100.0

Source: Weitzel (1993), Deutsches Handelsinstitut (Cologne)

Table 3.7 *Development of hypermarkets in Great Britain[a]*

Year	Number	Sales area 1000 sq.m.	Per cent change	Sales area per store (sq.m.)
1975	123	460.9	-	3747
1980	278	1025.7	122.5	3690
1985	432	1548.6	51.0	3585
1989	644	2308.1	49.0	3584

Source: Weitzel (1993), Institute for Retail Studies: Distributive Trade Profile 1990, calculations of the IFO Institute
[a]Hypermarkets and superstores = Verbrauchermärkte. Cumulative data on the basis of new opened stores.

Table 3.8 *Food retailing in 1990 in Germany by enterprises*

Structure of companies	Rewe Zentral AG	Aldi	Tengel-mann	Asko/ Schaper/ Coop	Spar AG	Total
No. of stores	7315	2250	3033	1021	6030	19649
Percentage	37.2	11.5	15.4	5.2	30.7	100
Sales area (1000 sq.m.)	4090	1350	1669	1381	1628	10118
Percentage	40.4	13.3	16.5	13.6	16.1	100
Turnover (£mn)	30700	23000	14109	10994	10460	89263
Percentage	34.4	25.8	15.8	12.3	11.7	100

Source: Weitzel (1993), Deutsches Handelsinstitut, Cologne

The five main companies in the UK food retailing sector were relatively similar in terms of sales area, 18–24 per cent (table 3.9). Data relate to 1990, since when there have been some changes (see table 3.10). Sainsbury is largest in terms of turnover but it achieves this with the highest ratio to sales area. Asda has concentrated on hypermarkets and hence has the largest average store size and the smallest number of stores among these top five firms.

Argyll and Gateway have much larger numbers of stores and hence smaller average store size. However, Argyll gets a markedly higher share of turnover from its stores. Gateway has been restructured; sixty of its largest stores have been acquired by Asda. At one stage it appeared that the company would be taken over by Tengelmann, which would have added considerable interest to our study as we have a particular concern with the behaviour of subsidiaries of the one country in the other. A&P, a Tengelmann subsidiary in the US, took a 20 per cent stake in the company, which was raised and then reduced to a low level – a rather short foray into the UK market.

There has been German activity in the sector and Aldi has thirty-one stores in the midlands and northern England. This is exploiting a gap in the sector as the major companies have a relatively small stake in the discount sector. Tesco, for example, has moved up market, increasing quality and moving away from a strategy which concentrated on low price. However, Gateway has moved into the discount sector with the launch of its Food Giant stores.

Table 3.9 *Food retailing, 1990, in Great Britain by enterprises*

Structure of companies	Sainsbury	Tesco	Argyll	Asda	Gateway	Total
No. of stores	303	376	761	191	756	2387
Percentage	12.7	15.7	31.9	8.0	31.7	100
Sales area (1000 sq.m.)	661	869	743	698	672	3643
Percentage	18.1	23.9	20.4	19.2	18.4	100
Turnover (£mn)	5400	4915	3920	3332	2370	19937
Percentage	27.1	24.6	19.7	16.7	11.9	100

Source: Weitzel (1993), Deutsches Handelsinstitut,Cologne

Table 3.10 *Leading UK grocers, 1990/91, by sales (with average outlet size)*

		£mn	sq.ft.
1	Tesco	6346.3	25159
2	Sainsbury	6208.4(a)	23247
3	Argyll (Safeway, Presto, Lo Cost, Galbraith)	4325.7	19390(b)
4	Asda	4142.6	40000
5	Isosceles (Gateway, Somerfield, Wellworth)	3118.7	9116(c)
6	Kwik Save (+ Lateshopper)	1784.5	
7	John Lewis (Waitrose)	995.7	12340
8	Wm Morrison	909.6	33347
9	Iceland	724.6	
10	Wm Low	384.0	12508

Source: Corporate Intelligence on Retailing (London 1992)
(a) Excludes Savacentre's grocery sales, estimated at £131 million in 1990/91.
(b) Safeway only.
(c) Gateway only.

Trends in the industry

The single market stimulus is imposed on an industry which was already changing. The response to the stimulus is affected by those trends. We have already noted the trend towards larger chains in food retailing. Large grocery chains managed to grow at almost twice the rate of overall food sales, by capturing market share from small chains and co-ops. Larger grocery outlets also raised margins by branching into non-food products, and in the largest outlets non-food sales approach 50 per cent of the total.

The clothing sector is also concentrated (table 3.11), although here there has been less of a trend towards rising store size. Some of the chains have retained separate names for the constituent companies acquired during the process of growth but the advantages of having chains of stores are largely similar in the two sectors: lower prices from bulk purchasing, better access to capital markets, scale economies in distribution (fixed costs can be spread over more outlets), scale economies in IT systems, in management (spreading the head office costs) and in 'goodwill' (it is easier to establish a new store if the firm's reputation is already well known), greater scope for market research and for spreading risks. Market research is required whatever the size of the organisation, but internal information becomes more valuable when the chain is larger and the range of information required rises less than proportionately with size. Similarly with many stores a number of risks will be regional or store specific and hence more readily absorbed.

In large stores it is possible to have much higher productivity, with respect to both turnover and floor space. Bowring (1990) suggests a fall of 30 per cent in staff requirements is possible between stores with less than 2,000 sq. ft. and those with more than 25,000 sq. ft. The discount stores do not follow this trend to the ever larger superstore, partly to keep rental costs down but also because they stock many fewer lines (1,000 in the case of Aldi, 2,000 for Kwiksave, compared with 10,000 in Gateway and nearer 20,000 in the more traditional stores like Sainsbury and Tesco).

The UK has done little explicitly to protect the smaller stores although planning rules can work in their favour. External factors like the growth of car ownership and the use of home freezers have worked against the small stores. The stores have therefore been following a strategy which can at best be described as survival, although they have been able to use devices such as longer opening hours and the convenience of their location to remain profitable. There are some niches as speciality stores but the large stores have even moved in on some of these by having within-store bakeries and specialist fishmongers. Collaboration has been one route employed, through purchasing groups, such as NRA, franchises from larger retailers, 7–11 probably being the best known

Table 3.11 *Womenswear market shares, 1990*

Company	Sales (£mn)	Share (%)
Marks and Spencer	1540	15.6
Mail Order firms	1200	12.1
Burton	1000	10.1
C&A (NL)	506	5.1
Sears	315	3.2
Storehouse	255	2.6
Littlewoods	230	2.3
Next	216	2.2
River Island/Chelsea Girl	210	2.1
Etam	160	1.6
Top 10	5422	56.9

Source: Mintel (1991) Retail Intelligence volume 3

example (the parent company is based in the US) and through links with wholesalers, for example, Spar. Booker, the largest of the food whole-salers, has close links with the purchasing groups VG, Mace and Circle K. Booker has indeed extended the chain backwards and now owns several food manufacturers. Nurdin and Peacock have some cash and carry outlets.

In clothing one particular route for smaller outlets has been offered by franchising, through groups such as Benetton, or Clarks in footwear. The larger stores have, however, been concentrating rather than diversifying their activities, divesting themselves of manufacturing activity in areas such as clothing and electrical goods (Burton is a well known example in the clothing sector, despite the fact that their original reputation was built on tailoring.) Manufacturing and retailing management skills have been widely thought too different to house within the single organisation. Transport services have been contracted out. Around 70 per cent was provided by independent contractors in the UK in 1990 compared with only 11 per cent in Germany (Institute of Grocery Distribution, 1990a and National Freight Corporation, 1989). However, while the scope of ownership may have been reduced, links between retailers and clothing and textile manufacturers have been increased. Retailers now exercise considerable control over their suppliers, specifying designs and production methods (Dawson and Shaw, 1989). Much of this is intended to improve the speed of response but the increasingly 'tied' relationship can act as a guarantee under which suppliers are prepared to undertake more substantial investment (Williamson, 1981).

In the large clothing stores, traditionally purchasing of stock was done by the manager of each department. By the 1970s, centralisation of buying operations had become the norm. This had the advantages for large retail groups of reducing costs, increasing their power over suppliers and centralising distribution. In the case of House of Fraser, decentralised buying continued until the early 1980s when it was replaced by 'own brand' lines. Management has become more centralised, with many of the decisions over store layout, sourcing, and so on, being centrally determined. In part this is a function of the strong rise in information technology, which has enabled a transformation of distribution systems. In food in particular, larger warehouses have been linked with daily direct data inputs collected via EPOS terminals at checkouts, themselves made more efficient by using scanning rather than typed in codes. On site stocks can therefore be reduced, deliveries concentrated out of trading hours and delivery times reduced. Scanning itself speeds up the check-out process thereby providing a further direct benefit to the customer. However, the overhead cost of installing these systems tends to mean that they are concentrated in the large chains.

Larger stores have also been seeking to reinforce their position by establishing 'own-brands'. This not only emphasises the company name but enables more price flexibility. There has been some diversification into related areas but on the whole development has been within the industry. Even competition has been kept within clear bounds, without drastic price-cutting wars. The market, particularly for food, has been characterised by a small number of major players, who recognise each other's strategies and hence have been able to expand while maintaining margins. Overseas expansion by UK food retailers has been limited and is as likely to be in North America as in Europe, in clear contrast with the cross-border operations that have been developing on the continent. Clothing companies have been rather more active, with the original wave in investment predating '1992'.

Food retailing, since it is dealing with a day-to-day necessity is much less cyclical than clothing. Thus food retailing did not rise markedly on the back of the boom in the UK in the second half of the 1980s. Nor did it fall away sharply in the recession which followed. Clothing on the other hand rose almost 10 per cent in 1987 alone and has fallen back as the economy has reversed. The share of food sales in consumers' expenditure has fallen from 15 per cent in 1983 to 12 per cent in 1990. This pattern of relatively slow growth in food sales will continue and, while clothing expenditure is likely to rise faster than the average as the recovery gets under way, it is sectors like domestic electrical appliances and DIY which have shown the fastest rates of growth in recent years.

Mergers and acquisitions

Although in general merger and acquisition is more a characteristic of the UK than of the German economy, retailing is an exception because it is to a large extent location specific. It is relatively difficult to gain market share from existing customer networks by setting up in a new location. An obvious exception is setting up out-of-town hypermarkets, which by offering free parking and a wide range of services under a single roof, provide a new attraction to customers. Incremental changes can also be made by adding facilities such as shops and cashpoints to petrol filling stations on main roads. However, it is only possible to gain sites in many instances by buying existing companies, aided by restraints on planning permission in Germany. This is not a matter of buying individual sites from competitors or from single site companies as these are not normally available but of buying the whole competitor with its network of mutiple stores. In Bavaria, for example, eleven regional trading firms with a turnover of DM6 billion were taken over between 1985 and 1990. The process is now coming to a halt as there is a lack of firms left to acquire.

German data on mergers and acquisitions is rather more sketchy than that available in the UK. However, a picture of behaviour in the 1980s can be built up from table 3.12. There has been a surge in acquisitions at the end of the period. In the first eight months of 1987, forty-two firms with a combined turnover of DM20 billion were taken over, compared with 178 firms with a turnover of DM12 billion during the whole of 1980–6. (The contrast is exaggerated by the turnover figures because of the increase in nominal spending in the sector as a whole during the period, with increases in both the price level and real activity.) Metro and Asko were most active. As a result Metro raised its turnover from DM7.5 billion in 1985 to DM19 billion in 1987, aided by taking a majority interest in Kaufhof, and to DM36 billion in 1991. Asko moved from a turnover of DM3 billion in 1985 to becoming the Asko-Schaper-Massa Group in 1987 with a turnover of DM11 billion, increasing to DM19 billion in 1991, after acquiring large portions of Coop AG. Metro and Asko are now themselves set to merge under terms agreed with the Bundeskartellamt.

Table 3.12 *Mergers and acquisitions[a] in German food retailing, 1980–7[b]*

Purchaser	Number of acquired companies and their turnover in DM million					
	1980		1981		1982	
	No.	Turnover	No.	Turnover	No.	Turnover
Leibbrand	5	185	10	128	19	345
Rewe-Group	2	212	3	156	3	250
Tengelmann	-	-	3	219	-	-
Coop AG	2	161	5	787	4	69
Edeka-Group	4	373	3	255	2	126
Metro	-	-	-	-	-	-
Sub-total	13	931	24	1545	28	790
Asko-Schaper	-	-	2	192	6	299
Others	4	435	11	698	5	975
Total	17	1366	37	2435	39	2064
	1983		1984		1985	
	No.	Turnover	No.	Turnover	No.	Turnover
Leibbrand	4	28	2	48	4	91
Rewe-Group	-	-	-	-	1	11
Tengelmann	2	21	-	-	5	167
Coop AG	1	13	-	-	1	4
Edeka-Group	3	28	-	-	1	16
Metro	-	-	-	-	-	-
Sub-total	10	90	2	48	12	289
Asko-Schaper	4	51	1	19	2	41
Others	5	187	9	1189	14	854
Total	19	328	12	1256	28	1184
	1986		1980-6		Jan-Aug 1987	
	No.	Turnover	No.	Turnover	No.	Turnover
Leibbrand	3	47	47	872	8	544
Rewe-Group	-	-	9	629	4	687
Tengelmann	2	24	12	431	4	305
Coop AG	5	409	18	1443	2	184
Edeka-Group	2	62	15	860	5	142
Metro	-	-	-	-	3	10058
Sub-total	12	542	101	4235	26	11920
Asko-Schaper	4	2064	19	2666	3	6747
Others	10	831	58	5169	13	1328
Total	26	3437	178	12070	42	19995

Source: Weitzel (1993), Bundeskartellamt, Berlin, published in *Lebensmittel-Zeitung*, 29 September 1987
[a]Without internal group acquisition. [b]Until August 1987.

Table 3.13 *Top twenty acquisitions and mergers by UK retailers, 1982–90*

Purchaser	Purchase	Sector of purchase	Year	Value (£mn)
Isosceles plc	Gateway	Grocery	1989	2200
Habitat Mothercare plc	British Home Stores	Mixed retailing	1985	1520
Boots Co plc	Ward White	DIY/Audio accessories	1989	900
Asda	61 Gateway stores	Grocery	1989	705
Dee Corporation plc	Fine Fare/ Shoppers Paradise	Grocery	1986	686
Argyll Group plc	Safeway	Grocery	1987	681
Management	Magnet	Furniture	1989	629
Alfayed Invest-ment Trust	House of Fraser	Department Stores	1987	615
Associated Dairies Group plc	MFI	Furniture/carpets	1985	615
Burton Group plc	Debenhams	Department stores	1985	566
Management	MFI	Furniture	1987	505
Sears plc	Freemans	Mail order	1988	477
Lowndes Group	Harris Queensway	Furniture/carpets	1988	450
Marks & Spencer plc	Brooks Brothers	Clothing	1988	440(a)
Thorn EMI plc	Rent A Center	TV rental	1987	371(a)
Next plc	Combined English Stores	Multi-sector	1987	340
Paternoster Stores (Consortium)	FW Woolworth	Multi-sector	1982	310
Next plc	Grattan	Mail order	1986	300
Grand Metro-politan plc	Pearle Health Services	Opticians	1985	248(a)
Wickes plc	Hunter	DIY/Builders merchants	1988	283

Source: Corporate Intelligence Group research, *The Retail Rankings*, 1992 Edition
(a) Overseas acquisitions.

Merger and acquisition activity in the UK continued at a substantial rate during the period (table 3.13). The process has now slowed and some transactions have been partly unwound as companies such as Next became overextended.

Cooperative alliances

One of the major distinguishing features between the UK and German markets is considerable development in Germany of links between companies which fall far short of mergers and acquisitions. The principal form of these alliances is through buying groups, which between them had a market share of 40–45 per cent compared with only 5 per cent in the UK (chart 3.1). These buying groups get the advantages of lower prices from larger scale purchases. These discounts also apply to advertising and a number of other central services, such as stock and cost control. According to Euromonitor about 7,500 independent food retailers in the UK are affiliated to the four leading groups (Mace Marketing Services, Londis (Holdings) Ltd, Spar (UK) Ltd and VG Distributors). It does in this case seem a little strange that this form of cooperation has not spread more widely in the UK given its popularity elsewhere in the EC. Perhaps this will be an area where continental experience will be followed as the result of the bringing together of the different markets.

Grouping together allows independent retailers to gain a corporate identity and hence compete more effectively with the large multiples. In general the German experience is that the smaller the stores involved the wider the range of services they use from the alliance. Intermediate size firms tend to use the purchasing arrangements but seek to maintain an independent identity. These linkages take the form of legal agreements. The more common arrangement in the UK is to use franchising. This is especially well developed in the light meals and car renting sectors. Two of the most notable successes of recent years – Benetton and the Body Shop – rely on franchise agreements. These franchising arrangements have the advantage that they are exempted from the general ban on cartels under Article 85 of the Treaty whereas trade groupings on the German pattern are subject to it.

Cross-border alliances

There has been relatively little extension of these systems of alliances across borders, although that might be expected within the single market. There have been linkages between national organisations, such as

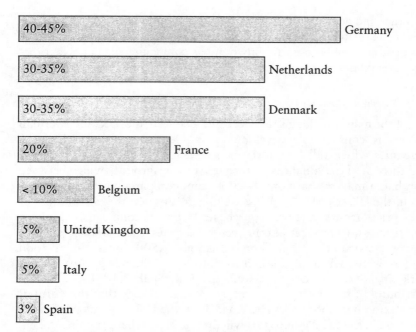

Chart 3.1 Market shares of purchasing groups, 1988
Source: Weitzel (1993), *Euromonitor*, M+M Eurodata, IFO Institüt, Munich

EXPERT in consumer electronics and consumer appliances and INTERSPORT. There is an incentive to form international purchasing groups because many of the main producers have themselves become multinational. It is the larger trading groups which have begun the process of putting international groups together, mainly since 1989 and as a direct consequence of the single market. One has been formed under Rewe Zentral, which includes GIB Group (Belgium), Paridoc/Docks de France, Vendex (Netherlands) and Coop (Switzerland).

Even more progress has been made by the European Retail Alliance (ERA) and Associated Marketing Services (AMS), who combine multiples from eleven European countries. Argyll, Ahold (Netherlands) and Groupe Casino (France) have equal shares in ERA and joint holdings in each other's companies. ERA has working groups on a number of areas including IT, distribution and logistics. The three ERA companies are also important partners in AMS. It is interesting that these are groupings of multiples giving horizontal integration in the industry rather than the more typical German style cooperative arrangements. Allkauf, the German partner in AMS, is involved with other alliances. AMS is concerned with only fairly general linkage arrangments and does not coordinate purchasing, which remains the responsibility of the individual members. AMS is a marketing service company working with selected manufacturers and suppliers in specific product areas.

The increasing currency stability of the 1980s may have helped encourage the development of links between retailers and suppliers as cross-country price comparisons became easier. The greater instability for the UK encourages switches in sourcing. The problems with the EMS since September 1992 and more acutely with the introduction of the 15 per cent bands for permitted fluctuation in early August 1993 may have reduced the attraction of alliances where devaluation seems likely. Clearly it depends which end of the transaction one is on as to who faces the potential gains or losses.

The role of regulation

One of the major sources of difference between the German and UK industries lies in the extent of regulation. German regulation is generally much more extensive. Larger stores have harsher regulation than smaller (Weitzel, 1993). This is ostensibly to deal with special problems such as the heavy traffic they generate but also to maintain the mix of retail outlets of various types and sizes. Measures such as planning controls are quite effective measures of protection for the smaller incumbents; nevertheless the number of large stores has grown steadily so that at best these arrangements delay rather than prevent entry.

A second major area of German regulation relates to packaging. Retailers are supposed to demand environmentally friendly or the re-use of packing materials from their suppliers. The regulation of 12 June 1991 obliges traders to take back and dispose of packaging materials. In order to arrange a network of collection and disposal sites in addition to the stores themselves, food manufacturers and the retailing groups have jointly set up the Duales System Deutschland – Gesellschaft für Abfallvermeidung und Sekundarrohstoffgewinnung mbH (DSD). Participants can put a green dot on their products to signify that the packaging will be taken back.

DSD aims to reduce waste, to encourage ecologically friendly packaging, to provide systematic information on how consumers can avoid wasting the materials and ensure their recycling and to promote re-usable beverage containers. Legislation supports this, requiring the provision of packaging bins in which the material to be re-used can be collected separately from household waste. It sets targets for the proportions of material to be collected by target dates; for example, 80 per cent of packaging materials must be collected by 1 July 1995. Firms, whether domestic or foreign, must offer adequate guarantees for the acceptance and recycling of these materials. By 1 December 1991 firms were obliged to take back and re-use packaging used for transport: pallets, barrels, boxes, cartons, and so on. This was supplemented on 1 April 1992 by the requirement to allow customers to remove and leave behind 'wrapping materials' on a self-service basis. Lastly, from 1 January 1993, firms have had to take back and demand deposits on containers for beverages, cleaning materials, detergents and paints.

The per item costs of these arrangements are quite small, ranging from 1–20 pfennigs, depending upon size (Weitzel, 1993). While in a sense this is non-discriminatory as all firms have to participate, the system is inevitably more difficult for foreign firms as they have to make arm's length arrangements, usually employing German agents. Insofar as they re-use materials themselves, then the amount in circulation will tend to be greater – because of the longer distance and hence time of supply and return – and the transport costs will be higher.

The third area of regulation in Germany, which is exciting considerable debate, is over shop opening hours. These are governed by the Shop Closing Hours Act, whose primary aim is protection of retailing employees from requirements to work excessive or unsocial hours. Since 1989 shops have been allowed to stay open until 8.30pm on Thursdays, provided they do not open for more than 64.5 hours in total. However, only about 10 per cent of firms have taken advantage of this opportunity and those which have appear to have rearranged their employees' working hours rather than increase employment or hours worked. However, the new arrangements have changed shopping patterns with a move towards shopping in city centres, particularly through multiple retailers. It is the smaller retailers in suburban and rural locations who appear to have lost out.

It would be wrong to think that Germany is more regulated in the retail sector than the UK. While the requirements of the Consumer Protection Act of 1967 and the Trade Description Act of 1968 on clear information about content and price are fairly similar to requirements elsewhere in the EC, the UK has greater restriction on advertising, particularly on tobacco and alcohol. Germany has no restrictions on alcohol advertising and only voluntary ones on tobacco. Secondly, planning restrictions are generally harsher in the UK. In Germany it is only the large-scale projects which are subject to considerable constraint. In the UK each local area has its own restrictions in addition to those imposed by the Town and Country Planning Act of 1971 and the larger cases have to be referred to the Department of the Environment. A company therefore requires considerable local knowledge, which implies an extra cost for foreign companies and the need to have considerable local assistance if they are to succeed in applications. All this in an environment where the incumbents, who are very much insiders, have every incentive to oppose these developments through official, legal and political channels.

The UK also has restrictions on shop opening hours. According to the 1950 Shops Act shops can be open on work days until 8pm and one night a week until 9pm. They should be closed on Sundays. However, de facto deregulation has occurred and fines, when imposed, are sufficiently small that they do not act as much of a deterrent.

The way forward is only partly determined by harmonising legislation required by the EC. Some small changes to labelling and advertising might be implemented. In the main the changes will be nationally driven and two trends can be expected, the one towards increased legislation on more environmentally favourable behaviour and the other on greater freedom to supply. The European Court has confirmed that it is the UK government which must resolve the issue of Sunday opening. In a series of preliminary rulings in 1991/92, the Court ruled that restrictions on Sunday opening hours were not contrary to Articles 30–34 of the Treaty of Rome. A further proposal for legislative change may be tabled in the UK Parliament in the near future.

Routes to change

In both the grocery and clothing sectors of retailing the larger firms appear to be following one or other of four main strategies in the face of the single market.

GROCERY

1   Concentrate on the home market, with little change in product mix, while expanding international sourcing, not just within Europe (for example, Budgen, Morrison, Low).
2   Concentrate on the home market, with little change in product mix but actively develop international purchasing through an information sharing alliance (for example, Argyll, Asda, Coop).

3   Develop sales outlets abroad, generally by acquisition of existing chains (US more common than Europe) (for example, Sainsbury, Tesco, Marks and Spencer).
4   Diversify within the UK market, using acquisitions or joint ventures to fill knowledge gaps (for example, Sainsbury, Asda).

CLOTHING

1   Expand selling activities abroad, starting with a low-cost entry method such as in-store concessions or mail-order. Subsequently set up independent outlets once knowledge of the market has been improved.
2   Diversify into new product areas at home, initially through existing stores but subsequently through new dedicated outlets.
3   Concentrate on new clothing trends in the UK, reducing lead times by improving relations with suppliers.
4   Exploit high quality and specialised niches in the domestic market.

The grocery sector

Grocery retailing has developed its own format which is not readily exportable to other sectors of retailing. The market is close to saturation, with a sequence of new stores set to open in the next two years. Acquisition of new sites is both slow and expensive, although there is some further scope for hypermarkets and discount stores. The UK does not have the continental option of trucking goods across borders or attracting foreign customers as a ready means of expansion. The emphasis has therefore tended to be on the home market, with only limited diversification except through the largest stores where non-food items now account for about half of turnover.

There has been some market entry (from Netto and Aldi) at the discount end of the market. However, while Argyll, Gateway and CRS are developing their own discount stores in parallel with their traditional stores, the other major companies have not followed suit as it can be difficult to integrate discount stores with the rest of the company's management and distribution systems (Tesco is trying some discount ranges within its existing stores). As profit margins are low, costs have to be trimmed to the bone. Some of the larger chains have been seeking greater market share by moving into the smaller, convenience store market, where margins are traditionally somewhat higher (Duke, 1990), although Budgens and Marks and Spencer have followed an intermediate path of opening 'neighbourhood' stores. Another variation of this strategy has been concentration on particular regions: for example Wm Low (Scotland) and Budgens (south-east England) have followed this route.

Attitudes have been rather defensive, with worries about the extent of differences in other markets. Elsewhere in the EC and in the US firms have been more aggressive. For example, after divesting itself of its northern European acquisitions, Carrefour (France) has moved into Spain, the Far East and South America, while Safeway (USA) has moved into Mexico and Saudi Arabia through joint ventures (Treadgold and Davies, 1988). It is argued that the high centralisation of the UK groups makes successful creation of subsidiaries more difficult (Treadgold, 1990a). Both Carrefour and GIB (Belgium) have implemented considerable local management power, while Habitat's failed West German operation attributed some of its problems to inadequate local discretion over purchasing, financing and sites.

International alliances are becoming more important for retailers who do not diversify or internationalise. However, while Argyll, Asda and Booker-McConnell have joined such groups (AMS, DEURO and Cooperation de Marketing, respectively) most continental chains have joined these or other groups. In part this may reflect the UK groups' earlier strategies of increasing size, severing links with manufacturing and developing own brands, which would make linking in with other groups a costly and less beneficial exercise.

The international alliances have gone to some trouble to disown the label 'purchasing group', if only because this could imply levels of collusion unacceptable to DG IV. In any case perishability means that many items have to be purchased in more decentralised supply chains. Sharing information enables the participants to increase quality, identify new products and follow best practice more readily. The gains from links with suppliers are also two-way as suppliers of own brands gain savings on promotion and distribution and reduced risk in the development of new products. Cost alone is not the reason for supply links and reliability can be developed by comparison with others. However, EDI and EPOS systems do benefit from coordinated purchasing and will aid future joint actions or links with common suppliers. Interestingly enough, much of the initial activity of these groupings has been in discussing proposed EC regulations and formulating a common response to them with appropriate lobbying tactics.

These alliances do not seem to prevent the members from competing against each other. Within AMS, Dansk Supermarked (via Netto) entered the UK in competition with Argyll before leaving the alliance in

1992 to pursue a new collaboration with Spar to develop Netto in Germany. Migros entered France in competition with Casino although they also left AMS at the end of 1992. The sharing of information is likely to ease market entry. However, the UK firms entering other markets have preferred vertical linkages to horizontal arrangements with other retailers. Indeed the real benefits of these large alliances are somewhat difficult to identify (Treadgold, 1990b) and may be chosen simply because of the great cost of the alternatives.

The propensity of UK companies to enter the US rather than other European markets seems in part due to difficulty of access both to companies and to sites but also because those markets require much larger changes to the trading formula. In any case the geographical barrier posed by the Channel means that UK overseas investments have to jump overseas and jumping the Atlantic is neither a great deal more expensive nor complex than jumping the Channel. Continental suppliers on the other hand can move readily across borders and hence have to make a step change to enter the US – not of course that this has prevented companies like Tengelmann from taking that step. The extent of comprehensive food retailing chains in the US is actually fairly limited and it is possible to purchase smaller groups and to make greenfield investments with greater ease. It has therefore been possible to enter with an immediate permanent large-scale presence and hence reap the advantages of economies of scale which are necessary to operate competitively there.

Product diversification nationally has been largely a complementary strategy with internationalisation. In both cases entry costs are high because methods need to be rather different. Acquisitions and joint ventures have been used in part because this is a straightforward means of obtaining the necessary knowledge of the new market area. One interesting example has been the joint venture by Tesco and Marks and Spencer in opening separate stores on the same sites in order both to make the new location viable and attract a wider range of customers than they would each individually obtain. DIY and home fittings have been among the commonest forms of diversification but the two businesses are largely separate, employing different technologies, with most of the economies of scale and scope only occurring at the head office. However, the company name does attract customers from one operation to the other. In practice, despite the saturation that has been rapidly appearing in this market, the new ventures have provided a rapid rate of return and have generally survived well in the economic downturn. They have therefore been able to move on to their own separate organic growth.

However, success in one diversification does not have any implications for likely success in another as the sectors are so different. A new strategy would be required for each entry with large separate managements involved. Thus for each step a fairly similar decision is faced between diversification and internationalisation.

The clothing sector

The experience of clothing is distinguished from food retailing in two important respects. Firstly the industry had over-expanded in high cost high street sites during the 1980s and has therefore been forced to sell off shops. Secondly, at the same time there has been much greater activity by new entrants and existing players from elsewhere within the EC (Benetton, C&A, Stefanel and Descamps) and from outside (for example, Hennes & Mauritz, Levi and The Gap). Entry has been motivated by perceived advantages in quality, price, style and in-store format. Although some have yet to get beyond London and the major cities, strong brand names and heavy advertising have enabled them to capture effective market share. There is also some suggestion that stronger vertical integration among some of these companies may have assisted their entry, UK companies having divested themselves of much of their manufacturing capability.

Unlike food retailing, it is much easier to enter foreign markets in the clothing sector on an 'experimental' basis. Labelling has become 'European', allowing a product to be sold in different markets. The role of fashion means that designs can be sold in a number of markets particularly at the higher value-added end of the market and do not require major local customisation. Internationalisation of supply is also helping in the development of trading links.

Two ready examples of this 'experimental' approach come through the opening of concessions within departmental stores and the use of mail order. Concessions draw immediately on a ready customer base and local knowledge, while avoiding the costs of site acquisition and promotion. Concessions are often short-run agreements which mean that the supplier is not locked into the arrangement. Mail order is relatively small in the UK (12 per cent of womenswear according to table 3.11) and focussed on particular sectors with over £1 billion turnover in 1990. Although the market on the continent has been rather different, nevertheless the order-processing and distribution technology are similar (including telephone and teletext shopping which has been rather more developed there). Entry has been facilitated by purchase, with Otto Versand buying Grattan and La Redoute gaining a controlling share in Empire.

One aspect holding back UK mail-order companies may be that they tend to be concentrated in the north of England and hence are slightly more isolated from the continent than other retailers. From the point of view of mailing and ordering this is of little consequence.

Franchising offers a route for quick market access without high capital cost, although with more limited managerial control, provided that there are clear means of maintaining quality control and franchisees are selected with great care. Burton for example abandoned its earlier venture in wholly-owned stores in northern Europe and has supplemented its concessions in Spain and Germany with franchising. Marks and Spencer also runs a large franchising operation in part because of the difficulties in expanding its network of new stores. Joint ventures have had some appeal, such as that between Sears and a French chain and activity within Europe has not precluded ventures further afield, like those of Marks and Spencer in North America and the Far East. Acquisition has proved more difficult, not just because of problems in identifying targets but in finding willing sellers.

Diversification has been followed most readily by the department stores, although Littlewoods and Marks and Spencer have made a number of 'piecemeal' diversifications into other services. In some cases companies have moved in the opposite direction, focussing on niches such as sportswear and outsize clothing. Others have followed a mixed strategy of using niches to protect parts of their operation while looking for new opportunities elsewhere.

Reflections

The response of the retailing sector in the UK and Germany has revealed some clear differences based on location, on structure and on previous strategies. The absence of a land border with the main markets has meant that the UK producers have not been involved in direct cross-border operations. Foreign operations have involved a major step outside existing markets and as a result there has been less distinction between the attractions of the North American and European markets. The concentrated nature of the UK suppliers and their rate of growth has meant that they have been able to sustain their own development without the network of vertical and horizontal relationships that has been developing in Germany. However, the process of growth in food retailing in the UK and the over expansion in clothing has meant that companies are relatively poorly placed for further internal or external growth.

German companies on the other hand have been able to make inroads into the UK market, in part because they have been able to offer a different format in discount stores, in part because they have larger financial resources, but mainly because there have been willing sellers and a more open market for acquisitions. Companies are pushed towards the acquisition route because of the barriers to greenfield expansion which occur through planning permission, the unwillingness to sell sites rather than businesses and the need for local knowledge. Nevertheless it does appear that UK companies have focussed rather more on domestic operations than their German counterparts, although the unification of Germany has diverted many companies away from their intended paths.

The clothing and food sectors of the industry have shown important differences. Not only is the expertise in food retailing difficult to transpose into other sectors, but it does not have the easier methods of experimental entry into other markets via concessions or mail-order, nor the ready ability to expand through franchising – links between independents in purchasing chains being the nearest equivalent.

The specific impact of 1992 has been relatively limited. It may have changed the pace of European strategies but it has not had much impact in encouraging new activity. Where the 1992 measures have run very much in line with industry trends in facilitating the development of Euro-brands and enabling concentration in labelling and detailed product content this has aided the way forward. However, technical differences remain and the new rules on returnable and recyclable packaging in Germany act as a barrier to outside entry and the development of manufactured food exports as well as cross-border retailing. Local differences such as shop closing hours have much less relevance to international competition except where consumers can cross the border. As a result one can expect considerable pressure on the German regulatory codes from border areas. Nevertheless tastes and habits appear to change only slowly and differences can persist for long periods with relatively limited competition among rules across the member states in this sector. Change in the industry has thus been very much one of continuing progression. While it may be relatively difficult to identify strong departures from pre-existing trends now after only six years of the single market programme, they may be much more obvious by the end of the decade.

4 The pharmaceuticals industry

The pharmaceuticals industry provides an interesting combination of features which make it ideal for our study. In the first place there is a strong industry in both the UK and Germany; indeed this is probably the best known of the few instances in manufacturing where the UK appears to outperform its German counterpart. Second, the industries are heavily regulated on a national basis and face strong national purchasers through the respective health service systems. These health services themselves have different structures, although they have common problems such as the need to contain costs. Third, the industry is characterised by large multinational firms already competing at the global level, which have the resources to change in response to a new regulatory environment. Lastly, the Commision has made it clear that it wishes to see substantial change in moving towards a single market in respect of both the licensing of drugs and their pricing. In this area, where consumer protection is so important, national sensitivities are likely to be at their highest. We therefore have the potential for change, clear differences between the two countries, and a wide range of single market and other EC regulatory changes in progress, in an industry with the ability to react and restructure at the international level.

In this chapter we begin with a brief overview of the industry and the main companies before moving on to its structure and performance. We focus in particular on the issues of pricing within the two countries and the central role of patents. The chapter is completed by an assessment of the vulnerability of the industry in each country to the opening of the market and the particular impact that the measures from the 1992 programme are likely to have in an industry where competition is global.

An overview of the industry and the issues

Although the present chapter is confined to the pharmaceuticals industry in Britain and Germany, this is highly restrictive as the industry is global in nature. Most of the world's top twenty firms (which together have over 50 per cent of the sales and over 85 per cent of R&D expenditure) operate in all the important markets in the world. The leading markets are the United States, with 29 per cent, Japan 20 per cent, Germany 8 per cent, France 7 per cent and Italy 7 per cent (Sharp, 1991). According to Burstall (1991) the UK market for pharmaceuticals is about 57 per cent of that in Germany, as shown in table 4.1, which would place it at between 4 and 5 per cent of the world market. If the world market shares of the member states of the EC were aggregated, their combined share would be some 30 per cent and would exceed even that of the US. Indeed, when the single European market is fully developed, the EC drug producers should be able to obtain all the advantages enjoyed by their American and Japanese rivals who already operate within unified markets. Such measures depend on drug prices which vary between countries and so the estimated world market shares should be regarded as indicating orders of magnitude rather than precise figures.

Expenditure also depends on the institutional arrangements for dispensing drugs in each country. In Britain, the National Health Service provides doctors with incentives to limit expenditure on drugs.[1] In the European Community, Germany tends to have high drug prices and France, Belgium and Italy tend to have low ones. Britain is a medium-price country. In 1989, the average retail price of drugs in West Germany was nearly 33 per cent higher than in the UK (Economist Intelligence Unit, 1991, p. 21). In the UK there is a Pharmaceutical Price Regulation Scheme (PPRS) under which producers are free to set whatever prices they wish for individual drugs providing the stipulated rate of profit is not exceeded.[2] In Germany there are constraints on drug prices. First, the retailers' margins are fixed. Secondly, there are maximum margins for wholesalers which in practice may exceed their actual margins. That is, the wholesalers pass on part of their margins to the retail chemist shops. Thirdly, there are reference prices for many drugs and the patient has to pay any excess of the actual price over the reference price.

Both Britain and Germany have negative lists of drugs which cannot be prescribed under the national or statutory health insurance schemes. Both require patients, with certain exceptions, to contribute towards the cost and both encourage the use of generics (out-of-patent drugs).[3]

Table 4.1. *Consumption of pharmaceuticals in Britain and Germany, 1988*

	Britain	Germany
Total expenditure, $US million	5410	9380
Per person, $US	89	153
% growth, 1983-6	21	3
% through hospitals	15	16
% through physicians	69	67
% over-the-counter (OTC)	16	17
Average cost (EC=100)	118	133
Volume per person (EC=100)	66	101

Source: Burstall (1991, Exhibit 1, p. 158)

The recent health reforms in Germany which linked patient co-payments to the excess of drug prices over their reference prices, together with negative lists and the closer monitoring of doctors' prescribing, are not part of the '1992' effects but they are nevertheless putting pressure on the German pharmaceutical industry. According to Paul Abrahams (*Financial Times*, 3 August 1993), health reforms launched in January 1993 led to the reduction of sales of pharmaceuticals by 11 per cent up to May 1993. German doctors have switched to prescribing cheaper generic drugs, with the result that the market share of the generic group increased by 20 per cent in the first half of 1993. Thus the effects of '1992' may be regarded as a subset of the many disturbances affecting the pharmaceutical industry in Britain and Germany. A comparison of pharmaceutical consumption in the two countries is given in table 4.1. It can be seen that total expenditure per person in Germany in 1988 was nearly 72 per cent more than in Britain. The average cost per person was nearly 13 per cent higher and the average volume per person was 53 per cent higher in Germany.

Research and development are of crucial importance in the production of ethical pharmaceuticals, where 'ethical' refers to a branded innovative medicine. The multinational pharmaceutical enterprises are footloose and the quality and cost of research influences the location of the research base (Casson, ed., 1991). According to the Club de Bruxelles (1991, p. 25) some 80 per cent of all research effort in the industry is concentrated in the United States, Japan, Switzerland, Germany, UK, France and Italy. Britain now accounts for 8 per cent of world expenditure on research and development on pharmaceuticals. As a proportion of the industry's gross output in Britain, R&D expenditure increased from 2.4 per cent in 1953 to over 16 per cent in 1990 (ABPI, 1992).

New research techniques are likely to accentuate the rise in R&D costs. Biotechnology, including the use of genetic engineering to clone proteins and to change them in order to eliminate unwanted side effects, will become increasingly important. Other factors making for increased costs include the public requirement for longer and more complicated testing. This upward pressure on costs, combined with the downward pressure on profit margins resulting from shorter effective patent lives and from government efforts to reduce the costs of health care to the state, affects drug companies worldwide. They are certainly important in the present analysis of the British and German pharmaceutical industries.

The official British definition of this industry contains more than the production of drugs and is as follows: SIC (1980) 2570, manufacture of products for therapeutic and prophylactic use (including veterinary) and chemicals for compounding into such products, including the same products subsequently used as additives in food and drink. The manufacture of saccharin, sutures, sticking plasters and dental consumables is included. This classification follows the NACE 257 classification used for EC statistics on the pharmaceuticals industry, which also includes additional products such as vegetable extracts, fish liver oils, dental cements, and plasters. The German definition also follows NACE 257. It should be noted that the definitions used in the trade sometimes differ from NACE 257, usually by excluding the manufacture of sticking plaster, dental consumables and so on. The present chapter uses the official NACE definition when comparing the British and German industries. When a smaller coverage, such as prescription medicines, is being used, this is stated.

Drug production itself has been further classified by Reuben and Burstall (1989) as shown by rows 1.1 to 2.2.3 in table 4.2. In addition, there is the OTC (over-the-counter) trade in row 3, which in 1987 represented 37 per cent of the pharmaceuticals market in West Germany and 22 per cent in the UK, according to the Economist Intelligence Unit (1991). More recent figures from ABPI (1992) put the OTC share of the British market in 1987 at 24 per cent, compared with 25 per cent in 1990.[4]

These estimates are based on OTC sales of £590 million in 1987 and £862 million in 1990, as shown in ABPI (1992, table 5, p. 14). Gross output of the whole NACE 257 industry in 1987 was £5010.3 million. The gross output of OTC products is not known. OTC sales include

Table 4.2 *Classification of drugs*

1	*Ethical pharmaceuticals (branded innovative medicines)*
1.1	True ethical pharmaceutical, protected by patent and marketed by its inventor
1.2	True patent-protected pharmaceutical, produced and marketed under licence by a company, not its inventor
1.3	Pirate ethical pharmaceuticals produced in countries where patent laws are lax or non-existent
2	*Multi-source drugs*
2.1	Out-of-patent pharmaceuticals marketed by their inventors under their brand names
2.2	True generics
	2.2.1 Out-of-patent pharmaceuticals marketed by non-originating companies under their own brand names
	2.2.2 Out-of-patent pharmaceuticals marketed by non-originating companies under a generic name plus a company name (or prefix or suffix)
	2.2.3 Out-of-patent pharmaceuticals marketed by non-originating companies under a generic name with minimum mention of the company's name, e.g. in small print on the label or by initials. These are illegal in most European countries since the doctor must specify the source
3	*Over-the-counter medicines (OTC) [These do not require a prescription]*

Source: Reuben and Burstall (1989)

imports, and the OTC gross output would include exports, hence the OTC sales figure cannot be used to measure OTC gross output. Nevertheless, the OTC sales figure is so small compared with the industry's gross output (about 12 per cent) that it is clear that the bulk of gross output of the industry relates to prescription medicines. Hence this chapter concentrates on the effects of '1992' on prescription medicines. However, special reference will be made to the OTC producers when discussing the effects of '1992' on the smaller businesses.

The total expenditure on ethical drugs is also influenced by the institutional arrangements for the payment of doctors. If they are paid on the basis of the number of patients on their lists, rather than on a fee per visit basis, there will be fewer visits per capita and hence fewer prescriptions per capita. In Britain the physicians' remuneration depends on the number of patients on their lists, although there are some service fees and bonus payments. In Germany, they are paid according to a points system with the number and value of points weighted towards basic services such as consultations and examinations. Hence, there will be more prescriptions per capita in Germany than in Britain. According to the international comparisons made by ABPI (1988), British patients receive on average 6.5 prescriptions per annum, compared with 11.2 for Germany, 35 for Japan, and 16.6 for the US.

The producers

Table 4.3 shows the production of the EC pharmaceutical industry, in million Ecus, 1980–7, compared with that in Japan and the US. It can be seen that over this period production in the US and in Japan increased more rapidly than in the EC. In 1980, EC production was more than twice that in Japan and about 30 per cent more than in the US. By 1987, EC production was some 68 per cent more than in Japan and 23 per cent more than in the US. The world's leading pharmaceutical companies are listed in appendix A to this chapter.

Since 1987 in the UK, the basic Census of Production reporting unit has been the business, which might be a company or an establishment, as explained in more detail in appendix A. Table 4.4 shows the size distribution of Census pharmaceutical businesses in 1987. The BSO in the UK also publishes distributions of local units (factories or sites) by employment, and of legal units (companies, partnerships, and so on) by turnover, for this industry which are discussed in detail in Hart (1992b).

Table 4.5 distributes the enterprises (all businesses under common ownership or control) by employment in 1987. The aggregation of businesses into enterprises explains why the number of observations, 352, is so far below the number in table 4.4, 402. It can be seen that the largest five enterprises have 35.2 per cent of the total employment in this industry, 47 per cent of total net output, and 51.5 per cent of gross value added at factor cost (defined as net output minus the cost of industrial services received, rates and the cost of licensing motor vehicles) and 38.4 per cent of total wages and salaries.

The Census of Production does not disclose any information which could be related to any individual firm, so we do not know the identities of the top five in table 4.5. However, other sources, including published accounts (Sharp, 1991, table 13.5, p.224, and *Acquisitions Monthly*,

Table 4.3 *Production of the pharmaceuticals industry in EC, Japan and the US, 1980–7*

	EC	Japan	US
1980	18601	9181	14273
1981	21199	12755	19987
1982	24234	13977	25207
1983	26585	17234	30791
1984	28952	19574	36704
1985	32397	21115	41058
1986	37775	20831	34915
1987	40442	24141	32722

Source: Club de Bruxelles (1991), table 7, annex, p. 8.

Table 4.4 *Size distribution of businesses by employment, pharmaceuticals, UK, 1987*

	n_j	L_j 000s	Q_j £mn	Q/L_j	E_j £mn	$(Q-E)/Q_j$ %
1-9	218	0.7				
10-19	41	0.5	113.6	26033	37.7	66.8
20-49	29	1.0				
50-99	29	2.1				
100-199	31	4.4	121.9	27790	39.3	67.8
200-299	9	2.2	63.1	28406	21.6	65.8
300-399	8	2.8	95.1	33389	28.9	69.6
400-499	5	2.4	79.9	33684	24.8	69.0
500-749	11	6.4	339.7	52719	68.8	79.7
750-1499	9	10.7	386.9	36071	121.2	68.7
1500-1999	5	8.5	291.7	34268	110.5	62.1
2000-2999	3	7.8	401.9	51209	101.1	74.8
3000 plus	4	21.5	1273.5	59266	278.7	78.1
Total	402	71.2	3167.3	44478	832.6	73.7

Source: *Business Monitor PA257,* Report on the Census of Production 1987, Pharmaceutical Products, table 4, p. 10.
L = employment; n = number of businesses; j = size class; Q = net output; E = wages and salaries (excluding employers' national insurance contributions).

Table 4.5 *Size distribution of enterprises by employment, pharmaceutical products (257), UK, 1987*

	n_j	L_j 000s	Q_j £mn	Q/L_j	E_j £mn	(Q-E)/Q_j %
1-99	277	4.0	102.4	25890	34.0	66.8
100-199	26	3.7	101.8	27240	33.4	67.2
200-499	17	5.8	200.5	34336	61.3	69.4
500-999	13	8.4	369.2	43934	85.9	76.7
1000-1499	5	6.2	249.1	39927	74.4	70.1
1500-1999	6	10.5	359.8	34273	135.3	62.4
2000-2999	3	7.4	293.1	39402	88.2	69.9
3000 plus	5	25.1	1491.3	59420	319.9	78.5
Total	352	71.2	3167.3	44478	832.6	73.7

Source: Central Statistical Office, Business Statistics Office. Report on the Census of Production 1987. Summary Volume *Business Monitor PA 1002*, table 13, p. 280
Note: Five largest enterprises by employment have 35.2 per cent of employment, 47 per cent of net output. 51.5 per cent of gross value added at factor cost, and 38.4 per cent of total wages and salaries.

Table 4.6. *Size distribution of businesses* (Unternehmen) *by employment, pharmaceuticals, Germany, 1987*

	n_j	L_j	Q_j DMmn	Q/L_j DM	E_j DMmn	(Q-E)/Q_j %
20-99	121	5601	859.1	153382	245.9	71.4
100-499	94	20090	3315.8	165049	1054.8	68.2
500 plus	43	65885	10415.4	158086	3827.0	63.3
Total	258	91576	14590.4	159326	5127.7	64.9

Source: *Statistisches Bundesamt* (1989), *Produzierendes Gewerbe*, Fachserie 4, Reihe 4.3.1, *Kostenstruktur der Unternehmen*, 1987, tables 3.1 (p. 30), 7 (p. 66), 8 (p. 72).
Note: j = size class; n = number of *Unternehmen*, L = *Beschäftige: Zusammen*; Q = *Nettoproduktionswert: Ingesamt*; E = *Bruttolohn- und Gehaltsumme: Zusammen* (*Sozialkosten* are excluded).

1989, p. 44) suggest they are now Glaxo, SmithKline Beecham, Ciba-Geigy, ICI, and Wellcome. Other possible candidates, such as Boots, Fisons and Reckitt and Colman are smaller. This is consistent with the list in the appendix.

For Germany, the size distribution corresponding to table 4.4 is shown in table 4.6. This relates to *Unternehmen* which approximate the British term, 'businesses' or units (sometimes companies, sometimes establishments), which make returns to the Business Statistics Office for the Census of Production. Note that this distribution is truncated, with all *Unternehmen* below twenty employees excluded. It is also extremely coarsely grouped, with only three size classes compared with the thirteen in table 4.4. Another limitation of these official statistics is that ownership is not revealed. A small business in Germany is often a free-standing unit selling primarily within Germany, whereas a small British business is often a subsidiary of a foreign multinational enterprise with all the financial and technical support that implies.[5] In fact, trade sources suggest that most of the 277 small British enterprises (those below 100 employees in table 4.5) manufacture generics, OTC products or the non-drug products included in the NACE category 257. This is important because the smaller enterprises have relatively low profitability, as shown below in the section on economic performance.

Sharp (1991) lists the following German firms in descending order of size in 1988–9: Hoechst-Roussel, Bayer, Boehringer-Ingelheim, Schering AG, E Merck, Knoll, and Boehringer-Mannheim. All are members of the Medizinisch-Pharmazeutische-Studiengesellschaft (MPS).

The average size of the German *Unternehmen* in table 4.6 is 355. But if the size distribution in table 4.5 is truncated at twenty employees to match table 4.6, the average British business above this size is 488, some 37 per cent larger than in Germany. Moreover, if those British businesses which were separate reporting units but owned by the same company were added together the British average size would be even larger. The conclusion to draw from the official data relating to NACE 257 is that the average British pharmaceuticals firm is larger, in terms of employment, than its German counterpart. It is not possible to measure the average size of businesses making prescription medicines using official NACE 257 data.

The production of prescription medicines is in two stages. The first is the production of the basic chemicals. The second is the formulation of these materials into dosage form. The formulation plants of the multinational enterprises, which dominate the industry, tend to be distributed across countries. Sometimes a multinational enterprise constructs a formulation plant in a host country to facilitate the marketing of its pharmaceuticals there. This tends to create excess capacity. Burstall and Reuben (1988) report that the European formulation plants of American multinationals often work at one third or one half of capacity. If this applies to all the 250 formulation plants in the EC it might be thought that the single European market would tend to reduce the number of formulation plants so that the excess capacity could be eliminated. Burstall and Reuben (1988) note this possibility but report that the multinational companies they interviewed thought there were sound non-economic reasons, such as preserving goodwill, why this would not happen. Nevertheless, Burstall and Reuben conclude that the effect of unification will be to strengthen the strong firms and make the weak firms even weaker.

The Economist Intelligence Unit (1991) notes the remark of the European Commission's vice-president, Martin Bangemann, that two hundred major pharmaceutical companies in Europe may be too many to compete effectively. The EIU reviews the acquisitions, mergers, joint ventures and collaboration between companies which have been taking place. Such activities are likely to be intensified with unification. The EIU also notes the likely entry of more Japanese companies, probably through greenfield investment rather than acquisition. The Japanese believe that when the new European registration system is working they might find it more difficult to obtain licences for their products unless they have their own plants in Europe.

Prices

In Germany and the UK there are constraints on the prices of prescription medicines as the result of regulations on profitability, as mentioned in the introduction. Such regulations differ between countries in the EC and there are signs that in future the Commission will monitor such regulations more closely. At the beginning of 1990 the Transparency Directive came into force. This was originally proposed by the Commission in 1986, following complaints that regulations in some member countries were unfair or discriminatory. The Transparency Directive is not a harmonisation measure as such but is a first step in that direction. It requires the appropriate authorities in member countries which have price or profit controls to:

- publish the criteria used;
- provide a statement to an applicant, where his proposal to set a price for a new product is rejected, giving objective and verifiable criteria for the rejection;

- make their decisions on proposals by companies within 180 days;
- review price freezes annually and avoid prolonging them unnecessarily;
- provide the Commission with details of the methods used to classify medicines, in either positive or negative lists, for reimbursement; and
- inform the Commission of the criteria for judging the fairness of transfer prices.

Discriminatory pricing and reimbursement schemes are contrary to the Treaty of Rome and the Transparency Directive may help to expose them. But this may depend on companies which are adversely affected being prepared to challenge the appropriate authorities in the courts, even though they will continue to depend on the decisions of such bodies in the future. The pharmaceutical companies appear to prefer a more complete liberalisation of the market for drugs.

According to Lynn (1991) the Commission has no plans for a common pricing policy, but it does plan to allow unfettered free trade in pharmaceuticals throughout the Community. At the moment it is possible for wholesalers to buy drugs in low-price countries and sell them in high-price markets, but they need licences and this trade – 'parallel imports' – amounts to only 1 to 1.5 per cent of European sales (Burstall, 1991). However, parallel imports are increasing and by 1987 reached between 5 and 10 per cent of the total drugs bill of the National Health Service in the UK. As time passes there will be fewer non-tariff barriers and such arbitrage may increase. Nevertheless, parallel importers will still need licences and in some cases pharmacists will still have the problem of being uncertain that the imported drugs offered to them are not counterfeit. Again, language barriers will continue and patients prefer instructions on the packet to be in a language they can understand. Hence, not all non-tariff barriers to trade will disappear and the growth of parallel imports may be constrained.

It might be possible in the short term for a company to differentiate its product, by selling it in one country as pills, in another as capsules, and in a third as injections, each with a different price and possibly a different brand name. But one would expect doctors to counter such moves very quickly by prescribing the cheapest form. Under another rule proposed by the Commission, manufacturers would no longer be allowed to issue promotional gifts to doctors, arrange promotional conferences or even advertise their drugs, thus limiting the scope for product differentiation. The Commission's proposal was subsequently modified and the proposed rules on advertising and so on, eventually submitted to the European Parliament for implementation on 1 January 1993, do not limit product differentiation.

It is also possible that some manufacturers simply will not market their drugs in low-price countries. This will create problems, especially if a new life-saving ethical drug is available only to those in a low-price country who can afford to import it. In the extreme, it is possible for a government to remove a patent from a manufacturer and give it to another who is prepared to manufacture it and sell it throughout the Community. But such action might have adverse effects on the incentives of companies to undertake the expensive research necessary to develop new drugs.

Completely free trade in pharmaceuticals would suit the manufacturers, but if present government policies on health care continue it would increase government expenditure considerably. Of course, such policies could change to place more of the costs on patients through private insurance. Perhaps the freeing of prices could be done gradually, beginning with older drugs. Perhaps those borderline cases (such as vitamins and tonics in Germany and tranquillisers in Britain) could be paid for by the patients. But the containment of government expenditure is really a separate issue concerning the politics of the allocation of expenditure between patients and taxpayers. The European Commission has entered the debate by proposing that member countries should relax controls on drug prices, should require insured patients to pay a significant share of drug costs, and should encourage pharmacists to use cheapest products (*Financial Times*, 29 February 1992). Subsequently, the European Commission shelved measures to harmonise drug prices in the Community. It recognised that the present dispersion of prices across member states runs counter to the most basic objects of the Treaty of Rome but the principle of subsidiarity, which fosters decision-making at the lowest possible level, favoured national rather than Community constraints on drug prices (*Financial Times*, 2 December 1992).

Economic performance

Measures of the comparative economic performance of the British and German pharmaceuticals industries may be obtained from the respective Censuses of Production, which of course relate to the official NACE 257 definition. Table 4.5 implies that the labour productivity (net output per head) of the top five enterprises in the UK was 33.5 per cent greater than the weighted average for the industry (0.47/0.352 = 1.335).

If gross value added at factor cost is used to measure output, the labour productivity of the top five was 46.3 per cent greater than the average (0.515/0.352 = 1.463). These results are consistent with the hypothesis that in the pharmaceuticals industry in the UK there is a small group of enterprises at the production frontier, well able to compete in a single European market, and a long tail of low productivity firms which might experience more difficulty.

This conclusion is supported by table 4.4, which shows that the largest businesses above 2,000 employees have higher labour productivity than those in the smaller size classes. The high net output per capita in class 500–749 is consistent with the high figure in class 500–999 in table 4.5, but it does not alter the general conclusion that in the UK the smallest firms have low labour productivity. The general conclusion from the German data in table 4.6 is similar; the smallest size class of businesses, with 20–99 employees, has the lowest weighted average labour productivity.

In principle, it is possible to compare the average labour productivities of British and German pharmaceutical businesses by using an appropriate exchange rate. The crude ratio of average productivities in tables 4.6 and 4.4 is given by 159326/44478 = 3.58. If the appropriate exchange rate is less that DM3.58 to £1, then average productivity is higher in Germany than in Britain. For example, if we use the average spot exchange rate in 1987 of 2.95, then average German productivity was 21 per cent higher than in Britain, since 3.58/2.95 = 1.21. But the spot rate might be misleading insofar as it is unduly influenced by short-term capital movements. Perhaps we should follow O'Mahony (1992) and use unit value ratios (UVR). But they are not available for pharmaceuticals and the nearest approximation is the 3.54 UVR for chemicals, which would suggest that average productivity was much the same in the two countries.

Against this, it might be argued that pharmaceuticals are a special case and cannot be represented by the chemicals UVR. The major part of production relates to patented ethical pharmaceuticals. By definition they are quite different from each other, within and between countries. Moreover, as noted earlier in this chapter, their prices (and hence their unit values) are constrained by the respective governments rather than being freely determined in the market. In the circumstances, a UVR for pharmaceuticals is not a legitimate concept and so we cannot compare average labour productivity between countries. Indeed, because of the unique properties of each pharmaceutical product it might not be reasonable to compare labour productivities between firms in the same country. In this industry, the brains of the research staff, rather than the productivity of manufacturing labour, govern the firm's economic performance and the research laboratories are excluded from the Census of Production data because they are not engaged in manufacturing.

But in any case, labour productivity by itself is an inadequate measure of economic performance. The Census of Production source at the foot of table 4.5 shows that the top five enterprises had a net capital expenditure of £202.2 million, which was 51.8 per cent of total net capital expenditure. Thus the top five enterprises had over 47 per cent greater investment per head (0.518/0.352 = 1.472) than the average. In such circumstances it is not surprising that their labour productivity was so high. To allow for their large capital inputs we need a measure of total factor productivity or at least a measure of profitability. The approximation usually adopted from Census of Production data is the gross profitability, $(Q-E)/Q$, where Q denotes net output and E denotes wages and salaries.[6] Using this statistic, the top five enterprises in table 4.5 had a profitability of 78.5 per cent. It is clear from table 4.5 that most enterprises, especially those with fewer than one hundred employees, were operating on much smaller profit margins.

The gross measure of profitability provided by $(Q-E)/Q$ in table 4.6 suggests that the largest German pharmaceutical businesses tend to be less profitable than the smaller ones. Furthermore, a comparison of tables 4.4 and 4.6 shows that the smaller German firms in class 20–99 employees have higher profitability at 71.4 per cent than the smaller British firms in the same size classes, which obtained 66.8 per cent. This supports the previous conclusion, based on labour productivity, that the smallest British pharmaceutical firms, which are probably mainly producing OTC medicines or generic drugs, are more vulnerable to the intensification of competition following the completion of the single European market.

Another indicator of comparative economic performance is provided by table 4.7 which shows UK exports and imports of pharmaceuticals 1980–90. It can be seen that the UK pharmaceuticals trade has a positive balance with the world but a negative balance with Germany. ABPI (1992) shows that UK pharmaceutical exports have grown very rapidly, compared with total manufacturing exports, since 1970. In terms of positive trade balances with the rest of the world, the Swiss pharmaceuticals industry has first rank, with Germany second, the UK third and the the US fourth.

A more detailed examination of such trade balances, decomposed into intra-EC and extra-EC trade, is used to classify industries by their

Table 4.7   *UK exports and imports of pharmaceutical products, 1980–90 (£mn)*

	Exports	Imports	Exports to Germany	Imports from Germany
1980	745	223	60	47
1985	1427	590	77	125
1987	1621	786	119	195
1988	1735	876	113	197
1989	2016	1062	121	221
1990	2259	1158	175	255

Source: ABPI (1992), tables 14 and 15
Figures relate to SITC Div 54 and include OTC and other pharmaceutical products. Exports are measured FOB (free-on-board). Imports are measured CIF (carriage, insurance and freight included).

degree of sensitivity to the single European market in Buigues *et al.* (1990). The average competitiveness of each industry is measured by a series of ratios, such as $X/(X+M)$, where X denotes exports and M denotes imports. The summary measures for UK and German pharmaceuticals are reported below in the section on vulnerability.

Patents

As shown in table 4.2, patents are extremely important in this industry. As soon as a drug is out of patent it faces competition from generics. The period of effective patent protection has been falling and is now probably below seven years. Patents are taken out at the end of the discovery stage, before the development stage, which lasts several years. During this time the patent life is steadily reduced before the drug can be sold on the market. Thus when it is finally marketed the unexpired patent life might be relatively short.

The European Patent Convention allows for a twenty-year life of a patent, whereas up to 1977 UK legislation had previously limited it to sixteen years. In March 1990, the EC proposed a new Supplementary Protection Certificate (SPC) for pharmaceuticals (or at least the fifty or so innovative drugs which are authorised annually), which would extend the effective duration of the patent to sixteen years from the date of marketing. The SPC would have a maximum duration of ten years. In contrast, the maximum extension in the US and Japan is five years

(Touche Ross, 1990). In December 1991 the Council of Ministers of the EC approved regulations which give an effective patent life of fifteen years although the maximum period of the SPC was made five years instead of ten years.

The effective patent life is of crucial importance to the drug companies even though there are some counter measures which they may take when their patents expire. Reuben and Burstall (1989) list several ways of extending the effective life of a patent. Three examples are given here. First, a long-acting formulation of an old drug is patentable and, because it reduces the frequency with which the drug has to be taken, it has a competitive advantage over the generic. Secondly, a drug coming out of patent may be replaced by another which has an identical effect but which requires a smaller dosage. Thirdly, the brand name or some other aspect of the original drug may protect it against competition from generics. For example, Fison's best-selling asthma drug, Intal, is still highly profitable although it is out-of-patent in the UK. Its brand name, and the difficulty competitors have had in designing a substitute aerosol inhaler, are still preserving Intal's profitability, as noted by Paul Abrahams in the *Financial Times*, 8 February 1992. Clearly drug companies with expired patents are not defenceless.

Patent protection enables a drug company to finance its research expenditure by charging higher prices than would arise under perfect competition. Research costs are escalating and, by its very nature, research is very risky; failure is frequent and the relatively few successes have to finance all the research – successful and unsuccessful. Burstall (1990, p. 14) cites the example of the seven German research-oriented companies which examined 280,000 compounds over the period 1972–81, 2,356 of which reached the development stage, but only forty-seven of which reached the market.

In such circumstances, it might be thought that the producers of generics would be able to undercut the ethical pharmaceutical companies because their prices do not have to cover research costs. Reuben and Burstall show that in practice this does not happen. Generic producers have low profitability and ethical drug firms can always compete with them by producing their own generics. Sharp (1991) states that some 70–80 per cent of generics are now made by the major companies. The danger to the ethical drug producers arises not because of price competition from generics but from regulations which favour the use of generics.

But in order to assess the effects of generics on drug prices in the UK, we really need a comprehensive economic and econometric analysis such as that recently published by Caves, Whinston and Hurwitz (1991) who investigated the effects of patent expiry in the relatively free American pharmaceuticals industry. They show that drug prices tend to rise immediately after patent expiry and before the entry of generics into the market. Even after the entry of generics the fall in price is modest. However, advertising expenditure is reduced sharply, which, they believe, causes a fall in the volume of sales in spite of the fall in prices. The 'goodwill' during the patented drug's life, and the doctors' habit of using brand names, tends to limit the competitive threat from generics. The net result is that the market for generics in the US remains 'embarrassingly small', to use the authors' description. It is possible that 'goodwill' and doctors' habits are not the only reasons for the small sales of generics. In a litigious society, American doctors have to bear in mind possible law suits if patients think, rightly or wrongly, that they have not been prescribed the most efficacious drug. This might lead to the prescription of new patented drugs rather than the cheaper generic forms of patent-expired drugs.

The period during which a patented drug can earn a monopoly price is also reduced by the entry of rival patented drugs into the market. Technological progress in the pharmaceuticals industry is very rapid as a result of the huge research programmes being undertaken. Computers accelerate chemical research and also aid the identification and targeting of diseases which are likely to offer economic returns on drugs which treat or prevent them. But research is expensive. Already some companies spend up to 15 per cent of sales on research and many companies are increasing their research expenditure by as much as 20 per cent per annum. New drugs are being developed at an unprecedented rate, not only to improve treatments, but also to compete with existing ethical pharmaceuticals. Indeed, it might be argued that too many drugs are being developed. To quote from Professor Wade's letter in the *Independent*, 12 November 1991, '... increasingly in the last thirty years excessive and inappropriate use of new antibiotic and chemotherapeutic remedies has been encouraged and has too often rendered them rapidly ineffective because of the widespread development of bacterial or parasitic resistance'.

Vulnerability

Gerstenberger (1990) regards the German pharmaceuticals industry as 'sensitive' to the single European market, grading it as minus 2, or clearly below average. In contrast, the Department of Trade and Industry (1990) gives the British pharmaceuticals industry a score of plus 4, well above average performance. These scores are based on measures of export performance and production specialisation at the industry level. But the degree of vulnerability differs between firms. It is likely that the experience of Glaxo will be quite different from that of the many small British firms producing generics. British drug companies are comparatively strong. Of the world's fifty best selling drugs, which account for nearly half of the total world market, 27.6 per cent originated in the UK, compared with 29.8 per cent for the rest of Western Europe, 29.8 per cent for the US and 12.8 per cent for Japan. The UK companies produce six of the world's twenty best selling pharmaceutical products, including the best seller. German companies produce three, and the leader of these is now out of patent (ABPI, 1992). The pharmaceutical industry in Germany faces problems. Not only are its major products going out of patent, but the recent health reforms mentioned in the introduction are increasing the pressure on the industry.

According to *Acquisitions Monthly* (1989), the single European market will encourage the import of cheaper generics into the more expensive markets, such as Germany. This will affect large German pharmaceutical manufacturers adversely. It refers to a report from Shearson Lehmann Hutton, securities analysts, which argues that the reduction of price differentials could lead to a fall in total sales of 5–10 per cent, although different prescription habits and drug presentation methods will limit the shrinkage. For example, in Germany, the prescribing doctor specifies the supplier as well as the drug, and this practice may favour German firms, thereby reducing the impact of imports. In any case, German generic prices are relatively cheap, which would also limit the effect of imported generics.

Reuben and Burstall note that the prescription habits of German doctors tend to be conservative, with the result that the proportion of older out-of-patent drugs is unusually large. Moreover, the German national health insurance agencies exert financial pressure on doctors to prescribe generics. Thus the present tendency for the use of generics in Germany to increase will be accentuated. Against this the ethical pharmaceutical companies might develop longer-acting formulations or smaller-dosage drugs, as mentioned above.

In the United Kingdom, branded drugs appearing on the blacklist cannot be prescribed on the National Health Service; their generic equivalents must be prescribed instead. For all other drugs, the doctors may still choose between generic and branded products.

Since the expiry date of each patent is known, it is possible to assess the vulnerability of each ethical manufacturer to competition from generics based on the life table of its portfolio of patents. For example, if the patent of a firm's major profit-earning drug expires in 1992, it will be vulnerable after 1992. Reuben and Burstall assess the vulnerability of the world's major drug companies. For example, in the period 1991–4 the following firms are included among the vulnerable: Beecham, Ciba-Geigy, Fisons, and Hoechst-Roussel. The slightly vulnerable include Boehringer Mannheim, Glaxo, ICI, and Reckitt and Colman. But these assessments are made against a background of global competition rather than European competition. The major drug companies are multinational and can spread risks between different countries.

The spreading of risks is vital. In many ways a firm's set of drugs is similar to a portfolio of shares on the stock market. The hope is that all will be profitable and more than cover the costs of research and development. But in reality some will be less profitable than others and, since the financial results are not known beforehand, it is advisable to have a portfolio of different drugs. The variance of the average profitability of the portfolio over time will be less than the variance of the profitability of any one of the drugs in it.

Those firms which cannot afford to finance a sufficiently large portfolio may undertake joint ventures with other drug companies or merge with another company. Thus *Acquisitions Monthly* predicted that the number of mergers would increase in response to the escalating research costs. The same theme was taken up by Jason Nisse in the *Independent*, 12 January 1991, although the emphasis was on mergers involving non-British companies.

The competitive threat from generics is easier to deal with. If necessary, the large manufacturers of ethical drugs can produce generics themselves: they have the technical expertise, the equipment and the skilled sales force to produce and market generics more efficiently than the smaller generic producers.

The effects of the single European market

The pharmaceuticals industry contains firms with different products, different labour productivities, different profitabilities and different vulnerabilities to the more intensive competition likely to arise with the completion of the single European market. The classification of industries by their degree of sensitivity to '1992' does not reveal the important effects on individual firms. It must not be assumed that the large British and German ethical pharmaceutical manufacturers will have the average sensitivity of the industry.

The escalation of research costs and intensification of competition between ethical drugs is independent of the single European market. The Treaty of Rome does not enable the European Commission to enforce price parity throughout the Community. But the pressure of taxpayers on governments to reduce the costs of their national health insurance schemes may be powerful enough to eliminate differential pricing of the same drug in different parts of the Community. Nevertheless, it will take time for drug prices to converge.

The harmonisation of drug regulations is another important effect of '1992'. The requirements of the national authorities are already similar in principle, but in practice differences remain. For example, although all agree that a decision on the safety of a new drug should be reached within 120 days, it takes Germany and the UK some two years to reach a decision, while Italy and Spain may take three years or more. The opportunity cost of such delays to the applicants is considerable and they would like the uniform 120-day rule to be followed in practice.

The Commission wants to create a European Medicines Agency. This would validate all drugs derived from biotechnology and would also be able to license conventional drugs submitted to it voluntarily by companies in member states. In practice, the primary responsibility for evaluation of drugs would remain with the existing Committee for Proprietary Medicines, which would be reconstituted and reinforced (Griffin, 1992). In addition, the national agencies would still be able to license conventional drugs. Approval in one member state would be submitted to other member states for confirmation. If two national agencies disagreed, the new central agency would act as arbiter. Harmonisation of drug regulations throughout the EC and indeed throughout the world could reduce costs of research and development and increase international trade in pharmaceuticals. Discussions are still in progress.

Conclusion

The pharmaceuticals industry, as defined by NACE 257, contains branded innovative medicines (ethical drugs), generics, OTC (over-the-counter) medicines and various other products such as dental consumables. Most of the output relates to the production of prescription medicines (ethical and generic drugs), which form the first subheading of these conclusions. The second relates to the whole pharmaceutical products industry (NACE 257).

Prescription medicines

The prosperity of individual British and German pharmaceutical companies after 1992 will be heavily dependent on patents, prices, and on the harmonisation of the regulations on drug evaluation. Agreement on the effective length of patent life has been reached. This will be fifteen years from the date of marketing a drug. The patents held by British pharmaceutical companies are more valuable, in terms of sales, than those of the German companies. The most valuable British patents also have more unexpired life. This augurs well for the British firms owning such patents.

National governments wish to limit their expenditure on drugs in their national health service or statutory insurance schemes and they are unlikely to agree to free market pricing. The regulation of profit margins will continue to constrain manufacturers' prices. Parallel imports are unlikely to have a major effect on national prices. The Commission's Transparency Directive proposed in 1986 came into force in 1990 and is designed to increase the information available on prices. This may eliminate some arrangements made between governments and companies on profit margins or prices. The recent health reforms in Germany, which link patient co-payments to reference prices, have added to the pressure on German pharmaceutical companies, though this is quite separate from the effects of 1992.

The discussions on the harmonisation of regulations on drug evaluation are still in progress. The move towards the centralisation of approval procedure in a European Medicines Agency, the reduction in administrative delays, and the improved transparency in licensing should reduce costs and facilitate competition.

Pharmaceutical products (NACE 257)

There is a wide dispersion of economic performance among British producers, whether measured by net output per capita and gross profitability from Census of Production data or by profitability on sales from company accounts. The dispersion seems to be much larger in Britain than in Germany, though the coarse size grouping in the German Census of Production might qualify this result.

The smallest British pharmaceutical enterprises, which are free-standing and not controlled by another company in Britain, have low labour productivity and low profitability. They include manufacturers of OTC products and appear to be particularly vulnerable to any intensification of competition after 1992. Those which are subsidiaries of overseas companies may have the backing of powerful parent companies, which may reduce their vulnerability. But such ownership is not reported in the Census size distributions. In any case, it is unlikely that even a powerful overseas company would provide unlimited support to a British subsidiary with poor economic performance.

Appendix A

The terms of reference of our research project relate to British and German companies. Nevertheless, the ranking of the world's top twenty companies by sales in 1990 is interesting because it shows the relative position of British and German enterprises in the global industry. It confirms that SmithKline Beecham in the UK is second to Glaxo, although the ranking is by world sales, not UK sales.

Changes in the sales ranking of the top fifteen pharmaceutical enterprises since 1977 are shown in table 4A.2. These changes indicate the degree of competition among the leading firms.

According to the European Commission (CEC, 1991b, table 5 p. 8–60), Johnson & Johnson of the US should be in the world's largest pharmaceutical enterprises, as shown in table 4A.1. The same source, table 6, pp. 8–60, adds Montedison (Italy), Akzo (Holland), and Sanofi (France) to Europe's largest pharmaceutical enterprises.

Tables 4A.1 and 4A.2 refer to the enterprise, which is a group of companies under common ownership or control. Hence there are more companies than enterprises.

The Central Statistical Office publishes a Directory of Manufacturing Business which lists local units with manufacturing activity. Non-manufacturing units, such as offices (sometimes including head offices) are omitted. The current Directory (1989, p. 127) refers to 457 local units in the pharmaceuticals products industry 2570 and lists 101 of them. The 1990 volume lists 16 more, making a total of 117. The remaining 340 local units are either small, and therefore excluded from the main analyses of the Census of Production, or have not consented to be included in the Directory.

Let us take Glaxo Holdings plc as an example. This is a multinational enterprise. The British manufacturing local units it owns or controls through subsidiary companies would be aggregated and entered as one enterprise in table 4.5. Each one of its manufacturing

Table 4A.1 *The leading pharmaceutical enterprises*

Company	Home country	Sales 1990 (£mn)	Growth 1990/89 (%)
Merck	US	3610	9.4
B-Meyers Squibb	US	3360	8.0
Glaxo	UK	2970	9.2
SmithKline Beecham	UK	2810	0.0
Hoechst	Germany	2600	18.2
Ciba-Geigy	Switzerland	2580	11.7
Johnson & Johnson	US	2360	12.4
AHP	US	2260	-3.0
Sandoz	Switzerland	2250	8.7
Eli Lilly	US	2090	16.8
Bayer	Germany	2090	8.3
Pfizer	US	2070	10.7
Rhone-Poulenc Rorer	France	2030	7.4
Roche	Switzerland	1950	19.6
Takeda	Japan	1500	-23.9
Schering-Plough	US	1490	6.4
ICI	UK	1390	8.6
Marion M-Dow	US	1370	3.0
Upjohn	US	1360	3.8
Wellcome	UK	1270	15.5

Source: *Financial Times*, Survey, 23 July 1991

subsidiaries, such as Glaxochem Ltd, would be entered as one legal unit. But Glaxochem itself would be recorded as five separate local units because it manufactures at five separate sites, namely at Montrose (Angus), Annan (Dumfriesshire), Greenford (Middlesex), Ulverston (Cumbria), and Bedlington (Northumberland).

The Census term 'business' used in table 4.4 refers to the unit which reports to the Census of Production. That is, one Census questionnaire relates to the activities of one 'business', which may be one or more local units or indeed all the local units of a company. It depends in part on how the company's accounting system is organised. For example, if the accounting system of Glaxochem is centralised and completes one questionnaire, it could form one 'business' in table 4.4. But if some or all of its local units have separate accounting systems, it could be entered

Table 4A.2 *The world's top fifteen pharmaceutical enterprises by rank, 1977–88/9*

Company	Country	1977	1982	1983	1984	1985	1986/7	1988/9
Hoechst	West Germany	1	1	1	3	3	2	3
Merck & Co	US	2	3	3	1	1	1	1
Bayer	West Germany	3	2	2	4	5	4	4
Ciba-Geigy	Switzer-land	4	5	5	5	4	3	5
Hoffman la Roche	Switzer-land	5	8	10	11	15	-	15
American Home Products	US	6	4	4	2	2	5	7
Warner-Lambert	US	7	14	13	14	7	11	12
Pfizer	US	8	6	6	6	6	7	11
Sandoz	Switzer-land	9	9	12	12	14	8	8
Eli Lilly	US	10	7	7	8	9	9	9
Upjohn	US	11	-	14	13	13	15	-
Boehringer	West Germany	12	15	-	-	-	-	-
Squibb(a)	US	13	-	-	-	-	-	-
Bristol Myers	US	14	10	9	9	10	13	13
Takeda	Japan	15	13	15	15	-	12	6
SmithKline(b)	US	-	11	11	10	12	14	-
Glaxo	UK	-	-	-	-	11	6	2
Abbott	US	-	12	8	7	8	10	10
Eastman Kodak(c)	US	-	-	-	-	-	-	14

Source: Economist Intelligence Unit (1991)
(a) Squibb merged with Bristol Myers during 1989; combining their sales would put them higher in the table, as with other mergers.
(b) SmithKline merged with Beecham early in 1989.
(c) Eastman Kodak acquired Sterling Drug in 1988.

as up to five 'businesses' in table 4.4. Of course, most firms are much smaller than Glaxo and operate on only one site. In such cases, the enter-prise, company, legal unit, local unit and business refer to the same undertaking. The unit corresponding to the 'business' in the German Census is the *Unternehmen* in table 4.6.

The Directory also lists some local units under the 2570 heading which are included in tables 4.4 and 4.5 but which might not be regarded as pharmaceuticals manufacturers. For example, Associated Dental Products of Swindon, English Grains (Holdings) of Burton-on-Trent and Tredegar. It is not possible to compile size distributions of manufacturers of branded innovative medicines, or of OTC products, from data published in the Census of Production.

Appendix B

The reference year of 1987 was used in this chapter because at the start of the whole research project this was the latest year for which information on the the German Census of Production was available to us. More recent data are now available. The size distributions of *Unternehmen* and of businesses for 1988 are shown in table 4B.1. That for Germany has four size classes compared with only three in table 4.6. The distribution for UK businesses has been compressed into the same four size classes for purposes of comparison. The average size of UK business was 503.5 employees, nearly 38 per cent larger than the average size of the German *Unternehmen*. Trade experts have questioned this result and it is true that the average size of the larger Brit-

Table 4B.1 *Size distribution of businesses by employment, pharmaceuticals, Germany and UK, 1988*

	Germany			UK		
L	n_j	L_j	L_j/n_j	n_j	L_j	L_j/n_j
20-49	78	2630	33.7	27	1000	37.0
50-99	40	2756	68.9	32	2200	68.8
100-499	97	21513	221.8	47	10500	223.4
500 plus	41	66556	1623.3	35	57300	1637.1
Total	256	93455	365.1	141	71000	503.5

Source: Germany Statistisches Bundesamt (1990) Produzierendes Gewerbe, Fachserie 4, Reihe 4.1.2
L = employment size class.
n_j = number of firms in class j.
L_j = employment in class j.

ish pharmaceutical business (those above 500 employees), at 1637 employees, is much the same as the 1623 of the German *Unternehemen*. But the UK has proportionately more large firms, with nearly 25 per cent above 500 employees compared with the German proportion of 16 per cent. It also has only 19 per cent between twenty and forty-nine employees compared with 30 per cent for Germany. Hence the UK average size of business is larger than that in Germany, when size is measured by employment.

5 The insurance industry

The eventual removal of non-tariff barriers to trade after the completion of the single European market is likely to have different effects on different industries in Britain and Germany. The present chapter deals with the likely effects on the insurance industry in Britain and Germany.

The world's largest insurance industry is in the US. It is followed by that in Japan with the German insurance industry ranked third and the British industry ranked fourth. This ranking of Germany and the UK must be qualified because it relates to domestic insurance business only and the UK overseas business is higher than that of German insurers (Datamonitor, 1992). In fact, the British insurance industry makes a large contribution to invisible exports. In 1986 and 1987 it was responsible for over 40 per cent of Britain's invisible exports (ABI, 1991, p. 39). As a result of the underwriting cycle and various catastrophes, the industry's overseas earnings have fallen in more recent years, so that by 1990 the share of insurance in invisible exports had fallen to just over 15 per cent.

Throughout the world this industry is regulated. There are many reasons for this. For example, the buyer of an insurance policy has to rely on the insurance company's capacity to pay any claim that he might make and this requires that the company is managed prudently. In turn, this necessitates the monitoring of its technical reserves, reinsurance arrangements and investment portfolio and because a national government finds it difficult to monitor the books of a foreign company it might require the company to maintain deposits and investments locally. This requirement can result in a non-tariff barrier to trade.[1]

The German insurance industry is far more regulated than its British counterpart (Finisinger *et al.*, 1985). With the completion of the single European market, the regulation of the insurance industry in Germany will be reduced since the German and the British regulations are likely to converge, although it may be many years before they are identical. Such modifications will intensify competition in insurance within the European Community and will affect British and German firms in different ways. The likely effects are the subject of this chapter.

The firms

Life assurance

The insurance industry is complex and may be sub-divided in many ways. The categories used here are life assurance, non-life insurance and reinsurance. Life companies provide life cover and pensions. Non-life companies deal with uncertain events, such as fire or accident, which may or may not be experienced by an individual or an institution. Companies selling both life and non-life products are termed 'composite'. Reinsurance is the insurance taken out by insurers to cover exceptionally large liabilities.

British firms receive some 30 per cent of total EC life and pension premiums compared with about 20 per cent of EC property and casuality premiums, according to EIU (1990). These estimates are subject to qualification but the basic conclusion that in Britain life business is even more important than non-life business still holds (Datamonitor, 1992, p. 225). For Germany, the opposite is true. In addition, there is a large health insurance sector in Germany which has about 14 per cent of total premiums and is shown separately in Datamonitor.

In Britain, until 1984, there were general tax reliefs given on premiums paid for qualifying life policies, so that life assurance became primarily a tax-efficient method of saving rather than a means of obtaining life cover. The 1984 budget changed this by removing tax reliefs on premiums on new life policies. The comparative tax-efficiency of saving through life assurance was further reduced by the introduction of Personal Equity Plans (PEPs), tenable from 1 January 1987. These enabled individuals to invest in British equities without paying income tax on dividends or capital gains tax on the shares and thus provided a tax-efficient method of saving up to the limit allowed. In addition, the introduction of the Tax Exempt Special Savings Account (TESSA)

Table 5.1 *Sizes of British insurance companies – life*

		Latest year £mn		
		Life funds	Premium income	Gross investment income
1	Prudential	32487	5190	2284
2	Standard Life	18484	3047	1221
3	Norwich Union	17484	2494	1199
4	Legal & General	14855	2600	1023
5	Commercial Union	9736	1164	706
6	Scottish Widows'	9432	1268	644
7	Sun Alliance	7416	861	552
8	Friends Provident	7379	1011	560
9	Sun Life	7283	1000	516
10	Eagle Star	6876	950	514

Source: Times Books (1992)

from January 1991 enabled individuals to receive tax-free interest from those banks or building societies deciding to operate such accounts. Clearly, life assurance is no longer such a tax-efficient way of saving. This is an important drawback for an industry which depends so much on tax reliefs.

However, investment in personal pension schemes is still tax-efficient. The provision of personal pensions, together with the spread of endowment mortgages to finance house purchase, has helped British life assurance companies to withstand the abolition of life assurance tax relief. But the British housing market is now depressed and so the life assurance industry is under some pressure. An article in the *Economist*, 20 July 1991, argues that, as a consequence, the number of life assurance companies will decline, with some being taken over by banks, building societies, or by insurers in other EC countries.

The ten largest British life companies are listed in table 5.1. The size measure used by the Times 1000 is life funds for the latest year, but premium income and gross investment income are also given. It can be seen that there are some changes in rank order when different size measures are used, but this does not affect Prudential and Standard Life which are ranked first and second on all three size measures. An alternative ranking by net premium income in 1990 is provided by Datamonitor (1992) which puts Standard Life first, Prudential

Table 5.2 Sizes of German insurance companies – life

		Premiums 1989 DM mn
1	Allianz Leben	6122.7
2	Hamburg - Mannheimer	2881.7
3	Volksfürsorge	2706.7
4	R&V Leben	1891.4
5	Victoria Leben	1665.3
6	Iduna	1554.0
7	Gerling - Konzern	1359.1
8	Aachener und Münchener	1259.2
9	Nürnberger Leben	1257.0
10	Alte Leipziger	1238.2

Source: Southall and Winlow (1992)

second, and places Equitable Life fourth, ahead of Legal and General. But these different rankings according to the size measure used must not mask the conclusion that the degree of concentration in this industry, as measured by the market share of the five largest firms, is low and indicates a competitive structure.

The ten largest German life companies are ranked by their 1989 premium income in Table 5.2. Allianz is by far the largest. An alternative source, Datamonitor (1992), ranks German companies by 1990 premiums with similar results, except that by 1990 Gerling-Konzern and Aachener und Münchener had changed places.

Non-life insurance

Companies providing non-life insurance depend on general economic growth: for example, more cars mean more motor insurance.[2] But the increase in the volume of insurance with economic growth in the 1970s and 1980s was not accompanied by an increase in income from underwriting. On the contrary, the profitability from underwriting was negative with a downward trend 1973–91, according to Harcus (1992). This downward trend seems larger than can be explained by the downward phase of the underwriting cycle. These underwriting losses were offset by income from investment until 1989, but in 1990 and 1991 underwriting losses were too large for this and overall losses were made. It might be argued that the appropriate rate of return to measure the economic performance of the insurance industry is the combined

Table 5.3 *Sizes of British insurance companies – non-life*

		Latest year £mn	
		Premium income	Gross investment income
1	Royal Insurance	3611	555
2	General Accident	3046	430
3	Sun Alliance	2513	361
4	Commercial Union	2432	306
5	Guardian Royal Exchange	2038	331
6	Eagle Star	1625	246
7	Norwich Union	1121	190
8	Prudential	1026	206
9	Municipal Mutual	572	93
10	Cornhill	504	51

Source: Times Books (1992)

Table 5.4 *Sizes of German insurance companies – non-life*

		Premiums 1989 DM mn
1	Allianz	6672.6
2	Colonia	2389.8
3	Gerling-Konzern	2224.6
4	R&V	1956.4
5	HUK-Coburg	1862.9
6	HDI	1648.5
7	Gothaer	1647.5
8	Frankfurter	1496.3
9	LVM Münster	1394.0
10	Victoria	1393.3

Source: Southall and Winlow (1992)

return from investment and underwriting and that this should be comparable with rates of return in other industries. But even if we take the sum of underwriting and investment income to measure profitability, the resulting series still shows a downward trend 1973–91.

The ten largest British non-life insurers are shown in table 5.3. An alternative source, Datamonitor (1992), puts Sun Alliance first, and

Table 5.5 *Leading European insurance companies by gross premium income, 1988*

1	Allianz (Germany)
2	Zurich (Switzerland)
3	UAP (France)
4	Prudential (UK)
5	Generali (Italy)
6	Royal Insurance (UK)
7	Winterthur (Switzerland)
8	Axa-Midi (France)
9	Nationale-Nederlanden (Holland)
10	Sun Alliance (UK)

Source: The *Economist*, 'European Insurance Survey', 24 February 1990

Royal second, by premiums in 1990. There are other slight differences in ranking but once again the degree of concentration is low, however measured, and is consistent with a competitive industry.

The ten largest German non-life insurers are shown in table 5.4. The alternative source, Datamonitor (1992), uses net premiums in 1989 to measure size and this time the differences between the rankings in the two sources are somewhat greater. Nevertheless, both sources show that Allianz is the clear leader and that the second company is less than half its size.

The leading European insurance companies in terms of gross premium income 1988 are shown in table 5.5. The Allianz is Europe's largest insurance company. In 1990 Allianz acquired 51 per cent (now 100 per cent) of Deutsche Versicherung, the former East German state monopoly, which involved it in heavy losses. Allianz informs us that losses were expected and were discounted in the acquisition price paid. This method was considerably cheaper than starting their own greenfield operation. Premiums in the Ostländer are lower than in the rest of Germany and the motor accident rate has increased sharply as a result of the combination of fast western cars, old East German Trabants and inadequate roads. In 1986 Allianz acquired a British insurer, Cornhill. Allianz has a 25 per cent stake in Münchener Ruck-versicherungs-Gesellschaft, the world's largest reinsurer. Together these two companies control Hermes, Germany's largest credit insurance company. In fact Allianz would be prevented by the German Cartel Office from taking over any more German companies and so it has acquired companies in Britain, France (Rhine et Moselle), Italy (Riunione Adriatica di Sicurta), Hungary, Spain, the US (Fireman's Fund). In 1991 it became the first European insurer to be authorised to form a subsidiary in the non-life sector in Japan. Allianz is firmly established in the global insurance market. In the words of its chairman, Wolfgang Schieren, 'The single European market is no longer an issue for us' (*International Management*, 1990).

Reinsurance

Reinsurance is the most international and least regulated part of the industry. The world's largest reinsurers are European: Münchener Re and Swiss Re. Lloyds of London is still a centre for reinsurance and for insuring large risks, especially marine and aviation. A century ago it had over 50 per cent of the world's non-life reinsurance business but now it has less than 25 per cent even of its speciality, marine insurance. Its basis of unlimited liability coupled with heavy losses in recent years have led to a considerable resignation of 'names'. Its business in the US is much larger than that in Europe, although it has opened six offices in Europe and so its European business is likely to grow.

But the effects of '1992' on Lloyds are of secondary importance compared with its need to undertake a fundamental reorganisation. This is being done and includes the introduction of companies with limited liability and the 'ring fencing' of the enormous losses before 1985. Lloyds names could face cash calls of up to £5 billion before March 1995 in order to finance this ring fencing. (*The Times*, September 16 1993, p. 23). This problem is accentuated by the fact that names still face demands for £1.25 billion for Lloyds' record loss in 1990 and, moreover, losses of £1 billion and £500 million are forecast for the underwriting years of 1991 and 1992. In many ways, Lloyds and Münchener Re typify the contrasting traditions of British and German capitalism discussed in Hart (1992c).

Groupings

The larger European players in the competition for insurance business are heavily involved in the acquisition, the purchase of minority interests or in the forging of other links with insurance companies in foreign countries. The Allianz acquisition policy has been noted already. Generali (Italy) is also an acquirer of foreign firms because its domestic expansion in Italy is constrained. A detailed list of seventy-two EC cross-border mergers and acquisitions between insurers, and of fifty-three mergers, joint ventures and cooperation agreements between insurers and banks in the EC (excluding the UK), is provided by Carter and Greenaway (1991), appendix C.

British insurance companies appear to be less 'European minded' and in any case feel that it is difficult to acquire companies on the continent, for reasons discussed in chapter 2. Indeed, British companies are takeover targets because of the relative ease of acquisition in Britain. Carter and Greenaway (1991) report the following acquisitions in recent years.

- Cornhill by the Allianz (1986)
- St Katherine acquired by St Paul (1987)
- Equity & Law Life by Compagnie du Midi (now Axa-Midi) (1987)
- Sentry (UK) by Assurances Générales de France (1988)
- Chandos (renamed Sirius) by Sirius (1989)
- General Portfolio Life by Générales de France (1989)
- London Life and Pearl by the Australian Mutual Provident Society (1989)
- National Insurance & Guarantee by Skandia (1989)
- Prolific Life by Hafnia (1989)
- Windsor Life by New York Life (1989)
- Pioneer Life by Swiss Life (1989)
- the UK and Irish portfolios of National Employers Mutual by AGF (1990)
- Victory Re by Nederlandse Reassurantie Groep (1990)

International cooperation between national insurers is also achieved through minority interests in a company's shares. Fondiaria (Italy), Royal (UK) and AGF (France) had such interests in the German Aachener und Münchener Beteiligungs (AMB) until Royal announced in December 1991 that it wished to sell its 18.6 per cent stake in AMB in order to reduce its debts. At the same time, the state-owned AGF (Assurances Générales de France) wanted to increase its holding in AMB in order to obtain sufficient voting rights to influence the management of AMB. This attempt was resisted by AMB, who prefer their less hostile relationship with Fondiaria, Italy's second-largest insurer, and Royal. We understand that there is still a link between AGF and AMB and that the then chairman of AMB, who resisted AGF, has since left. But the relationship between the German, Italian and British companies was strengthened in February 1992 by the formation of a Luxembourg holding company, EPIC European Partners for Insurance Cooperation S.A., jointly owned by AMB, Fondiaria, and Royal. EPIC will be managed by executives from each of the three parent companies and will aim to increase business outside Germany, Italy and the UK. Each of the three is second largest in its home country and they believe that there is a good chance of increasing their market shares in other countries through EPIC. At the same time, Royal's sale of two Dutch companies, Royal Nederland and Royal Leven, to EPIC for £225 million provided a net addition of £166 million to its resources, thereby increasing its solvency ratio by about 5 per cent.

Equally important is the development of closer relationships between the banks and the insurance companies. The Germans call this development *Allfinanz*, while the French dub it *bancassurance*. As a result of the more favourable tax treatment of savings in life assurance policies, there has been a switch from bank deposits to life assurance, which improves the competitive position of the insurers. There is a real need to increase life assurance because the ageing German population will make it impossible for the State to finance pensions in the next century on the same scale as at present. At the same time the commercial banks have large networks of branches and are in a good position to sell insurance policies to customers. For example, Lloyds Abbey (an insurance company owned by Lloyds Bank) has found that insurance salespersons targeting Lloyds Bank customers are four times as successful as those trying to sell to other people, on whom Lloyds Bank does not hold any financial information. Thus the banks and building societies have the distribution network needed by the insurers, especially for the simple consumer products.[3] It might be more difficult for the banks to sell the more sophisticated products. These tendencies foster *bancassurance*, which can take several forms: start-ups, acquisitions, mergers, joint-ventures, and marketing agreements.

The starting of insurance companies by banks is not new. In 1967 the British bank TSB set up a life assurance business. Some 95 per cent of its insurance business comes from its bank branches. More recently, the Deutsche Bank and the French bank Credit Agricole have created insurance subsidiaries. In the other direction, Gothaer acquired the Berliner Bank and the Spanish insurer Mapfre set up its own retail banking business.

Acquisitions are also important. In 1988 Lloyds Bank acquired a controlling interest in Abbey Life. In the opposite direction, the German insurer Aachener und Münchener acquired the Bank für Gemeinwirtschaft.

Mergers are often less expensive than acquisitions. Holland's fourth largest life insurer, Amev, merged with its biggest savings bank, VSP Groep. One of Europe's biggest bank insurers was created in Holland in

1991 with the merger between Nationale Nederlanden and Postbank. Share swapping is also used. In France, the largest insurer, UAP, swapped 10 per cent of its shares with BNP.

Joint ventures are common in Britain and in the rest of the EC. In Britain, Commercial Union and Midland Bank formed a joint life-assurance undertaking, while Natwest has formed a new joint venture with Clerical Medical. Scottish Equitable is linked to the Royal Bank of Scotland. Standard Life bought 35 per cent of the Bank of Scotland in 1986 and had a tied agency with the Halifax Building Society. In August 1993 the Halifax Building Society announced that this link would be broken from the end of 1994 when its 700 branches would sell only the policies written by its subsidiary, Halifax Life. Harcus (1992) cites a Datamonitor survey of UK building society managers revealing expectations that, by 1995, 74 per cent of branches will be selling property insurance and 34 per cent motor insurance. Whether these branches will be selling policies under joint ventures with insurance companies is another matter. It is possible that by then many more building societies will abandon links with insurers and sell only through their own insurance subsidiaries. In addition to Halifax, the Woolwich, the National & Provincial and Britannia have life companies. *Bancassurance* is changing its form as it develops.

A good example of a marketing agreement is that between Allianz and the Dresdner Bank, Germany's second largest bank. Allianz has an extensive system of tied agents and Dresdner has its branch network. The links between the two are designed to exploit each other's customer base. These links have attracted the attention of the German Cartels office which ruled that Allianz should reduce its shareholding in Dresdner from 22.3 per cent to about 19 per cent (*Financial Times*, 23 May 1992). However this decision was reversed on appeal and no divestment was required.

There is competition between the insurers, building societies and the banks. All are in the money management business, collecting it from customers, investing it, and earning a profit from it after paying customers benefits or interest. The money management business is quite general and industrial companies are also involved in it. Indeed, large non-insurance companies may decide to insure themselves, possibly by acquiring or creating an insurance company. Self insurance of property and casualty risks is growing, though it is usually coupled with reinsurance to cover catastrophe or substantial claims. This development represents another source of competition for insurance companies. Carter and Greenaway (1991, page 43) report that in the US possibly one third of commercial non-life premiums have been lost to insurers as the result of 'self-insurance'. They also note that larger firms may also administer their own pension schemes.

Regulation and European integration

The regulation of the insurance industry in the UK is undertaken by the Department of Trade and Industry, which negotiates with its EC counterparts on the harmonisation of regulations. The outcome is a series of European Commission directives which are eventually implemented by national governments. A very helpful summary of these directives up to May 1991 is provided by the House of Lords (1991) European Communities Committee, Sub-Committee A, Chairman's Third Draft Report E/91/A 119. It is worth quoting at length.

> Negotiations in the Council to complete an effective European market in insurance have taken place since the 1960s. The Reinsurance Directive (1964) removed barriers to establishment and provision of services in reinsurance. The First Non-Life Directive (1973) and Life Directive (1979) enabled insurers to set up branches in other member states, subject to authorisation and supervision by the host state. These Directives also laid down the conditions for authorisation in member states and the rules on calculation of minimum solvency margins for firms carrying on insurance business.
>
> Some real progress towards freedom to provide insurance services was made in the Second Non-Life Directive (1988) and Life Directive (1990). These Directives lay down two distinct regimes under which insurers can offer insurance services in one member state from an establishment in another. In non-life insurance a distinction is drawn between 'large risks', where the policy holder is normally a substantial commercial undertaking and 'mass risks', where the policy holder is normally an individual or small undertaking. For life insurance the distinction is between transactions entered into by the policy holder on his 'own initiative' and those initiated by an intermediary or insurer. In the case of large risks and own initiative business the insurer is subject only to control by the home state authorities. In the other cases, member states may, if they wish, require host state authorisation. The United Kingdom did not implement this option. These distinctions reflect decisions of the European Court of Justice on

the extent to which a 'protectionist' regime could be justified in the insurance field. The Second Non-Life Services Directive came into force in 1990. The Second Life Directive is due to come into force in 1993.

Other single market measures which have already been agreed include the 1976 Insurance Intermediaries Directive, which allowed intermediaries to conduct business in other member states based on an agreement that equivalent experience should be acceptable in place of formal qualifications in member states where these would otherwise be required. The 1978 Coinsurance Directive prevents member states from requiring lead insurers to be established in the state where the risk is situated, and from requiring additional authorisation for coinsurers authorised in other member states. Four Motor Insurance Directives have set up a Community-wide regime for compulsory motor insurance and compensation schemes and have integrated motor insurance into the general non-life framework. The 1987 Legal Expenses and Credit and Surety Directives introduced certain safeguards for these classes of insurers but prevented member states from requiring them to be conducted by specialised insurers.

The basic problem is that existing regulations differ so widely between member countries that negotiations will take time to produce an integrated single European market in insurance. In Germany there were regulations on policy wordings, premium levels, claims handling and new insurance products had to be approved by existing insurers before they could be marketed. The latter regulation enabled incumbent insurers to ban a new product or, if they liked it, to copy it before it entered the market. But changes are taking place. Prior authorisation of new products by the BAV is being phased out. Again, the regulation of premium levels by BAV, which enabled marginal insurers to stay in business and thereby provide protection for their clients, is also on the way out. From 1994 the powers of BAV will be cut significantly (Städtler, 1992). However, restrictions continue elsewhere. In France insurance on property has to be placed with a French authorised insurer. In France, Germany, Italy and Spain, rates on mandatory motor insurance are controlled. Britain does not have corresponding regulations. Indeed, the relatively relaxed regulatory framework in Britain is traditional. As it adapts to the directives emanating from Brussels, this tradition will change.

The Third Life and Non-Life Directives, which largely replace the First and Second Directives on insurance, have two aims. These are, first, to enable an insurance company in one member state to establish branches or provide services on the basis of a single licence, subject to the supervision by the authorities of the member state which issued the licence and secondly, to afford insurance buyers access to the widest possible Community insurance market so they can choose the most suitable product (Department of Trade and Industry, 1991a,b). Member states have two years to implement the measures into national legislation. In practice, member states tend to fall behind the scheduled implementation. The House of Lords (1991) noted that only 20 per cent of national legislation required to transpose existing insurance directives into national law had been adopted (paragraph 46).

Moreover, it is clear that the free access of customers to insurance products of firms in other member states is subject to safeguards. For example, '... it is for the Member State in which the risk is situated to ensure that there is nothing to prevent the marketing within its territory of all insurance products offered for sale within the Community as long *as they do not conflict with the legal provisions protecting the general good in force in the Member States...*' (paragraph 20, Third Council Directive on Non-Life Insurance).

The creation of a common market within which insurers in the EC can compete fairly is the aim of the negotiations. This process is long and arduous, but the negotiators seem to be moving steadily towards their target, even if they will not reach it for many years after 1992. Allowing for the time lags between the formal adoption of the Third Directives and their implementation, they 'will probably not be completely applied everywhere until the end of the century' (Pool, 1992). Even then the precise interpretation of the 'general good' clauses in some member states may lead to a further postponement of the single European market for insurance.

But while the European Commission's Directives are very important in the creation of a single European market for insurance, there are other influences on the relative growth of British and German insurance companies which are even more important. This was emphasised in the evidence to the House of Commons Trade and Industry Committee (House of Commons, 1989) provided by Mr T. J. Palmer (Legal and General Group) and Mr M. Butt (Eagle Star Insurance Co.). The British industry is global in outlook and any European policy of 'reciprocity', which led to non-European countries such as the US restricting the writing of American business by European firms, would adversely affect British firms. Hence, British firms oppose 'reciprocity', the idea that the Community should seek reciprocity of access to non-European countries, defined in terms of comparative volumes of trade or identity of legislation and standards. The automatic provision of reciprocity in Community law, as noted by the House of Commons Select Committee (1989, p. xxxiii), might have damaged the UK's position in world markets. In the US, retaliation was being prepared. There was even a suggestion that reciprocity was being advocated in Paris and other continental centres in the belief that it would reduce the comparative advantage of London. Nevertheless, this committee concluded that reserve powers to implement reciprocity, rather than an automatic reciprocity, could be a useful bargaining tool in the GATT negotiations to persuade some countries to open their markets. The Third Directives do not amend or delete the reciprocity provisions in the Second Directives and it will still be possible to exclude subsidiaries of non-Community countries on the grounds that their home countries do not grant adequate reciprocal rights to Community insurers. The government takes the view that the reciprocity provisions are designed to improve market access to third countries and it 'would be concerned if they had the opposite effect' (Government response to House of Lords, 1991, paragraph 15).

Another barrier to trade in insurance between member countries is created by exchange rate risk: it would be risky for a German firm to take out a policy with a British company in £ sterling, or for a British firm to provide it in Deutschmarks, when the £/DM rate can fluctuate. The return of Britain to the European Exchange Rate Mechanism would restrict such risks, but they could be eliminated entirely by a single European currency. Under such conditions, British firms think that they would have a competitive edge, particularly in life assurance. Thus the removal of exchange-rate risk would be a more important step towards a single market than are some of the Commission's insurance directives. But at the moment it seems that the introduction of a single European currency and the elimination of exchange-rate risk will not take place for many years.

British firms also argued that the Financial Services Act (1986) imposed costs upon them which were not borne by their continental competitors. For example, in his evidence to the House of Commons Committee (p. 97), Mr Butt (Chairman of Eagle Star) stated that in 1988 his company incurred some £3–4 million extra regulatory costs, which were equivalent to 5 per cent of life assurance business expenses. The committee recognised that the FSA was designed to protect consumers' interests but concluded that its costs should be closely monitored. A level playing field in the Community is still a distant target and measures which accentuate its uneven nature may have to be modified.

The single European market

In the European insurance market, life assurance accounts for just under half of the total direct business (that is, excluding reinsurance) and non-life insurance has just over the remaining half of total premium income. The British and Irish spend more on life assurance than most of their fellow members of the EC, partly because their state pensions are smaller proportions of their final salaries. Some 80 per cent of German life assurance premiums are paid on endowment policies, which attract tax breaks. In Britain, some 45 per cent of life assurance premiums are paid on 'unit linked' policies which are just as tax efficient as endowment policies. It is thought that the British life assurance companies have an exportable knowledge of life, pensions and savings products. According to a survey by the Bank of England (1989), many other European countries have insufficient life assurance, so that there is considerable potential business in the life sector in the longer run.

The non-life sector in most member states is regarded as providing less scope for expansion. However, there is still some potential: for example, most households, even in the UK and Germany, do not have sufficient household contents insurance (Datamonitor, 1992). Again, there may be niches, such as flood insurance in Germany, which may be opened to competition from insurers. However, market conditions vary considerably between countries (for example, Germany has more legal expenses insurance than Britain) and risks differ (young Germans are more likely to be killed in road accidents than are young Britons). Thus specialist knowledge of national insurance markets is essential and this entry barrier will continue after 1992. Cultural barriers, including language and tradition, will continue to be important.[4] The Financial Services Act, with its burden of compliance costs, might act as a barrier to the entry of foreign firms into the British market.

The extent to which insurers are allowed to deduct amounts placed to reserves from taxable income also differs between member states. UK insurance companies are unable to make tax deductible transfers to equalisation and catastrophe reserves, unlike their competitors in Germany, France, Italy and the Netherlands. This is disputed by the Inland Revenue who have produced counter arguments to show that in some respects British insurers face more favourable tax rules than do

German insurers: for example, British corporation tax rates are much lower. Thus British insurers may have a competitive disadvantage, which is increased by the more favourable tax regimes in EC havens such as Dublin and Luxembourg. The different tax laws in different countries also affect the sale of tax-based products. Clearly, these must be specific to each country while tax systems differ: there is no scope for a uniform tax-based product being marketed from any one country.

Conclusion

The upshot is that the development of the single European market, as the result of the implementation of a series of EC directives, will facilitate competition between insurers. At best, it may act as a catalyst to the growth of the insurance firms in the longer run. German insurers reporting to the Economist Intelligence Unit (1990) thought that German policyholders might benefit from the broader product range but the quality of service was unlikely to be improved. British insurers were sceptical about any benefits from '1992'; they already compete with foreign insurers who have set up in this country.

The formation of the European Economic Area (EEA) between the twelve EC members and the EFTA members with the exception of Switzerland frees all movements of goods, services, capital and people in almost all of western Europe from 1993. This includes insurance and so the large Swiss parent insurance companies will be outside the EEA bloc.

Nevertheless, the most important competition is global, rather than European, and arises from the increasing liaison between insurers, banks and other financial services such as building societies. All are in the business of money management: they receive money from customers and make a profit on lending it for a higher return than they pay their 'depositors'. Non-life insurance finances its underwriting losses from investment income. Most of the life assurance business is concerned with methods of saving rather than with assuring lives. The business interests and expertise of the insurers and the banks are converging and this is likely to continue across Europe and indeed across the world.

The survey by Arthur Anderson for the Economist Intelligence Unit (1990) suggests that this trend will increase concentration among the EC's 4600 insurers. The number of British companies accounting for 80 per cent of life and pensions premiums is expected to halve by 1995. The number of European insurers dealing with property and casualty insurance is also expected to fall, as the result of falling profit margins and acquisitions by the larger companies. Thus their argument is that the effects of '1992' will favour the larger British and German insurance companies: many of the medium and small companies will disappear. This survey also revealed that British insurers expected Japanese companies to increase their share of the European insurance market. This view is shared by Carter and Greenaway (1991, p. 55) who point out that most of the large Japanese non-life insurers are already established in the London market. They suggest that the acquisition of a stake in Sphere Drake by Dai Tokyo Fire and Marine in 1987 might herald the acquisition of British insurers by Japanese companies. Perhaps joint ventures will be preferred. British insurers have much to offer and the Royal Group's recent acquisition of a 24.9 per cent stake in NICEL, Nissan Fire and Marine's European company, might be the first of many joint ventures between Japanese and British insurers.

The fact that in the insurance industry competition is global does not mean that as the result of the '1992' Directives, British and German insurers will increase their provision of insurance to each other's country directly. It is more likely that insurance will continue to be written locally by agents or subsidiaries of insurers in the other country, because a local presence is necessary in order to inspire confidence in claims-paying ability.[5] Furthermore, access to an efficient distribution network is vital. In practice this means the branches of banks and/or building societies. Hence, insurers will continue to form joint ventures, or mergers with banks and building societies in order to grow. Cooperation and alliances would have happened without the formation of a single European market. Both British and German firms share the view that '1992' by itself is unlikely to produce dramatic effects on the growth of their companies, especially when the actual implementation of the Third Non-Life and Life Directives throughout the Community and the formation of a freely competitive insurance market is unlikely to occur this century.

6   The machine tool industry

Machine tools form one of the forty 'sensitive' sectors identified in *European Economy* (1990) by the European Commission. It is clear why. Europe is a major exporter worldwide yet trade within the Community is at a lower scale than would be expected on the grounds of purchasing power and the distances over which the goods have to be transported. Furthermore, in comparison with Japan and the United States, the average size of plants is relatively small and productivity relatively low. *Prima facie*, therefore, large changes might be expected from the single market.

The German and UK industries are clearly different. The German industry is second in size only to Japan's, nearly five times as large as its UK counterpart and is clearly internationally competitive. Gerstenberger (1990) ranks it in the group of sensitive industries most likely to gain from the completion of the internal market. The UK Department of Trade and Industry (1990) was much less optimistic in its assessment of the UK industry. We would therefore expect to see important differences in their performance and reaction to the single market.

In practice the outcome has been far more complex. The UK industry has indeed found itself in difficulty but this has far more to do with the recession since 1989 than with direct elements of the single market programme. Capital goods always exhibit more substantial fluctuations in demand than the economy at large and machine tools as sources of capital goods reflect such fluctuation even more markedly (chart 6.1). The German industry is also now suffering, with layoffs being made for the first time in many companies' histories. While this might be ascribable to the problems of German unification, it is not reasonable to lay it all at the door of the single market.

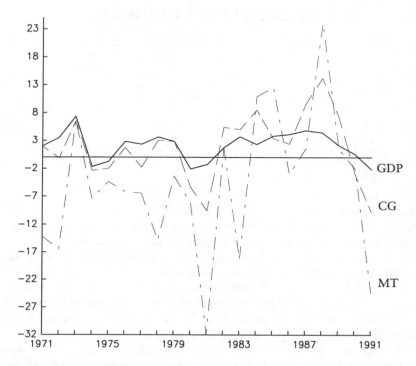

Chart 6.1 Annual percentage change UK GDP, capital goods (CG) and
machine tools (MT)
Sources: CSO Blue Book, MTTA

However, the machine tool industry also provides a clear example of
the difference between the technical and theoretical opportunities offered by the single market and those available in practice. As our analysis shows, the huge variety of products in the industry and its considerable existing level of internationalisation means that the extent of actual
'inefficiency' is considerably less than that implied by the small scale of
many existing firms (see also Mayes *et al.*, 1991). The limited extent of
worldwide demand for many specialist products makes it impossible to
reap all possible scale economies. We, therefore, begin our analysis
with a description of the industry and the processes of change affecting it
before moving on to the impact of the single market and the way it has
stimulated change in the industry.

The nature of machine tools

Machine tools can be distinguished in a variety of ways. As defined by the official Standard Industrial Classification (NACE 322), they can be categorised as either metal cutting or metal forming machines, depending on their function. There are, in addition, machine tools for working with other materials, which form a different sector of the market, outside the context of this chapter. Metal cutting itself comprises turning, drilling, gear cutting, grinding, broaching, screwing, tapping, threading, milling, boring, sawing, honing, lapping, planing, shaping and slotting. In addition, physico and chemical cutting comprises a sub-sector of metal cutting and must be considered as a different process from conventional cutting methods. Metal forming consists of punching, bending and forming, hydraulic, pneumatic or mechanical pressing, pinching, shearing, forging and stamping. (See Economist Intelligence Unit, 1985 for a detailed description of the industry.)

There is thus considerable product variety; indeed, many machine tools are custom built. The industry has changed markedly over recent years to meet purchasing industries' demands for improved quality, reduced labour requirements and faster production methods. Machine tool manufacturers have responded by developing numerically controlled (NC) machines. We use this term to denote both NC machines and the more sophisticated computer numerically controlled machines (CNC) since there is no distinction in the available statistics. Nearly all new generation machines are CNC. These machines combine electronics and computer control with precision positioning and machine drive systems to achieve a high standard of tooling through automatic operations. Most CNC machines can be linked to a flexible manufacturing system (FMS), containing several machines controlled by a master computer coordinating the operations. The flow of workpieces in the system is facilitated by transport machines, which automatically transfer parts between specific operations. While such sophisticated manufacturing techniques are becoming more widely used, clearly the introduction of NC machines and the associated automation requires a high level of investment. Levels of investment by manufacturing industries thus remain a dominant factor in demand for the EC machine tool sector.

Structure of the market

The EC machine tool industry is essentially a varied array of national

Table 6.1 *World shares of machine tool production, 1990*

		Production (per cent)
1	Japan	23.3
2	West Germany	18.9
3	USSR	9.8
4	Italy	8.5
5	Switzerland	6.8
6	US	6.7
7	UK	3.7

Source: *American Machinist*. Data based on US$ values

industries, with varying regional concentrations of production and product specialisation within a highly competitive world market.

Japan is the world's largest producer of machine tools and components (see table 6.1 for figures on 1990). The West German machine tool industry ranks a close second. In addition, in 1990 the former GDR ranked ninth with 2.3 per cent of production. However, it is not possible merely to add these two numbers together to get the impression that the German share is now near to 21.2 per cent because much of the industry in the new Länder is being run down as its major markets in the former CMEA dry up. By contrast, the UK industry ranks seventh (in addition, Japan and Germany are the main suppliers to the UK machine tool industry itself and to the UK market as a whole), although the UK industry remains the main component supplier in the domestic market.

Despite the large US machine tool industry and Japanese attempts to increase its world market share, the European machine tool manufacturers continue to be the biggest supplier. A third of the world's output comes from the European Community, nearly half as much again as Japan, the world's largest single producer (see table 6.2), although the decision of some Japanese manufacturers to set up operations within the Community has undoubtedly contributed to the output figures of the EC.

On current estimates of the machine tool production for 1991 the world market experienced a fall in orders as the recession deepened. The largest decline in consumption probably came in the former USSR, although estimates from the new countries that have replaced it are not yet reliable. It is clear, however, that with the demise of Comecon, EC and Pacific-rim countries have been able to increase their share of world output.

Table 6.2 *World machine tool production; trade and consumption*

Rank	Country	Production			Trade			Apparent consumption
		Total	Cutting	Forming	Export	Import	Balance	
1	Japan	11.6	9.4	2.2	4.0	0.7	3.3	8.3
2	Germany	8.8	6.1	2.8	5.1	2.3	2.8	6.0
3	Italy	3.5	2.4	1.1	1.6	0.9	0.7	2.8
4	US	3.3	2.3	1.0	0.9	2.0	-1.1	4.4
5	Switzerland	2.0	1.5	0.5	1.7	0.4	1.3	0.7
6	Russia(a)	3.2	1.8	1.4	0.4	0.1	0.3	2.8
7	China	1.4	1.1	0.3	0.2	0.6	-0.4	1.8
8	UK	1.3	0.8	0.5	0.7	0.8	-0.1	1.4
9	Ukraine(a)	1.3	0.7	0.6	0.0	0.1	-0.1	1.4
10	France	1.0	0.7	0.3	0.4	0.7	-0.3	1.3
	World total	42.9	30.5	12.5	18.8	15.2	3.6	39.3

Source: *American Machinist*
Notes: Exports > Production indicates significant re-export trade.
(a) Rough estimates from fragmentary data.

The community's machine tool industry represents only a quarter of 1 per cent of GDP (and a similar proportion in Japan); however, machine tool production is almost twice as important to the German economy, although this in turn is small compared with the 0.9 per cent in Switzerland (see table 6.3). In the last decade, German production has been more important than the whole of the rest of the community (Mayes *et al.*, 1991), contributing 56 per cent of machine tool production. Italy, the UK, France and Spain contributed 21.8 per cent, 8.1 per cent, 6.4 per cent and 4.7 per cent of total production respectively.

Germany exported 58 per cent of production, while Italy also had a trade surplus amounting to 20 per cent of production. The UK and Spain have small deficits of 5 per cent and 8 per cent respectively, while France has a more considerable deficit of 70 per cent. In addition, Switzerland, with the third largest output in Europe, has a significant impact on the community machine tool market, since it exports three-quarters of its machine tools to other European countries. (The German, Austrian and Swiss industries have considerable similarities, although the Swiss industry specialises in precision machines suitable for watch-making.)

Table 6.3 *Shares of machine tool production in GDP, 1991(%)*

France	0.1
Germany	0.5
UK	0.1
Italy	0.3
EC (eight largest only)	0.3
Japan	0.3
US	0.1
Switzerland	0.9

Source: CECIMO

In terms of world trade, the influence of the Community is even more significant, since it comprises 42 per cent of the total (Mayes *et al.*, 1991). This is largely because the US and the former USSR, although both large producers of machine tools, are in the main concerned with satisfying domestic demand and have shares of export demand of only 4.4 per cent and 2.1 per cent.

Owing to the high degree of specialisation in the machine tool industry, it is characterised by intra-industry trade. Despite being the world's largest exporter of machine tools, Germany imported nearly a third of its requirements, while the US imported nearly half of its requirements, making it a net importer by as much as a third of its production. Taking the balance divided by total trade as a measure of intra-industry trade gives a value of 0.4. This ratio would be 1 if there were no specialisation in the industry and zero if specialisation were total; 0.4 thus indicates considerable intra-industry specialisation. The EC as a whole imports nearly half of its requirements and has a net export surplus of some 15 per cent of its needs. (The change in fortunes of the last couple of years has strengthened the US trade position while weakening that of the EC.)

The pattern of German imports (see table 6.4) is markedly different from that of the UK, principally because over 25 per cent of German imports come from Switzerland compared with 5 per cent from the UK. This pattern has not been substantially affected by the early years of the single market programme although the Swiss share of German imports has declined by 15 per cent (4½ percentage points). The German share of the UK market has risen by 3 points while the UK share of the German market has also risen. Exports to the EC have, on the other hand, increased their share markedly, by 20 per cent for the UK and by 10 per

Table 6.4 *Imports of metal-working machine tools*

	UK			Germany		
	Shares %		Diff.	Shares %		Diff.
	1985	1990	90-85	1985	1990	90-85
World	100	100		100	100	
OECD total	94.81	94.56	-0.25	93.80	92.30	-1.49
OECD Europe	62.59	61.24	-1.35	71.65	72.69	1.03
EC 12	50.14	51.64	1.50	32.47	37.08	4.61
of which:						
France	3.67	4.23	0.57	6.02	6.09	0.08
Germany	28.65	31.70	3.05			
Italy	7.37	5.84	-1.54	11.46	13.74	2.28
UK				5.58	6.52	0.95
Bel/Lux	3.87	3.67	-0.20	2.75	2.04	-0.72
Netherlands	2.48	2.57	0.08	2.49	3.35	0.86
EFTA	12.53	9.50	-3.03	39.16	35.37	-3.79
of which:						
Austria	0.93	0.91	-0.23	4.52	5.89	1.37
Sweden	3.04	2.80	-0.28	3.25	2.67	-0.58
Switzerland	7.99	5.37	-2.62	30.94	26.39	-4.55
US	15.89	13.92	-1.98	5.55	4.66	-0.88
Japan	15.84	15.64	-0.20	16.51	14.72	-1.78
Canada	0.38	3.53	3.15	0.04	0.10	0.06
Non-OECD	5.19	5.43	0.24	6.20	7.69	1.50
of which:						
Comecon	1.34	1.15	-0.18	2.94	2.89	-0.05
USSR	0.13	0.24	0.11	0.70	0.44	-0.27
OPEC			no data available			

Source: OECD Trade Statistics Series C
Note: figures include sales of parts and accessories.

cent for Germany. An increased share of sales going to Germany explains the largest portion of the UK increase but the UK share of German exports has not changed. This change in pattern is perhaps rather surprising. Germany has reinforced its traditional markets and despite being hit substantially by a decline in the share of its sales going to the former Comecon countries (a 4 percentage point reduction) it has not expanded its exports in the EC in the same way that the UK has. Even

Table 6.5 *Exports of metal-working machine tools*

	UK			Germany		
	Shares %		Diff.	Shares %		Diff.
	1985	1990	90-85	1985	1990	90-85
World	100	100		100	100	
OECD total	69.98	76.52	6.54	62.87	71.63	8.76
OECD Europe	34.77	55.66	20.88	44.42	57.04	12.62
EC 12	26.76	47.68	20.92	27.71	38.68	10.97
of which:						
France	4.94	7.73	2.79	6.90	11.32	4.43
Germany	9.21	16.31	7.10			
Italy	1.94	4.78	2.85	4.01	7.50	3.49
UK				6.48	6.33	-0.14
Bel/Lux	3.17	8.07	4.89	2.91	3.04	0.13
Netherlands	2.12	2.86	0.74	3.90	3.94	0.05
EFTA	7.54	7.58	0.04	15.93	17.76	1.83
of which:						
Austria	0.39	1.01	0.62	4.20	5.23	1.02
Sweden	2.82	3.14	0.32	3.89	3.60	-0.30
Switzerland	2.28	2.37	0.86	5.73	7.35	1.63
US	25.50	16.26	-9.24	12.95	9.43	-3.52
Japan	1.52	1.72	0.20	2.46	3.64	1.18
Canada	4.66	1.27	-3.40	1.63	1.00	-0.63
Non-OECD	30.02	23.48	-6.55	37.13	28.37	-8.76
of which:						
Comecon	3.67	4.81	1.14	14.30	10.27	-4.03
USSR	2.47	3.40	0.93	8.50	6.15	-2.35
OPEC	5.67	7.44	1.77	12.04	7.02	-5.02

Source: OECD Trade Statistics series C
Note: charts include sales of parts and accessories.

though the latter is operating from a smaller base, the smaller German percentage increase is actually larger in absolute terms. The principal decline in UK export shares occured in North America (9 percentage points for the US and 3½ points for Canada) in a period when sterling's value was at its highest. While imports are strongly European oriented, exports cover a wide range of destinations, over a quarter of which are outside the OECD (see table 6.5).

Table 6.6 *The ten largest machine tool companies, 1992*

Rank	Company	Sales ($mn)	Rank in 1990
1	Amada (Japan)	1331	1
2	Fanuc (Japan)	1027	3
3	Yamazaki (Japan)	995	2
4	Okuma (Japan)	848	4
5	Thyssen (Germany)	685	-
6	Mori Seiki (Japan)	684	6
7	Toyoda (Japan)	566	9
8	Komatsu (Japan)	532	7
9	Pittler (Germany)	527	-
10	Toshiba (Japan)	476	-

Source: *American Machinist*. Charts based on company accounts

Concentration in the industry

Although there are some large firms, the machine tool industry is not very concentrated. However, none of the ten largest machine tool companies in the world is British. Eight are Japanese and two are German (see table 6.6). This German presence is recent and is the result of amalgamations of companies. There were no German firms in the top ten in 1986 (Mayes *et al.*, 1991). The Japanese have specialised in multi-function CNC machines with a large market and as a result have developed companies which are large by comparison with the rest of the machine tool industry. German companies by contrast tend to be more specialised. So while their market shares of their particular segments may be larger than those of the main Japanese companies they can achieve this with a smaller company size.

Concentration in the UK industry

The UK machine tool industry has undergone cyclical fluctuations over the past few decades, due mainly to a failure of the manufacturing sector as a whole to invest in manufacturing equipment and to anticipate demand in the early 1980s. These problems have led to a lack of competitiveness by many UK companies. As large engineering groups sold off their machine tool subsidiaries in response to these factors in recent years, the UK machine tool industry has re-aligned itself, often as the result of management buy-outs, so that the situation in the UK industry is generally one where companies manufacture only two or three products as is common in other countries.

The trend for UK manufacturers to concentrate on a limited product range is not a new one. Rather, the situation is one in which different markets exist within the machine tool industry. Some manufacturers specialise in advanced machines, often at high cost, which are supplied specifically to individual customers, particularly in the automotive and aeronautical manufacturing industries. Newall Manufacturing Technology, for example, produces specialist grinding machines for the aerospace industry in small numbers. Yamazaki, on the other hand, operates on a considerably larger scale and has the capacity to manufacture approximately one hundred machines per month at its Worcester plant mostly for export to other parts of the EC.

While specialist markets are not new phenomena for the machine tool industry, a number of British manufacturers have benefited from specialisation recently: Jones and Shipman have concentrated activities on CNC grinding machines, Newall on grinding machines, Edwards Pearson on hydraulic shears and presses, Colchester and TS Harrison on CNC and conventional lathes, and Cardinal Broach on broaching machines and tooling.

The growth of sales of CNC machines over the last ten years has changed their status from that of niche market products. The 'volume market' now largely consists of standard CNC machine production rather than manual machines, which were previously thought of as the volume production sector in the UK.

Following a period of rationalisation in the 1980s, the UK machine tool industry now mainly consists of small- and medium-sized companies producing high quality, advanced machines in relatively small numbers. With a limited machine tool industry, the UK has not been able to sustain a higher share of world production. However, despite the contraction of British-owned companies, the presence of Japanese and US-owned companies in the UK is growing.

Japanese and US machine tool companies continue to set up manufacturing bases in the EC, a trend reinforced, but not initially motivated by, the single market programme. Following the success of Yamazaki in Worcester, Japanese investment in a UK manufacturing base can be expected to increase, probably in the form of self-contained enterprises rather than joint ventures. As Japanese-owned motor manufacturing develops, other supplying companies will tend to be drawn in to support them.

Despite the inroads which Japanese companies are making in the US market, the performance of American-owned companies in the UK, such as Cincinnati Milacron, Bridgeport and Cross & Trecker (now

Table 6.7 *Leading UK machine tool manufacturers, 1991*

Parent company and company	Sales (£mn)
Yamazaki Magak Corporation (Japan)	
Yamazaki Machining UK Ltd	61.9
Cincinnati Milacron Inc (US)	
Cincinnati Milacron UK Ltd	60.1
600 Group plc	
Colchester Lathe Co Ltd	29.6
TS Harrison & Sons Ltd	14.1
Startrite Machine Tool Co Ltd	7.7
Bridgeport Machines Inc (US)	
Bridgeport Machines Ltd	38.6
Brooke Tool Engineering (Holdings) plc (a)	28.8
Jones & Shipman plc	22.4
FMT Holdings plc	19.8
Giddings and Lewis Ltd (US)	
Giddings and Lewis Ltd	12.1
Marbaix (Holdings) Ltd	
Marbaix Lapointe Ltd	16.3
Frederick Pollard & Co Ltd	14.9
Dolk Industries Holdings BV (Netherlands)	
Edwards Pearson Ltd	12.1
Wickman Machine Tool Manufacturing Co Ltd	11.5
Monarch Machine Tool Co (US)	
Dean Smith and Grace Ltd	9.4
Gildemeister AG (Germany)	
Gildemeister (UK) Ltd	9.3

Source: Keynote Report (1992)
(a) Includes sales of non-machine tool production.

Giddings & Lewis), remains strong. The contribution of US parent companies in providing the finance for R&D facilities is probably a crucial factor for the success of UK subsidiaries. Nevertheless, it is impossible to generalise about the reliance of UK manufacturers on product knowledge from their US parent companies. In the case of Cincinnati Milacron, the Sabre family of machines produced in Birmingham was certainly the result of R&D and new product knowledge derived from the UK subsidiary, while the Maxim family of products was developed separately in the United States.

The situation is different in the case of Yamazaki in Worcester, where the machines manufactured are designed and developed in Japan, albeit with engineering development for the specifications of individual customers done in the UK.

With regard to research and development in the UK, a structured programme of collaborative research projects was agreed by the Department of Trade and Industry and AMTRI (the Advanced Manufacturing Technology Research Institute) in 1990. The first project is in advanced spindle research, with the aim of developing and testing high performance spindle system technology.

The UK machine tool industry is highly fragmented, with small firms producing specialist equipment, often for individual clients. During the 1980s, the trend in the UK was for demerger and management buyouts, rather than concentration into large engineering conglomerates. This trend followed on from problems which a number of large UK companies, in particular Alfred Herbert, faced in the 1970s. After a period of expansion (carried out with financial and political support from the government) and concentration on the mass-production of basic products, Alfred Herbert went into receivership in 1980.

During the 1970s, the size of machine tool companies in the UK was on average smaller than in West Germany over the same period (Prais, 1981), although there is no evidence that large plants are required for success in the machine tool industry, nor that the gains from centralised marketing and financing in a firm of that size are proven.

Demergers and management buyouts have resulted in a situation where no UK machine tool manufacturer employs over 600 workers, and only three internationally sizeable companies remain listed on the stock market: 600 Group, B Elliott, and Jones and Shipman (Keynote, 1990). Of these three companies, only Jones and Shipman (who recently acquired Brown & Sharpe (USA) to expand its product range of grinding machines) is involved solely in the manufacture of machine tools.

Because of the high degree of specialisation in the industry, links with manufacturers in other countries are important (Mayes *et al.*, 1991) although cooperation is just as likely to be with non-EC companies as with Community-based manufacturers.

Concentration in the German industry

Unlike their UK counterparts, German machine tool manufacturers tend

Table 6.8 *Structure of the German industry, 1989*

Size of establishment (employees)	No. employed (%)
1-19	0.4
20-49	9.7
50-99	12.4
100-199	14.8
200-299	10.7
300-399	7.3
400-499	8.4
500-999	20.2
1000-	16.0

Source: Statistische Bundesamt, Fachserie 4, Reihe 4.2.1, 1989

to be privately owned companies, although more recently some (Hermle, Maho, Montanwerke Walter, Traub) have become publicly registered companies. Levels of merger and acquisition activity are low, although it has been made easier by the increasing number of M&A experts in Germany.[1]

The private structure of German firms has both advantages and disadvantages. It predisposes companies to internal, rather than external, growth and to 100 per cent ownership of subsidiaries. Private ownership also makes it more difficult to raise finance, but it does make the company more immune to external pressures, particularly pressures for short-run performance.

In Germany, collaboration tends to be at the domestic level, with linkages primarily being with local firms, university and research institutions, industry associations and banks, rather than with firms in other EC member states or in third countries. This trend was stimulated in the 1980s by federal government investment in R&D initiatives. The Sonderprogram Fertigungstechnik (Special Programme for Manufacturing Technology) between 1980 and 1983 provided funding to companies, universities and research institutes for R&D in the field of factory automation. This programme was followed by the Production Initiative 1984–8, which provided DM530 million for R&D in high-technology industries, particularly CAD-CAM and robotics. Federal government financial support for R&D initiatives continues; in 1991 the German machine tool industry received support in the region of DM1.3 million for joint industrial research at a pre-competitive stage.

Table 6.9 *Regional distribution of West German machine tool industry, 1988*

Region	No. of firms (%)	No. of employees (%)	Output (%)
Schleswig-Holstein, West Berlin, Rheinland-Pfalz	2.3	1.8	1.7
Hamburg	2.3	1.3	1.7
Niedersachsen	4.7	2.1	2.1
Nordrhein-Westfalen	35.1	22.3	21.6
Hessen	8.2	5.9	4.9
Baden-Württemburg	34.5	46.3	48.3
Bayern	12.9	20.3	19.7
Total	100.0	100.0	100.0
Total numbers	171	54446	8247.31(a)

Source: VDMA (as at end-December, 1988)
(a) DM million.

This level of government funding for R&D contributed to the strong links which now exist between universities and companies in Germany, particularly in the Baden-Württemberg area, where the greatest concentration of machine tool companies exists, and to a lesser extent in Nordrhein Westfalen. Graduate students and visiting fellows from the specialist research institutes also play an important role in technology transfer, carrying technical know-how into German industry. The Max Planck Institutes conduct basic research in the physical and social sciences and are predominantly funded by the public sector, while the Fraunhofer Institutes are more directly involved in applied contract research, particularly in production technologies, materials and engineering. R&D funding from industry now constitutes one-third of Fraunhofer financing resources as German firms seek to utilise the Institute's expertise.

A new element in intra-company collaboration within Germany is the growing level of east–west company affiliations. As the state-owned companies of East Germany attempt to compete in the new competitive environment of the EC, it has been their counterparts in West Germany who have been keen to develop linkages. Such linkages are even more important for East German companies, in order to adapt to western market forces. Overall, however, the expansion of the German market has not provided much opportunity for the production or

Table 6.10 *East–west German machine tool company linkages*

West German company	East German company
Maho AG	Maho Seebach GmbH
Schiess AG	Aschersleben
Trumpf GmbH & Co	Niles GmbH
Gebr. Hoffmann AG & Co	Union Gera GmbH
	Union Sachsische Werkzeugmaschinen GmbH
	Niles GmbH
	BWF GmbH
	Werkzeugmaschinenfabrik
	Glauchau GmbH
	Leipziger Drehmaschinen GmbH
EX-CELL-O Holding AG	Werkzeugmaschinenfabrik Vogtland GmbH
Boehringer GmbH	Herrmann Matern Werkzeugmaschinenfabrik
Pittler Maschinenfabrik AG	Neue Magdeburger Werkzeugmaschinen GmbH

Source: IFO Institute

sale of German machine tools, even if expansion into a new market has helped offset economic slowdown in the west.

While there are clear advantages for large companies in terms of production facilities, R&D, and marketing power, it is not necessarily the case that UK and German firms will see merger and acquisition as the most effective way to meet the challenge of Japanese producers. Collaboration and other forms of linkage are viable strategic responses for European firms, albeit smaller than their Japanese competitors, seeking to meet the challenge of the single market. Size is therefore not the only determinant of competitiveness for German and UK machine tool manufacturers.

Since 1988, pricing policy has changed as a result of the single market as parallel importing has become a serious threat. In the past, for example, Italy was a high price market as it was not possible to obtain satisfactory domestic components, although good local suppliers have now been found by some machine tool manufacturers. Market unification has occurred principally through the action of larger companies with the resources to open purchasing offices in a number of countries, enabling them to buy in one country and ship to another.

Type of products

The general trends in machine tool design have been moves to increase productivity and accuracy. Improved cutting materials have extended the period of time that machine tools can work without repair. Basic modular tools can be marketed, which may then be adapted to suit individual customer needs, enabling manufacturing costs for machine tool producers to be kept down.

In addition, developments in manufacturing industry as a whole clearly have a direct impact on the requirements which machine tool manufacturers must meet. Successful operation of Just-In-Time (JIT) manufacturing systems requires closer design specification for machines, and consequently closer liaison between machine tool manufacturers and their customers.

Machine tool manufacturers will increasingly take into account technological developments in cutting materials. Carbide, composite and ceramic cutting materials will become more common, as will 3D laser machining. In addition to being able to machine materials which were previously difficult to cut, newer cutting materials have the advantage of decreasing machine tool wear and increasing accuracy.

As machine tool technology rapidly develops and faster or higher quality machines come on to the market, machine life is likely to become shorter. This is a trend driven by computer technology, together with new developments in the use of lasers, high speed machines, and the need to cut ceramics. While actual machine reliability can be maintained for longer periods, it is computer technology which is increasingly determining the length of machine life. Older machines which cannot compete with newer models will tend to be replaced after ten years or less, although some manual machines will be retained to carry out small jobs. This will clearly have implications for the financing of new investment. Payback periods will need to be shorter, and reliability will be an important factor as 24-hour manufacturing processes become more commonplace. Even so, in Germany instances of 24-hour manufacturing processes are limited, in particular because of prohibitively high wage costs.

The use of computer numerically controlled (CNC) machines will increase. However, despite the high degree of sophistication achieved, in 1990 CNC equipment still accounted for little more than 10 per cent (by volume) of machine tools installed in the UK (Keynote, 1990). The same is also true of the rate of CNC machine tool installation in other countries, including Japan.

Complete integration of engineering systems is a longer-term aim for many companies given the high levels of investment required to achieve the complete networking of mainframe computers, PCs, CAD/

Table 6.11 *Machine tool sales by UK manufacturers, 1980–92 (excludes estimates of contributions by small firms)*

Year	Total sales £mn	NC as % of total	non-NC as % of total		Parts and accessories as % of total
			Cutting	Forming	
1980	589	15	54	15	16
1981	436	19	51	12	19
1982	425	23	44	14	18
1983	346	25	38	14	24
1984	373	32	31	13	24
1985	431	33	29	14	23
1986	489	35	29	13	22
1987	478	37	29	12	22
1988	608	44	26	11	19
1989	700	49	20	11	20
1990	700	51	18	11	19
1991	532	45	16	15	24
1992	405	47	15	16	22

Source: Business Monitor PQ3221/MTTA. (Percentages may not add up to 100 because of rounding)

CAM workstations, CNC software and CNC machine tools. Such developments are likely to require an increasing sophistication of CNC machine tools to facilitate fully integrated manufacturing processes.

As table 6.11 shows, sales of NC machine tools relative to those of non-NC machines have grown steadily over the past decade, particularly during a period of strong private investment in the late 1980s. As the cost of NC machine tools falls in real terms, their use will become even more widespread. The increased use of NC machine tools also has implications for training and employment strategies of UK manufacturers. Although the number of manual workers employed in the machine tool manufacturing industry is set to fall further as a result of new technologies, the increased use of computer-controlled equipment will require a highly skilled, well trained workforce. A response to the training needs of the machine tools sector will be necessary from firms, national governments and the European Community.

Main markets

Until the current economic recession led to a fall in domestic demand, the latter half of the 1980s had been characterised by continued growth for the British machine tool industry, which provided the financial stability for companies to invest in new manufacturing techniques. However, as demand has fallen in the early 1990s, UK investment levels in machine tool equipment have fallen accordingly. Latest estimates from the Machine Tools Technologies Association (MTTA, 1993) show that production of machine tools in the UK fell in 1992 to approximately £590 million, accompanied by a decline in exports to £330 million. These figures indicate that current production levels in the UK are the lowest in real terms since 1984.

The German machine tool industry has established a dominant world market position based on sales in a large and healthy home market, coupled with successful export strategies and product innovation. Its decline has occurred later.

Competitiveness

In a major study on the competitiveness of the EC machine tool sector, produced for the European Commission (WS Atkins et al., 1990), 'net export ratio' was used as an indicator for competitiveness in the machine tool sector, with an indicator ranging from +1 to −1 with positive figures indicating 'net exports'.

Overall, the study showed that the EC lost some of its international competitiveness in the 1980s. German machine tool manufacturers had faced strong competition from imports in their domestic markets, increased their share of intra-EC trade, but suffered a reduction in their share of non-EC markets.

In contrast, the UK machine tool industry was reported to have suffered a 40 per cent fall in production and in domestic demand between 1980 and 1983 before recovering in the latter half of the decade. While the UK share of world production fell during the 1980s, its international performance remained broadly stable, with exports to other EC countries increasing from 28 per cent to 35 per cent between 1980 and 1988 (WS Atkins et al., 1990).

The European machine tool industry regarded itself as being already highly competitive before the start of the single market programme, particularly in the more specialised products, despite the challenge of

Table 6.12 *Indicators of competitiveness: Germany*

Indicator	1980	1988
Import ratio	31.00%	34.00%
Export ratio	58.00%	59.00%
Net export ratio	0.54	0.48
Share of world production	18.10%	18.20%

Source: VDW Database, IFO Institute

Table 6.13 *Indicators of competitiveness: UK*

Indicator	1980	1988
Import ratio	47.00%	47.00%
Export ratio	49.00%	46.00%
Net export ratio	0.04	-0.03
Share of world production	6.20%	4.00%

Source: VDW Database, IFO Institute

non-EC manufacturers. One therefore has to ask how the 1992 process will impinge on that position.

However, although Gerstenberger (1990) characterises the German machine tool industry as having a strong competitive position in the single market, during the 1980s German machine tool manufacturers did lose market share to competitors from East Asia, and in particular Japan. This trend is likely to continue within the single European market (Gerstenberger, 1990).

Productivity

The relative performance of the industry in the two countries is illustrated by table 6.14, showing the growth in productivity for machine tool manufacturing in Germany and the UK between 1975 and 1989. The figures differ from those covering the period 1975–87 since they show that the UK has been improving relative to Germany in both machine tools and mechanical engineering. This may be due to the fact that 1989 was a boom year for machine tool sales in the UK. What is noticeable is that productivity for machine tools in both countries has grown more slowly than for mechanical engineering, which in turn has grown more slowly than total manufacturing. It is of course the comparison

Table 6.14 *Productivity[a] growth rates, 1975–89, per cent per annum*

	Germany	UK
Machine tools	1.25	1.75
Mechanical engineering	1.85	2.09
Total manufacturing	2.62	3.84

Levels: mechanical engineering and total manufacturing from O'Mahony (1992) p. 50. Machine tools: output and employment for UK from 'Annual Report on the Census of Production' (1987), CSO, and Germany from 'Kostenstrukturen der Unternehmen im Investitionsgüterproduzierenden Gewerbe' (1987), Statistiches Bundesamt, converted to common currency using purchasing power parity for machine tools for 1985, unpublished from OECD, brought forward to 1989 using producer price indices from 'Annual Abstract of Statistics', 1989, CSO, for UK and 'Statistisches Jahrbuch', 1988, Statistisches Bundesamt for Germany. Annual average hours as for mechanical engineering.
[a]Productivity is defined as real output per worker hour.

with the same industry in third countries which will give a view of competitiveness. Similarly differences in productivity levels give an indication of the scope for efficiency improvement, merely by adopting existing best practice without the need to innovate.

The single European market

Since many European machine tool manufacturers are world market leaders already operating on an international scale, it is difficult to evaluate the extent to which intra-Community trade was hindered by barriers before the '1992' programme. Partly because Europe itself is a major market for machine tools, absorbing 30 per cent of world production, the need for manufacturers to operate in an international market has already become a necessity. Many machine tool companies already operate distribution networks through collaborative agreements or subsidiaries in order to achieve Community-wide sales. Nevertheless, the European Commission's single market programme has the intention of removing existing physical, technical and fiscal barriers to intra-community trade. Many of these measures will have an impact, in varying degrees, on the EC machine tools sector.

Removal of physical barriers

The long timescale necessary for building a large machine reduces the importance of costs often associated with border delays, which are a particular problem for perishable goods with a short product life. The removal of customs and administrative controls on the industries is thus unlikely to be very important. Machines also tend to have a high value added against which the costs of barriers are small (Mayes *et al.*, 1991). Fast delivery for replacement and spare parts is extremely important, but apart from this area just-in-time production methods are not a major concern for the industry. Furthermore, some EC machine tool manufacturers have complained that the extra burden imposed by the Community requirement to provide additional data on exports will actually offset any cost benefits which may result from the removal of border restrictions.

While the motivation of Japanese companies to locate production within the Community comes in part from a desire to establish a European manufacturing base and benefit from the removal of border controls, the advantages of removing frontier barriers to intra-EC trade are not expected to be great for UK and German machine tool manufacturers. Nevertheless, the overall effect of removing physical barriers to the free movement of goods in the EC is likely to facilitate increased levels of intra-Community trade in the future and hence spill over into demand for machine tools as part of a general expansion.

Removal of technical barriers

Although differences in technical standards between member states continue to cause some problems, particularly with regard to product safety (usually overcome by changing machine specifications), the Machinery Directive, which was adopted in June 1989 and came into force on 1 January 1993, should ensure that all machine tools sold in the Community satisfy wide-ranging health and safety requirements. In some cases they will be subject to type-examination by an approved body (the DTI has yet to designate an approved body in the UK), and carry a 'CE' mark and other information which generally relates to the manufacturer. The process will largely be one of self-certification by manufacturers of machine tools, with the exception of two or three types of machine listed in the directive, which are considered to be particularly dangerous. While the directive does not specifically remove barriers to trade which previously existed, it is anticipated that common EC health and safety provisions for machine tools will reduce costs in administration and those associated with adaptation of machines for other EC markets, although it is still unclear how liability will be defined in the case of imported goods.

To complement the Machinery Directive, the Commission has also proposed a directive on used machinery. If adopted, the directive would apply to used machinery involving a change of user and, as with the Machinery Directive, would ensure that machinery is put into service only if a certain level of safety is guaranteed. However, there are now indications that the proposal for a directive on used machinery will be dropped by the Commission following strong opposition by the majority of member states. At a meeting in Brussels in June 1992, seven member states objected to the draft in principle and only Spain and Italy supported it.

The work of the European standards body (CEN) is also eradicating many of the differences that do exist between national product standards. However, it must be pointed out that the very fact that machine tools are often to the specifications of individual customers reduces the importance of common safety standards.

Environmental standards are of particular concern to machine tool manufacturers only to the extent that non-EC manufacturers can avoid certain regulations and hence have a price advantage in markets outside the Community. Product liability is also a considerable problem since, in addition to having to say more about products and translate manuals into other languages, it can result in the performance levels of machines being described as well below their technical limits. The constraints on the production process and on the product itself are very limited.

A further significant element of the removal of technical barriers may be its impact on consumer industries. As a convergence of consumer demand across the community begins to develop, a reduction in the number of machine tools needed from rationalisation of production may entail a loss of machine tool makers. However, this is a second step as in the original change itself investment will be required to set up the new production lines. As Burridge and Mayes (1993b) indicate, it is likely to be the capital goods industries that are one of the main beneficiaries from integration, as reorganisation involves a measure of re-equipment. However, this may generate a further cycle in the machine tool industry as any surge in investment is likely to result in some overshooting in capacity as more suppliers hope to benefit from the improved market than can actually succeed. A pattern followed by most bouts of deregulation and market opening – the overshooting from the

'Big-Bang' in financial services in the UK is still not fully offset and the ensuing contraction has helped add to the unusual pattern of the current recession with its emphasis on service industries and the southeast rather than on the heartlands of manufacturing as has been the case in the other postwar business cycles.

Free movement of labour and mutual recognition of engineering qualifications in the single market should reduce some of the shortage of skilled labour, which has been an existing problem in the sector, until the recent recessions in the UK and Germany, that is. The First General Directive on the recognition of professional qualifications (awarded on completion of education and training of at least three years' duration, normally to degree standard) was adopted in December 1988. All member states were due to implement the directive by 4 January 1991 (although only four member states had transposed it into national legislation by 1992). A second general directive on the recognition of professional qualifications (awarded on completion of education and training of less than three years' duration) was adopted in June 1992.

Both these directives have implications for the free movement of engineers involved in the machine tool industry throughout the Community by enabling an engineer, qualified in one member state, to work in another member state without having to requalify. Instead, the principle of mutual recognition of qualifications will prevail, subject to only limited exceptions.

However, the impact of free movement of skilled engineers in the Community, with subsequent implications for the reallocation of manpower resources in the machine tool industry, presupposes that there is a surplus of labour in some areas of the Community and a deficit in others. With the exception of the short-run impact of the recessions in the UK and Germany no such surplus of appropriately skilled labour exists in the Community at the moment, and in the future available manpower resources will be largely dependent on the willingness of both the Commission and member states to invest in training and retraining programmes for the engineering workforce in response to technology innovation and transfer. Even allowing for these factors, language barriers will continue to be a significant barrier to the free movement of workers. As for the possibilities of company relocation, labour costs alone are too small a percentage of total costs to provide a sufficient incentive to move production, except in extreme cases.

Labour market issues will generally be important only where no language problems exist or where this source can be found in close proximity to the manufacturer's base. Alsace-Lorraine, for example, offers German machine tool manufacturers in Baden-Württemburg cheaper energy sources together with a German speaking workforce, located closer than many parts of Germany itself.

Removal of fiscal barriers

The 'removal' of fiscal barriers to intra-Community trade in the single market will have a minimal effect on the machine tool industry. The degree to which harmonisation will take place is in any case minimal. VAT differences are not of great importance for such capital inputs. However, as Matthews and Mayes (1993) point out, the current system still acts as one of the restraints on cross-border leasing. Leasing is widely used for some machine tools in the UK and Germany. Differences in corporate tax remain and while competition among rules may reduce the discrepancies if companies move their operations across borders in response to them in any substantial numbers, further progress seems relatively unlikely in the short run. The impact from changes in fiscal regulations will come primarily from capital mobility, where any reduction in capital cost is likely to stimulate investment, increasing company expenditure in machine tool equipment. However, world market demand is more significant than demand within the Community.

It was clear from the companies we interviewed that the impact of reducing exchange-rate fluctuations planned in the run-up to economic and monetary union, although largely an indirect facet of the '1992' programme, is likely to be greater than other aspects of fiscal integration. Exchange-rate fluctuations cause reductions in potential sales in the industry within the EC first because of transactions cost in conversion but also because of uncertainty, which leads companies to price higher to cover the risk. Sometimes this is included in contracts, where price renegotiation could be demanded by one or other party if exchange rates were to change by more than 2.25 per cent (in effect if they were driven outside their then ERM bands).[2] Progress towards economic and monetary union as originally planned would therefore tend to reduce uncertainty and, ultimately, transactions costs. All this has been substantially upset first by the devaluation of September 1992 and then by the widening of the permitted bands of fluctuation to ±15 per cent. The relative position of sterling and the DM has changed again, with convergence looking a much more distant prospect.

Overall impact

In general, the single market programme will have a positive impact on the machine tool industry in both Britain and Germany, reducing the small level of technical fragmentation which does still exist in the market, lowering costs and encouraging linkages between specialised producers in areas such as marketing and technical cooperation. The benefits of such linkages were undoubtedly a motivating factor in the recent agreement between Maho and Bridgeport on the manufacture of machine tools in Germany and the UK. However, the scope for technical economies of scale is limited by the size of the world market rather than by existing barriers in the European market. Thus economies of scale technically available may not be realised simply because of the smallness of the global market.

Since Europeanisation of the machine tool industry was largely undertaken in the 1970s, the single market does not offer great opportunities to move into new markets. It may even be the case that, in some cases, local sales facilities operate most effectively with the backup of local assembly and support operations to provide an efficient service to customers. This is particularly true when customers are small undertakings, which buy relatively infrequently and need considerable support. From the perspective of the seller, this also necessitates a wide customer base in a particular region.

In Buigues et al. (1990), machine tools were identified as likely to be one of the industries sensitive to completion of the single market, since the industry was protected by a moderate level of non-tariff barriers and those barriers either prevented economies of scale or allowed large price discrepancies to remain between member states.

The impact of '1992' on the machine tool sector in UK and Germany is, however, unlikely to be dramatic since it has been an open market for a number of years. Mayes et al. (1991) argued that the fragmented structure of the machine tools sector is not primarily due to barriers to trade of a physical, fiscal or technical nature, but to factors which will not be so substantially affected by closer integration. This is not to say that the industry will not be affected by the 1992 programme – an increase in the rate of European investment is expected, particularly in the early response of companies to the single European market. Even so, the overall response of UK and German manufacturers to the '1992' programme cannot be expected to have a significant impact on the sector.

Trade with non-EC countries

Globalisation of the machine tool industry is every bit as important as Europeanisation. Markets outside Europe, particularly on the Pacific rim, are exhibiting faster growth and offer potential in terms of both sales and production. This trend towards globalisation highlights the importance of international, as well as European, standardisation. The standard for CNC, for example, is set by Japan, and in particular by the Fanuc company.

Similarly, the adoption of a modular approach which enables common components to be fitted to many machines, and so allows considerable economies of scale, can be attributed to Japanese rather than European influence. Much of the scope for economies of scale by standardising components across machines and among suppliers has already been achieved and would have continued even without the impetus of the single market. The machine tool industry itself is contributing to the reduction in the scope for economies of scale through developing the ability to retool rapidly and hence reduce cost efficient batch sizes and operate on an individually customised basis.[3] As machine tools are themselves extensively used in the production of machine tools, these cost gains can be expected to raise the efficiency of the smaller producers. Some scope for economies of scale in purchasing, marketing and organisation remains. Hence we are only discussing a reduction in the expected scope of this form of cost reduction, not its elimination as suggested by Pratten (1988).

The potential markets for machine tool products in eastern Europe are expected to develop slowly as levels of investment remain low in the early years. Since reconstruction will involve substantial investment in up-to-date western technologies, machine tool demand can be expected to be high, especially since it is likely that the countries will want engineering to resume its role as a major employer (in order to exploit the skills available and to focus on higher value-added activities). Germany is clearly better placed geographically to take advantage of this increase in demand, particularly in Bohemia, although Hungary is also likely to have strong links with the Austrian machine tool industry. Since both the former GDR and USSR were large producers of standardised machine tools, their own machine tool industries may develop as investment and technology improves in these economies. This will clearly have a long-term impact on the external and internal markets of Community machine tool manufacturers. Competition will be greatest where these tools are the closest substitutes for existing production, which could affect the UK more than Germany.

Despite the universal impact of some single market measures throughout the Community, clearly the effects of '1992' on the machine tool industries in the UK and Germany will differ. This is particularly true in the case of non-EC ('third country') investment in the two countries. The UK machine tools sector has traditionally received high levels of foreign investment, since many companies are publicly quoted on the stock exchange. Together with a general decline in the domestic machine tool industry over the last twenty years, this has resulted in third country ownership of UK companies in significant numbers, particularly by US firms. Generally, third country control of UK manufacturers has been considered a viable strategy for non-EC firms anxious to establish a production base inside the Community before the advent of the single market at the beginning of 1993, particularly because of fears of a 'Fortress Europe' policy. Indeed much of this from both Japan and the US predates the single market programme as such.

Concerns over Community policies towards non-EC producers have also been a motivating factor behind the decision of Japanese motor manufacturers (Honda, Nissan, Toyota) to site their European operations in the UK. Language is also a motivating factor for Japanese firms who locate their European operations in the UK, particularly if they have already established a manufacturing base in the US. We have already noted that the motor industry is the biggest purchaser of machine tools. The expansion of the UK motor industry is thus increasing demand for machine tools. Although this new demand is likely to be met from traditional Japanese sources in the early years, as time progresses it is likely to lead to increased demand for the UK industry and to the setting up of new facilities by the Japanese manufacturers themselves. Other Community member states are also experiencing the arrival of Japanese machine tool manufacturers: Amada and Toyoda have both established production plants in France through acquisition of French companies, and further investment is clearly likely in Germany. Overall, the situation is one where 'regional' strategies are being adopted in the world market for machine tools: by dividing the potential world market into US, Japanese and European sectors, major players in the machine tools sector now recognise the need to establish a manufacturing capacity within the European Community.

7   Conclusions

When this research started in 1989, enthusiasm for the single European market was high and the German and British economies had been enjoying substantial economic growth. There were problems on the horizon with some sort of linkage with East Germany and an expected downturn in the UK. With '1992' on everyone's lips we expected to find a strong role for the single market programme as a stimulus for change in industry in the two countries. While that expectation has been fulfilled, '1992' is only one of the forces for change and it has been firmly replaced at the top of the agenda by unification in Germany and the recession in the UK. Indeed the coordinated deflation in pursuit of nominal convergence has meant that many companies restructuring in the hope of more rapid expansion of the market have had their fingers burnt.

Although the experience in *Sharpbenders* (Grinyer *et al.*, 1988) had been that it was much more common for threats to work as a force for change than for opportunities, we looked for the role of the single European market as an opportunity for major change in companies' behaviour. It is a testament to the perceived importance of the 1992 programme that it was so widely cited as a contributory factor in the process of change.

The European Commission takes an optimistic view of the impact of the single market (Sutherland *et al.*, 1993). They compare growth in the period since 1987 with the trend of earlier years. Since growth in this period exceeds the trend they argue that at least some of this better performance must be due to the single market. By their estimates an effect of around 2 per cent of GDP has been recorded – approaching half of the total static gain suggested by Catinat *et al.* (1988) in 'The Costs of Non-Europe' for the entire process. Some anticipation of the effect seems highly likely but the particular amount might be thought large. In any case this form of methodology is unlikely to be repeated by the Commission in the future as the current recession will in effect eliminate the gain. A more plausible technique is to 'harmonise' the growth performance of the EC according to economic performance elsewhere (Kreinin, 1973; Plummer, 1993). The US is the obvious choice and this results in a much more modest view of the success of the single market, but it still implies that there was indeed a surge of activity in the early years after the launch of the programme. It is unlikely that none of this was due to the single market process.

The stimulus to change

In their different ways, all four industries we considered in detail reflected a weaker role for the single market than might have been expected from the textbook arguments presented in the Cecchini Report and 'The economics of 1992'. In the case of machine tools, firms felt that the single market did not offer them much that had not been available before. Firms, particularly in Germany, had regarded Europe as a single market for some time. What the single market programme was doing was facilitating the realisation of that vision. The physical, technical and fiscal barriers were not regarded as insurmountable and the contribution to reducing costs was not thought to be substantial. The existence of the 1992 programme had encouraged the development of linkages among firms across borders and accelerated the process of standardisation of parts. However, in many respects, the most effective competitive threats had come not from within the EC but from outside with the pressure from Japan.

In insurance, there was a general feeling that the 1992 programme did not address many of the most important factors which helped segment the market. However, there were clear differences between the retail and other parts of the market. Reaching individual clients requires a large local network, which can be set up from scratch or accessed through cooperation with another institution which already possesses a suitable network, such as a bank or building society. In the main these linkages have been on a national basis, strengthening the grip of the existing players. Getting round this implies purchase of an existing company, which had indeed occurred in the UK with the purchase of Cornhill by Allianz and Eagle Star by Axa Midi, for example. Even though these cross-national links were being established, on the whole the markets were being developed separately so that a 'multi-domestic' rather than a single market was emerging. Axa on the other hand was taking considerable steps to unify aspects of the European operations.

Even at the retail level there had been progress in direct selling by companies such as Direct Line which were able to cut out a complete layer in the structure. Thus to some extent we felt that the existing industry was arguing that its position was more secure than it was. The German industry in particular, with its more highly regulated background, had the opportunity for extensive change, some of which would depend upon the actions of the dominant market leader, Allianz.

In pharmaceuticals, by contrast, the main restriction on the impact of the single market was that the most important changes were yet to be implemented. The system of mutual recognition and testing of preparations at a European level is set to come in during 1995. In any event the structure of the industry remains dominated by the purchasing systems practised by the national health services. Although these are all assailed by the common problem of rapidly rising costs there is little indication of moves towards a single market in health care. The 'single market' is achieved by trying to ensure equal treatment for citizens from other Community states with the domestic population.

Retailing again, with the exception of mail-order and franchising, requires operation in a physical location in the other country if it is to address that market. Cross-border shopping is only a major activity where there is a land border and substantial centres of population near the border. This then acts as an important factor differentiating Germany from the UK. The UK has only the limited land border in Ireland, where strict controls remain for reasons of security. Germany on the other hand has extensive borders with five other member states opening it to competition at the margin on a much more extensive basis.

Otherwise entry has to occur through purchase of existing stores or through developing new sites. Neither of these is easy. The first requires willing sellers and the second local knowledge and considerable effort to overcome planning restrictions. Nevertheless, limited entry is now occurring, particularly in the UK with the establishment of cut-price own grocery stores stocking a limited range of goods. Aldi, as a German company, is especially interesting from the point of view of the present study.

Taken together, therefore, although the stimulus to change may be weaker than that first envisaged, it is proving a substantial force in both the UK and Germany. Although the single market may be a common destination for the two countries (and indeed the Community as a whole) the actions required to get there depend upon the starting points, which are by no means equal. Our study therefore reveals not just different responses to the stimulus from the single market programme but different stimuli – greater changes are required in some cases to comply with harmonised regulations.

An uneven starting point

In a simple sense one would expect that the impact on British industry might be greater than that on German industry, simply because British industry is less well integrated in the European system in terms of trading pattern. As shown in chapter 2, a larger proportion of the UK's exports and imports are extra- rather than intra-Community. However, in absolute terms, Germany is a more important extra-Community trader. There is no specific reason for expecting that the ultimate structures will be similar, merely that German shares have been more stable in recent years, while the Community content of UK trade continues to rise.

Trade is by no means the only characteristic of internationalisation of industry and UK industry is much more international in the sense that existing levels of ownership of firms in other member states are higher than for Germany and foreign ownership of firms in the UK is also higher.

Nevertheless, our analysis of the structure of industry in chapter 2 reveals that in general most British industries are more inefficient than their German counterparts, with specific exceptions such as pharmaceuticals and some areas of business and financial services (see Smith, 1992, for example). To some extent this difference occurs not just because British firms in general are less efficient but because there is a longer tail of inefficient firms in the UK.

Routes to change

The scope for difference in response is relatively limited. In the introduction we suggested that three main mechanisms were available for achieving change: external growth, internal growth and relocation. We came across relatively few examples of existing activity actually being shifted in order to exploit an improved cost structure in the single market, which may reflect the smallness of our sample and the limited coverage. However, expansion plans and actions did suggest a considerable reorientation, whether by merger and acquisition or investment in new plant and machinery.

In insurance, for example, there has been a surge in linkages between insurance companies and other financial institutions – banks in Germany and banks and building societies in the UK. However, the motivation is confused as the principal stimulus in the case of the UK was not the single market proposals but the Financial Services Act, which had a dramatic effect on agency arrangements. Agents had to decide whether they wanted to be independent or tied. It was no longer possible for agents to mix the arrangement. Insurance companies wishing to protect their network had an incentive to conclude agency agreements with those who already had networks for other financial activities as the rules segmenting markets were relaxed. The UK was thus making foreign entry more difficult before the single market started. Entry into insurance therefore had to be largely in terms of merger or outright purchase of existing UK companies. This has certainly occurred and although it is on a small scale it is more extensive than entry into the German market. One simple reason for this is that UK companies have gone through a period of poor profitability which limits the ability to finance purchases and makes them more vulnerable to takeover. Of course the same does not apply to other purchasers in the German market. The more limited takeover activity in Germany and the more national character of the new relationships in part reflects the relative difficulty of open-market takeovers. Takeovers within Germany are almost invariably by consent. This does not mean that there are no takeovers of companies that were not in some sense 'for sale'. A good offer could be persuasive but making such an offer successfully requires the ability to identify the principal owners of the company and to value it accurately. As such companies are typically not publicly quoted and do not have to make extensive annual returns there is a clear asymmetry between the UK and Germany.

Other features of corporate governance in Germany make takeovers more difficult and less attractive. The enshrined position of workforce and other directors on the supervisory board can mean that it is not possible to obtain sufficient control of the company to make sweeping changes in the short run. The role of banks as shareholders in their own right and as holders of proxies for others can make it more difficult to purchase shares and provide a readier defence through financial assistance or the organisation of alternative sources of help.

Special factors can also affect the balance of activity as in the case of Allianz in the insurance industry, which had reached the point where further acquisitions within Germany would not have been permitted because its share of the market was too high. Further growth therefore either had to be through internal expansion in Germany or expansion outside the country (the opportunity to purchase Deutsche Versicherung upon the unification of Germany was an unexpected bonus). As a result it made a string of purchases aimed at making it a world player not just a European one.

There was no specific trend among German rather than British companies to form cross-border alliances, although this practice was more common within Germany, particularly in the retailing industry. This tightening of the link with suppliers or the downstream distribution helps strengthen a company's grip on the market. Although for a long time companies like Marks and Spencer have pursued such strategies in the UK, it has been competition and example from Japanese companies which has generated the response, rather than a lead from the single market.

In areas such as railway equipment (one of the subjects of an earlier study in Mayes *et al.*, 1991) the ready formation of coalitions of suppliers to bid for large public procurement contracts has been a feature of German responses in the single market (in contrast to the mergers and acquisitions which have involved the main companies in most of the other member states, including the UK).

This degree of collaborative behaviour, revealed above in the links between banks and companies, and the ability to find national partners in the face of foreign acquisitions, is part of a wider element of mutual support or at least conformity to unofficial rules of behaviour which effectively limit competition. This is not illegal collusive behaviour under either German or European law but what has been described by Sir Kenneth Berrill and others as 'tribalism'. It is reflected in the role of trade associations, membership of which is often compulsory, which gives a ready basis for mutual contact in a framework of assistance and for the establishment of formal and informal codes of behaviour. This more measured capitalism has strengthened German companies in their defence of the home market and by consequence aided them in expansion elsewhere.

However, while this more 'corporatist' approach may have eased the process of economic adjustment, particularly since this process of consensus has included trade unions and workforce representatives in large firms and many small ones, it may be impeding microeconomic adjustment to the single market. German companies in the insurance industry, for example, were worried that more innovative approaches, such as direct selling led by foreign companies, might gain a market niche. Similarly they were concerned that they would be outperformed in the field of techniques of portfolio management. This had led to some limited specialisation of functions among German and UK companies (Gentle, 1993). German firms were also losing out in cross-border shopping because of their lack of flexibility in opening hours (in sharp contrast to the flexibility in the UK which has actually resulted in opening hours which are illegal but occur because the law is not enforced by common consent).[1]

In general, however, the examples which were produced were the exception rather than the rule. The German propensity to have more extensive and harsher regulations (illustrated particularly in chapter 3 on retailing) had not resulted in any extensive action by German companies to relocate their operations where the rules were weaker. The fears of social dumping, expressed by Streeck in Mayes et al. (1993) for example, therefore seemed somewhat unwarranted. We came across only one example of a company relocating part of its production outside Germany (in the machine tool industry) where this involved both rationalisation to avoid duplication and taking advantage of lower labour costs in France.[2]

In general the pattern of behaviour has been to protect the level of employment in existing plants. It was interesting to note that, except in retail operations (both retailing and insurance) where being close to the customer is essential, most companies had not taken the opportunity to invest in the new Länder although they had considered the possibility and several were keeping a continuing watch on developments. However, the problems of obsolescence of equipment, agreements to raise wages to western levels and the poor quality of infrastructure and work skills meant that such investment was not so attractive as it might at first have appeared. The low response is not therefore a good indicator of the willingness to relocate. However, the mere existence of this potential opportunity to expand production in the new Länder is a clear disincentive to considering alternatives outside Germany. Substantial private investment from west to east has of course taken place in German industry as a whole (IFO, 1993).

During the period studied there was a lack of strong incentives to alter behaviour from regulatory changes emanating from the single market programme. The pharmaceutical industry in Germany was far more exercised by the changes in the German purchasing regime in its struggle to control costs than it was by the changes scheduled for 1995 for simplifying the registration of drugs for use throughout the Community. That change is still to come. In a separate study of the leasing industry (Matthews and Mayes, 1993) the lack of action was shown very clearly because the single market programme was not tackling the main factors which led to segmentation, namely tax differences and the need for local knowledge and contacts (and, to a lesser extent, differences in accounting practices). New products were finding their way into the German industry as a result of international exposure, particularly to the more developed US and UK industries, but this was more part of a continuing process of internationalisation which predates the single market and has not been substantially influenced by it.

Part of the problem has been that after the initial stimulus given by the announcement of the single market there has not been a strong string of regulatory changes and other measures to increase competition that have transformed the market. The process has been sufficiently attenuated that there is no sufficient discrete kick to the system to stimulate marked changes in behaviour beyond a general build up of measures leading to continuing change. The rate of this pressure has not been noticeably greater than other spurs to action from increases in international competition from imports, product innovation, technical and organisational change and the arrival of new competitors in the domestic market as a result of foreign direct investment (although the single market has itself acted as a stimulus to the latter).

This is in sharp contrast to the pressures from the recession, from 1989 in the UK and more recently in Germany, which has had a considerable impact on companies, prompting internal restructuring to reduce costs. It is noticeable in the UK that unemployment rose more quickly in the downturn and has started to fall much earlier in the upturn than would have been expected from previous experience. The single market might provide a marginal contribution to this change in behaviour but the basic influence is domestically generated.

Looking to the future

The experience of the period since the second half of 1992 has emphasised that the German and British economies still show fundamental differences. Both countries were slow to ratify the Maastricht Treaty, which commits them to seeking to achieve economic and monetary union by the end of the century. The possibility of starting in 1997 is offered in the treaty but the widely held view at present is that the EC will do well if it achieves EMU by the 'final' date of 1 January 1999, and then only for some of the member states. Indeed, the intergovernmental conference planned for 1996 may decide to extend the timetable. If both are to join EMU they have to show considerable convergence in the sense of achieving similar rates of price inflation and interest rates, being able to hold their exchange rates within the bounds laid down by the ERM for two years and to keep the ratios of the public deficit and debt to GDP below 3 per cent and 60 per cent respectively. (The exact convergence criteria set out in the Maastricht Treaty are explained and discussed in Britton and Mayes (1992).) However, achieving and maintaining that convergence requires a far wider measure of convergence in the two economies.

As Britton and Mayes (1992) and Mayes (1993a) explain, convergence has five further main facets if economies are to function similarly. Economies can diverge because they have different economic structures, institutions, policies, behavioural responses or real standards of living. If the divergence in these facets is too great then nominal convergence is likely to be because the responses to external shocks will be too different. Enduring disparities are possible because one may offset another. For example, similar levels of wage inflation can be achieved through a flexible system of bargaining at plant level or inflexible centralised negotiation among the social partners. Such centralised agreements require the institutional or behavioural mechanisms to ensure that they are carried out in practice. Although this is rather a caricature of the British and German systems, their approach to wage bargaining has been substantially different and in the past has generated very varied outcomes.

In our discussions up to now we have explored the extent of divergence between the British and German economies in these five facets of behaviour and shown that despite differences there has been considerable convergence in recent years. The single market has been an unusual 'shock' to the system in the sense that it is designed to achieve responses which lead to greater convergence. It thus encourages differential responses among the member states in pursuit of this single aim.

Our research has shown that, although the structures of the British and German economies continue to differ, with a substantially greater emphasis on manufacturing in Germany, particularly in engineering, the structures are converging. The UK's pattern of trade is substantially more concentrated on its European partners than it was even a decade ago. Real disparities have also narrowed. Productivity differentials in manufacturing have been reduced and as the recovery develops during 1993 the gap should begin to narrow further. This is not to say that the discrepancies will be eliminated nor that there is any question of the UK achieving German levels of GDP per head or unemployment in the foreseeable future. Substantial differences in these variables are quite consistent with the satisfactory operation of a mature EMU like that in the UK. Nevertheless, unless the UK does something quite striking to narrow the gap in the effort devoted to developing human capital through vocational education and training we cannot see convergence proceeding at a rate the UK will find satisfactory.

The institutional, policy and behavioural distinctions between the two countries are, however, more striking and do lead to serious questions about the degree to which successful convergence will actually be achieved. Our study has placed considerable evidence on corporate governance in both the traditional sense of the term (Hart, 1992a) and in a rather broader framework (Woolcock, 1993). In our view these differences help explain why the two economies respond differently to the same external pressures. From the point of view of economic efficiency we would like to see more convergence in the two systems. The UK could do with institutional structures which permit a rather longer-term view to be taken of the process of corporate growth and evolution. A more supportive relationship among firms, financial institutions, the layers of government and research and training/educational institutions would be of considerable benefit. Even within companies the need for development of structures has been recognised with, *inter alia*, the Cadbury Report, although there is more scope for change (Hart, 1992a). Germany on the other hand needs to have a rather more open market for corporate control if the single market is to develop on a balanced basis.

The wider differences are revealed by the regulatory structures and what is described as 'Ordnungspolitik' (see the chapters by Hager and Streeck in Hager *et al.*, 1993, for example and also Bulmer, 1993). To an extent closer integration through the removal of barriers under the single market programme is bringing these closer together (as illustrated in the case of doctors and lawyers by Brazier *et al.*,1993) but the pace of change is relatively slow. We do not yet understand how this process of 'competition among rules' will develop in the context of the single market. Some systems will coexist, some will drive out others while some may result in convergence on some new, compromise system.

Compromise between Anglo-Saxon and continental systems has been difficult to achieve in many areas. We have noted in the case of accounting systems that coexistence appears to be the route although the European professional body (FEE) argued for convergence on the international (Anglo-Saxon) standards (Matthews and Mayes, 1993). In insurance there has been a substantial measure of convergence and the same seems likely in pharmaceuticals. Nevertheless there is still a clear debate about whether the market should or indeed can decide in a framework based on deregulation on whether a new regulatory system should be negotiated outside the market, thereby avoiding the problems of 'competition among rules' altogether. The fear on the one hand is that competition will lead to the domination of the least onerous systems as with 'social dumping' or the 'Delaware' approach to company regulation. The fear on the other is that the more restrictive systems will dominate as they confer monopoly rents on companies. Thus the more 'protected' German companies would gain a competitive advantage over their British rivals.

Our research suggests that some of the worst fears about a 'rush for the bottom' have not been borne out in practice in the experience of British and German industry, particularly in the field of social dumping. However, some of the strongest elements of social protection are being eroded in the EC. The great difficulty in firing people in Spain has resulted in many new employees being taken on under temporary rather than permanent contracts. Competition among rules in this instance may emphasise the distinction between 'outsiders' and 'insiders' in the labour force (Calmfors and Driffill, 1988) and hence lead to a reappraisal of policy. German firms do actually appear to have benefited in areas such as environmental protection, where German legislation has led the European trend. German companies have adapted earlier and have developed techologies and techniques which they can export as others also seek to change. Insofar as German standards are nearer to the eventual European standard, German companies gain an edge over their British counterparts. Similarly in areas such as financial services, where the destination appears closer to UK behaviour, the adjustment costs may be lower for UK companies.

The experience of the limited range of industries we have studied suggests that the balance may be in favour of Germany but that in many respects the single market will be incomplete as the differences will not be resolved. In part this is because they have not been addressed as in the case of aspects of fiscal harmonisation (Matthews and Mayes, 1993) or because they cannot readily be addressed by regulatory means as in the case of the need for local knowledge and presence for retail operation that deal directly with individual consumers or small firms. However, it is also because some of the legislation is either ineffective or yet to be implemented as in the well known use of tachographs

(Butt-Phillip, 1988).

Much of the stimulus to change in British and German industry offered by the single market is still to come as we have yet to see many of the market measures take effect. The European Commission has realised this in the Sutherland Report (1993) which seeks more effective means for implementing the market measures. It is doubtful if these suggestions go far enough, Mayes (1993b) and Dehousse *et al.* (1992) suggest that the EC may need to adopt an approach similar to that in the US using executive agencies if subsidiarity is not to result in non-enforcement rather than a flexible means of achieving the variety of response necessary in the various member states for convergence. Britain and Germany have contrasting economic systems and our study suggests that much will be required if the single market is actually to be the stimulus to change in British and German industry originally hoped for. Certainly more fundamental convergence is required if EMU is to be achievable by the end of the century. The recovery as interest rates fall and more flexibility is permitted in the EMS is likely to generate a more favourable environment for renewed change in both countries.

Notes

1 ROUTES TO CHANGE

1 The European standards organisations CEN (European Committee for Standardisation) and CENELEC (European Committee for Electrotechnical Standardisation) comprise the respective national standards bodies of the EC and EFTA countries. ETSI (European Telecommunications Standards Institute) is a separate body dealing with standards relating to the telecommunications sector and includes amongst its members representatives of twenty-one countries, national telecom administrations and public operators as well as producers and service users.
2 Although tariffs on manufactured goods traded between member states were eliminated early in the Community's life it was still necessary to get customs clearance to establish whether excise duty or VAT were payable, whether the goods were permitted for import, subject to quota from their country of origin, and so on, all of which created an administrative barrier.
3 The external feedback was assumed not estimated by a full run of the OEF world model. See Burridge *et al.* (1991) for description of the world and industry models and their use.
4 There is one well-known exception set out in detail in Grinyer and Spender (1979) in which Central and Sherwood sold one of its most famous businesses, Izal, because this enabled them to get a good price for it. (Since it was already performing well there was not the scope for such a dramatic change in performance as could be obtained from other parts of the company after the necessary reorganisation and investment.)

2 THE UK AND GERMAN ECONOMIES

1 This difference is particularly important when spelt out in absolute terms as it means that German manufacturing is virtually double the size of that in the UK.

2   Some of Porter's description seems a caricature, with remarks about things being 'not done' and 'gentlemanly' not really sounding like a description of the 1980s. However, the broad analysis conforms with many other analyses, such as that of the House of Lords Committee on Overseas Trade (1985).

3   It is interesting to note, despite the popular views, that both the UK and Germany have received very similar proportions of investment from Japan as they have from all sources (38 per cent of Japanese investment accumulated over 1951–89 went to the UK and 8 per cent to Germany compared with the 40 per cent and 6.2 per cent figures shown for total investment over 1980–9 in chart 2.2).

4   Direct comparisons are difficult to make as the mismatch in categories even in the OECD data in table 2.4 indicates. Therefore subsequent figures in this section on German services are drawn from *European Economy*, no 5, supplement A, May 1993.

5   These medians are drawn on the basis of employment not number of firms, that is, half of employment lies above and below the median not half of the firms.

6   The data shown in table 2.12, drawn from O'Mahony (1993) are not those officially published, because, as explained above, the two countries use different assumptions about the life of assets and the way they depreciate (OECD, 1993). They are a new computation on a common base.

7   It can also be argued that the rapid fall in corporation tax to 34 per cent in the UK compared with 50 per cent in Germany led multinationals to use transfer pricing to shift as much of their profits as possible to the UK. Profit and hence the rate of return may also be exaggerated in the UK relative to Germany as UK companies report primarily to shareholders whereas German accounts are addressed more to the tax authorities and creditors.

8   The figures O'Mahony uses for productivity are based on the output and employment estimates from the *Annual Census of Production* in the UK and the *Kostenstruktur im Berghaus und Verarbeitendes Gewerbe* in Germany. Use of national accounts estimates in the UK would add some 15 per cent to the gap between British and German levels as they show manufacturing output 6 per cent lower and employment 7 per cent higher, reflecting the use of different enquiries. She argues plausibly that while one or other method may be better at estimating the aggregate variables, the ratio ought to be estimated using precisely the same sample of companies. (The Central Statistical Office in the UK is currently trying to eliminate the source of these discrepancies between the Employment and Production censuses by creating a common register of businesses.)

9   In any case there are several reasons for avoiding the production function approach; first because the function may not be identified (Walters, 1968). In perfect competition all firms would operate identically with equal inputs, scale and efficiency hence showing only a single vector of observations, differing only randomly from case to case. Insofar as departures are observed from this perfectly competitive ideal this will tend to be because a single production

function is inappropriate because products and inputs are not homogeneous or are inaccurately measured. Secondly, in parallel with the production function there is a simple accounting identity between valued added, Q (output, Y, multiplied by price, P) and wages (the wage, E, multiplied by the number of wage earners, L) and profits (the volume of capital, K, multiplied by the rate of return on it, R):

$$Q \equiv YP \equiv LE + KR.$$

Hence estimating a simple production function, $Y = f(L,K)$ would be in danger of merely estimating this identity instead (Hart and Shipman, 1991a).

10 Financed by the Leverhulme Foundation.

11 What was then the Business Statistics Office, BSO (now part of the Central Statistical Office, CSO), calculated the distribution of Net Output per head, NOPH, for the main orders of manufacturing industry over the years 1963–79 following a request from NEDO, the National Economic Development Office. A thorough analysis of these data has recently been published by Sheryl Bailey in Caves et al. (1992). Unfortunately these data are truncated because small firms with fewer than twenty employees are not sampled in the UK's Annual Census of Production (ACOP). The 'census' also uses a less than 100 per cent sample for businesses below 100 employees.

12 Value-added is defined slightly differently from net output as used here (see Mayes et al., 1991) but not enough to alter the conclusions drawn here.

13 The standard deviation divided by the mean.

14 In that study it appeared that the occurrence of dispersion was influenced by a similar range of factors in each country: concentration ratios, openness to international trade, product heterogeneity, spatial dispersion and the rate of structural change in the industry (see the summary of all the studies in Caves et al., 1992, chapter 1).

15 Other economists believe that the size distribution of shareholdings of a company, and hence the distribution of votes, constrains management. A wide dispersion of shareholdings gives managers more scope to pursue their own ends rather than those of the shareholders. For example, Leech and Leahy (1991) show that ownership structure affects the profitability and growth of British companies.

16 For example, average research and development expenditure per employee in Britain is only 35 per cent of that in Germany (1,530 in Britain compared with 4,320 in Germany, as shown in the International Comparisons of R&D expenditure in The Independent, 10 June 1991, p. 20).

17 Department of Trade and Industry (1989) provides a comprehensive description of the barriers to takeover in Germany.

18 These results drawn from Kumar (1984) are based on a series of cohort studies of 824–1,747 industrial and commercial companies.

19 It is important to recall that the data for merger activity in individual years can be distorted by one or two major acquisitions or the 'incorrect' classification of deals because of the specific sector of the merger vehicle used. (A subsidiary may be used to mount a bid.)

20 The emphasis placed by British observers on the role of German banks in the growth of German companies has a long history. Alfred Marshall's writings on the subject in his *Industry and Trade* (1919) are cited by both Shonfield (1965) and Prais (1981). Shonfield argued that the *Aufsichtsrat* is an important channel for the banks' influence as a result of their direct and indirect control of voting.

21 Commercially oriented graduate engineers are employed by German banks in departments dealing with large investment projects. But the numbers involved are very small. For example, our colleague, G. Weitzel of IFO-Institute, Munich, informs us that the Deutsche Bank employs some twenty-six staff in this category.

22 But Veba AG acquired Feldmuehle Nobel in 1989 after Friedrich and Gert Flick had made an unsuccessful contested bid in 1988 and had secretly sold a 40 per cent stake in the company to Veba. See Franks and Mayer (1990a), Appendix B2. Jenkinson and Mayer (1992) state that there have been four hostile takeovers in Germany since 1945. Baums (1993) qualifies this result and claims that there have been no successful public hostile takeovers.

23 Rose (1991) shows that gross corporate saving as a percentage of gross national product was much the same in Britain and Germany over the period 1960–87, though it was lower in Britain in 1988–9. But the share of gross profit in gross national product tends to be lower in Germany than in Britain (OECD *National Accounts*, 1990, table 14). Hence the share of corporate saving in profit tends to be higher in Germany than in Britain, which is consistent with the findings of Mayer and Alexander (1990).

24 The Commission's BACH database on companies (Laudy, 1991) indicates that German firms raise more finance from retentions and bank loans than their UK counterparts who make more use of equity.

25 It should be recalled that on average only around 5 per cent of successful mergers and acquisitions are hostile. We are grateful to a referee for this point.

26 Those mergers and acquisitions which are attempted in Germany will also attract fees and other costs. Hence the gap between the two countries is less than 7 per cent even though the German figure remains unknown.

27 Even in the case of Germany, Bühner (1991) estimates that for takeovers among the largest 500 firms over the period 1973–85, the average cumulative loss for acquiring shareholders was 10 per cent after two years. The figure was near zero for horizontal mergers where some extension of the product range was involved and a loss of over 20 per cent for conglomerate mergers. However, it is this former category of horizontal mergers which might be thought most likely in the exploitation of the opportunities offered by the single market.

4   THE PHARMACEUTICALS INDUSTRY

1 Under the PACT system British doctors are sent information each quarter on their prescribing levels and costs compared to national and area averages.

There will be firm prescription budgets for regional and area levels and indicative budgets for local practices. This is discussed by Bosanquet (1991).

2   The PPRS dates from 1957, when it was known as the Voluntary Price Regulation Scheme, even though profits rather than prices were regulated. Under the current scheme operated by the Department of Health, companies supplying the National Health Service submit annual financial returns on the costs and profits of their NHS sales. At the moment, profitability on capital in the range 17–20 per cent is regarded as reasonable. This scheme is being re-negotiated (*Financial Times*, 28 December 1992).

3   The exemptions from patients' contributions are important. An economic appraisal of patients' co-payments for prescribed medicines in the European Community is provided by Griffin (1992).

4   The large pharmaceutical manufacturers are planning to expand OTC sales. At one time Glaxo planned to switch its best-selling drug, Zantac (used for ulcers, indigestion, heartburn) from prescription to OTC in Japan (*Financial Times*, 23 January 1993). SmithKline Beecham, Merck, Wellcome and Ciba-Geigy are also aiming to increase their OTC trade (*The Independent*, 1 February 1993). Glaxo, Wellcome and the American company Warner-Lambert announced (*The Independent*, 29 July 1993) a joint venture to form the world's largest OTC pharmaceutical company to sell well-known non-prescription drugs, including Zantac.

5   It is also true that some German firms are split into several small *Unternehmen* (usually GmbHs) in order to reduce taxation and to get below the threshold size requiring the establishment of a works council.

6   The Census of Production measure of gross profitability is quite different from the profitability on capital or on turnover which is normally obtained from company accounts. For example, in 1987 the worldwide gross profitability on turnover of Glaxo Holdings in £ million was $(55 + 665)/1,741$ or about 41.4 per cent. This result may be obtained from the published accounts by adding depreciation to trading profit and dividing by turnover. Net output, Q, may be estimated by adding depreciation, trading profit, wages and salaries, social security payments, pensions and directors' fees to give £1,081 million. E is £361 million. Hence, $(Q - E)/Q$ is 66.6 per cent. This may be compared with the profitability measures in table 4.5 which relate to UK production only. That is, non-manufacturing establishments such as research laboratories are excluded. Glaxo is the largest enterprise in the top five in table 4.5 and must dominate the domestic weighted average of $(Q - E)/Q$ of 78.5 per cent. But this does not imply that its domestic profitability exceeds its world profitability of 66.6 per cent. In fact comparisons of such profitability measures should really be restricted to manufacturing enterprises of different sizes within table 4.5.

5   THE INSURANCE INDUSTRY

1   Foreign insurers might be able to overcome this barrier by using letters of credit

to satisfy local requirements while maintaining deposits at home to earn higher interest rates.

2   It is also influenced by social trends such as the tendency for increased litigation which in turn leads to more legal expenses insurance.

3   The insurers may try to avoid creating a distribution network by selling direct to the client. Insurers such as Direct Line (owned by Royal Bank of Scotland), Churchill (owned by Winterthur) and the Insurance Service (subsidiary of Royal Insurance) engage in such direct selling (Harcus 1992; *The Times*, 11 September 1993, p. 26).

4   Cultural barriers are important not only for customers in different countries but also for the insurance firms. A successful joint venture between two firms based in different countries requires managers at each level to overcome the difficulties arising from their different traditions, education and training. Cultural differences also exist between different financial industries in the same country. For example, the insurance industry is based on selling (insurance products are 'sold' rather than 'bought') whereas the commercial banks have no tradition of hard selling. This cultural difference has to be faced by any development of *bancassurance*.

5   It might be argued that because of the differences between national markets, the competition between the multinational insurers should be termed 'multi-domestic' rather than 'global'.

6   THE MACHINE TOOL INDUSTRY

1   When the Austrian company Voest bought Steinel to provide an EC manufacturing base this was something of an exception.

2   We only came across this clause in our interviews in Germany. This was not mentioned in our interviews in the UK but it was not an explicit question. (Our research strategy was to pilot our methodology in the UK first, where interviewing costs were lower before proceeding to the German phase for each industry.) However, in subsequent work on public purchasing (Mayes and Webb, 1993) we have found this clause in twenty-seven contracts with the public sector.

3   In a related study (Mayes and Young, 1993), set-up costs for machine tools were said to have fallen by as much as 85 per cent in two years in some instances.

7   CONCLUSIONS

1   This is a clear example of the sort of evolutionary pressure for regulating change which is expected under the concept of 'competition among rules' in the single market, although in this instance it is the continental example (not from Germany!) rather than direct competitive pressure which is responsible.

2   'Social dumping' was originally largely feared as being the siting of production by German owned companies outside Germany, without regard as to whether the output would then be exported back to Germany. However the concept

would equally well apply to foreign investment which would otherwise have come to Germany but for the high employer cost of social benefits. Our study did not attempt to investigate this latter possibility. Ironically it was wage costs rather than non-wage labour costs which were cited as a contributory factor to the specific investment outside Germany which we explored. However, the distinction was not probed during the interview.

References

3i plc UK (1992), *The Role of the Finance Director – Part 3, Corporate Governance*, April, 3i, 91 Waterloo Road, London SE1 8XP.

ABI (Association of British Insurers) (1991), Insurance Statistics 1986–1990 London.

ABPI (1988), *Parliamentary Briefing 1*, The Association of the British Pharmaceutical Industry, London.

ABPI (1992) 'Pharma Facts and Figures', The Association of the British Pharmaceutical Industry, London.

Acquisitions Monthly (1989), 'Escalating R & D costs put drugs companies under merger pressure', November, pp. 44–7.

Ambramovitz, M. (1986) 'Catching-up, forging ahead and falling behind', *Journal of Economic History*, 46, pp. 385–406.

American Machinist (1992), World Machine Tool Output Survey, February.

American Machinist (1993), World Machine Tool Output Survey, March.

Aitken, N.D. (1973) 'The effect of the EEC and EFTA on European trade: a temporal cross-section analysis', *American Economic Review*, 63(5), December, pp. 881–92.

WS Atkins Management Consultants *et al.* (1990), *Strategic Study on the Machine Tool Industry*, Commission of the European Communities, May.

Audretsch, D.B. (1993), 'Industrial policy and international competitiveness' in Nicolaides, P. (ed.), *Industrial Policy in the European Community: A Necessary Response to Economic Integration*, The Hague, Nijhoff.

Baldwin, R. (1989) 'The growth effects of 1992', *Economic Policy*, 9, pp. 248–70.

Baldwin, R. (1990) 'On the micro-economics of the European monetary union' in *European Economy*, 'The Economics of EMU', Special Issue.

Ball, J. (1991), 'Short termism – myth or reality?,' National Westminster Bank Review, August, pp. 20-30.

Bank of England (1989), 'The single European market. Survey of the UK financial services industry'.

226

Bannock, G. (1981), 'The clearing banks and small firms', *Lloyds Bank Review*, October.

Barnett, C. (1986), *The Audit of War: the illusion and reality of Britain as a great nation*, London, Macmillan.

Barro, R.J. and Sala-i-Martin, X. (1991), 'Convergence across states and regions', *Brookings Papers on Economic Activity*, 1991 (1), pp 107–182.

Barro, R.J. and Sala-i-Martin, X. (1992), 'Convergence', *Journal of Political Economy*, 1992, 100(2), pp. 1072–85.

Baumol, W.J., Panzar, J.C. and Willig, R.D. (1988), *Contestable Markets and the Theory of Industry Structure*, San Diego, Academic Press.

Baums, T. (1993), 'Foreign financial investments in German firms – selected legal and policy issues', paper given to COST A7 meeting, Brussels, September.

Bhattacharyya, S. (1979), 'Imperfect information, dividend policy and the "bird in the hand fallacy"', *Bell Journal of Economics* 10, pp. 259–70.

Bosanquet, N. (1991), 'European pharmaceuticals in the 1990's: how real will be the global ambitions', *European Business Journal*, 3, pp. 24–30.

Boston Consulting Group (BCG) (1985), 'Strategic study of the machine tool industry', Commission of the European Communities, February.

Bowring J.A. (1990), 'Food retailing 1990.' Institute of Grocery Distribution.

Brazier, M., Lovecy, J. and Moran, M. (1993), 'Professional regulation and the single European market: a study of the regulation of doctors and lawyers in England and France', University of Manchester, mimeo.

Britton, A. and Mayes, D.G. (1992), *Achieving Monetary Union*, London, Sage.

Bühner, R. (1991), 'The success of mergers in Germany', *International Journal of Industrial Organisation*, 9, pp. 513–32.

Buigues, P. and Ilzkowitz, F. (1988), 'The sectoral impact of the internal market', Commission of the European Communities, EC Brussels II/335/88-EN.

Buigues, P., Ilzkowitz, F. and Lebrun, J.-F. (1990), 'The impact of the internal market by industrial sector' in *European Economy*, special edition.

Bulmer, S. (1993), 'Community government and regulatory regimes', paper for the European Community Studies Association, May 27–9, Washington DC.

Burridge, M., Dhar. S., Mayes, D., Meen, G., Neal, E., Tyrell, G. and Walker, J. (1991), 'Oxford Economic Forecasting's system of models', *Economic Modelling*, 8, pp. 227–413.

Burridge, M. and Mayes, D.G. (1992), 'The implications for firms and industry of the adoption of the Ecu as the single currency in the EC', report to the European Commission, summarised in *De Pecunia*, (5), August 1993, pp. 115–25.

Burridge, M. and Mayes, D. (1993a), 'The impact of internal market programme on European economic structure and performance', report to the European Parliament.

Burridge, M. and Mayes, D. (1993b), 'Industrial change for 1992' in Driver, C. and Dunne, P. (eds), *Structural Change in the UK Economy*, Cambridge, Cambridge University Press.

Burstall, M.L. (1990), '1992 and the regulation of the pharmaceutical industry', London, The Institute of Economic Affairs Health and Welfare Unit, Health Series no. 9.

Burstall, M.L. (1991), 'Europe after 1992: implications for pharmaceuticals', *Health Affairs*, 10, (3), pp. 157–71.

Burstall, M.L. and Reuben, B.G. (1988), 'The cost of non-Europe in the pharmaceutical industry', report for the Commission of the European Communities, Economists Advisory Group, London.

Business Statistics Office (1990), *Retailing 1987*, Business Monitor SDA 25.

Butt-Phillip, A. (1988),'The application of the EEC regulations on drivers' hours and tacographs' in Siedentof, H., and Ziller, J. (eds), *Making European Policies Work: The Implementation of Community Legislation in the Member States, Vol. I: Comparative Synthesis*, London, Sage, pp. 88–129.

Cable, J. (1985), 'Capital market information and industrial performance: the role of West German banks', *Economic Journal*, 95, pp. 118–32.

Calmfors, L. and Driffill, J. (1988), 'Centralisation of wage bargaining and macroeconomic performance', *Economic Policy*, 6, pp. 13–61.

Carter, R.L. and Greenaway, D. (1991), 'The implications for the insurance industry of economic and monetary union in the European Community', Report to Association of British Insurers.

Casson, M.C. (ed) (1991), *Global Research Strategy and International Competitiveness*, Oxford, Blackwell.

Catinat, M., Donnie, E. and Italianer, A. (1988), 'Macro-economic consequences of the completion of the internal market: the modelling evidence' in *Studies on the Economics of Integration, vol. 2, Research on the Costs of Non-Europe*, Brussels/Luxembourg, Commission of the European Communities.

Caves, R.E. *et al.* (1992), *Industrial Efficiency in Six Nations*, Cambridge, Mass., MIT Press.

Caves, R.E., Whinston, M.D. and Hurwitz, M.A. (1991), 'Patent expiration, entry and competition in the U.S. pharmaceutical industry', Brookings Papers, pp. 1–66.

Cecchini, P. (ed) (1988), *1992: The European Challenge*, Wildwood House.

Club de Bruxelles (1991), 'The pharmaceutical industry in the single European market', issued from 10 rue du College, Saint-Michel, B1150 Bruxelles.

Commission of the European Communities (1985) *Completing the Internal Market*, White Paper, COM (85) 310.

Commission of the European Communities (1991), *Panorama of EC Industry 1991–1992*.

Corporate Intelligence Group (1990), *Food Distribution in Europe in the 1990s*.

Cosh, A., Hughes, A. and Singh, A. (1990), 'Takeovers and short-termism in the UK', Institute for Public Policy Research, Paper no. 3, London.

Daly, A., Hitchens, D.M.W.N. and Wagner, K. (1985), 'Productivity, machinery and skills in a sample of British and German manufacuturing plants', *National Institute Economic Review*, February, pp. 48–61.

Datamonitor (1992), *European Insurers. A market report*, Datamonitor, London.

Davies, G., Kilpatrick, A. and Mayes, D.G. (1988), 'Fiscal policy simulations – a comparison of UK models', *Applied Economics*, 20, pp. 1613–34.

Dawson, J. and Shaw, S. (1989), 'Horizontal competition in retailing and structure of manufacturer-retailer relationships' in Pellegrini, C. and Reddy, S. (eds), *Retail and Marketing Channels*, London, Routledge.

Dehousse, R., Joerges, C., Mayone, G. and Synder, F. (1992), 'Europe after 1992: new regulatory strategies', European University Institute Working Paper in Law, no. 92/31.

Dell, E. and Mayes, D.G. (1989), '1992 and the environment for European industry', occasional paper, Centre for European Policy Studies, Brussels, 3 July.

Department of Trade and Industry (1989), *Barriers to Takeovers in the EC*, report prepared by Coopers and Lybrand.

Department of Trade and Industry (1990) 'United Kingdom' in Buigues *et al.*

Department of Trade and Industry (1991a), *EC Third Non-Life Insurance (Framework) Directive*, DTI London.

Department of Trade and Industry (1991b), *European Commission Proposal for a Third Life Insurance Directive (the Life Framework Directive)*, DTI London.

Dosi, G., Pavitt, K. and Soete, L. (1990), *The Economics of Technical Change and International Change and International Trade*, Brighton, Harvester-Wheatsheaf.

Dowrick, S. and Nguyen, D.T. (1989), 'OECD comparative economic growth 1950–1985: Catching up and convergence', *American Economic Review*, 79, pp. 1010–30.

Duke, R. (1990), 'Post-saturation competition in UK grocery retailing', School of Business and Economic Studies, University of Leeds, Discussion Paper 90/9.

Economist (various issues), 'European Insurance', 24 Feb. 1990; 'Banking Brief', 20 Oct. 1990; also 17 Nov. 90; 'British Life Assurance', 20 July 1991; also 9 Feb. 1991 and 16 March 1991.

Economist Intelligence Unit (1985), European Trends Special Series, Report Nos 1–4 by Market and Industry Analysts, Brussels.

Economist Intelligence Unit (1990), *Insurance in a Changing Europe 1990–95*, Special Report no. 2068 by Arthur Anderson Consulting.

Economist Intelligence Unit (1991), *Europe's Pharmaceutical Industry: Tackling the Single Market*, Special Report no. 2085.

Edwards, J.S. and Fischer, K. (1991), 'Banks, finance and investment in West Germany since 1970', Centre for Economic Policy Research, Discussion Paper 497.

Eltis, W. (1992), 'The Financial Foundations of Success', Esmeé Fairburn Lecture, Lancaster University, November.

Euromonitor (1991), European Marketing Data and Statistics, 26th Edition.

European Economy, Special Edition (1990).

Eurostat (1988), 'Purchasing power parities and gross domestic product in real terms: results 1985', Statistical Office of the European Communities, Luxembourg.

Fairburn, J. and Kay, J. (eds) (1989), *Mergers and Merger Policy*, Oxford, Oxford

University Press.

Financial Times (1992), various issues.

Finisinger, J., Hammond, E., and Tapp, J. (1985), *Insurance: Competition or Regulation*, London, Institute of Fiscal Studies.

Franks, J. and Harris, R.S. (1989), 'Shareholder wealth effects of UK takeovers: implications for merger policy' in Fairburn and Kay (eds).

Franks, J. and Mayer, C. (1990a), 'Capital markets and corporate control: a study of France, Germany and the UK', *Economic Policy*, April, pp. 189-225.

Franks, J. and Mayer, C. (1990b), 'Takeovers and the correction of managerial failure', London Business School and City University Business School, mimeo.

Freeman, C., Sharp, M. and Walker, W. (1991), *Technology and the Future of Europe*, London, Pinter.

Fukao, M. (1993) 'International integration of financial markets and the cost of capital', OECD Economics Department Working Paper, no. 128.

Gasiorek, M., Smith, A. and Venables, A.J. (1992), '1992: trade and welfare – general equilibrium model', chapter 2 in Winters (ed).

Gentle, C. (1993), *Financial Services Industry*, Aldershot, Avebury.

George, (1989), 'Do we need a merger policy' in Fairburn and Kay (eds), *Mergers and Merger Policy*, pp. 281–300

Gerstenberger, W. (1990), 'Federal Republic of Germany' in Buigues *et al.*

Gerum, E. with Steinmann, H. and Fees, W. (1987), 'Wertsystem der Unternehmensführung und Mitbestimmung – Einige empirische Befunde' (with English summary), *Zeitschrift für Betriebswirfschaft*, 57(4), April.

Griffin, T.D. (1992), 'An economist's view of patient co-payment for prescribed medicines in the European Community', *International Pharmacy Journal*, 6.

Grinyer, P.H., Mayes, D.G. and McKiernan, P. (1988), *Sharpbenders*, Oxford, Blackwell.

Grinyer, P.H. and McKiernan, P. (1993), 'Organisational entropy after sustaining superior performance from recovery: the case of the sharpbenders', paper given to a NIESR conference, 14 January.

Grinyer, P.H. and Spender, J.G. (1979), *Turnabout: the Fall and Rise of the Newton Chambers Group*, London, Associated Press.

Hager, W., Knight, Sir A., Mayes, D.G. and Streeck, W. (1993), *Public Interest and Market Pressures: Problems for the 1992 Programme*, London, Macmillan.

Harcus, I. (1992), 'Insurers see little respite', *Management Consultancy*, April, p. 20.

Hart, P.E. (1988), *Youth Unemployment in Great Britain*, Cambridge, Cambridge University Press.

Hart, P.E. (1992a), 'Corporate governance in Britain and Germany', NIESR Discussion Paper, no. 31.

Hart, P.E. (1992b), 'The effects of "1992" on the pharmaceutical industry in Britain and Germany', NIESR Discussion Paper, no. 8.

Hart, P.E. (1992c), 'The effects of "1992" on the insurance industry in Britain and Germany', NIESR Discussion Paper, no. 18.

Hart, P.E. and Shipman, A. (1991a), 'The variation of productivity within British and German industries', NIESR Discussion Paper no. 203.

Hart, P.E. and Shipman, A. (1991b), 'Skills shortages in Britain and Germany', *International Journal of Manpower*, 12, pp. 18–27.

Hart, P.E. and Shipman, A. (1992), 'The variation of productivity within British and German industries', *Journal of Industrial Economics*, December, 40(4), pp. 417–28.

Hitchens, D.M.W.N., Wagner, K. and Birnie, J.E. (1990), *Closing the Productivity Gap: A Comparison of Northern Ireland, the Republic of Ireland, Britain and West Germany*, Portsmouth, Avebury.

Hooper, P. and Larin, K.A. (1989), 'International comparisons of labour costs in manufacturing', *The Review of Income and Wealth*, Series 35, no. 4, December.

House of Commons (1989), Trade and Industry Committee, *Fifth Report, Financial Services and the Single European Market*, HC256, London, HMSO.

House of Lords (1985), *Report from the Select Committee on Overseas Trade*, HL 238 I–III, London, HMSO.

House of Lords (1991), European Communities Committee. Sub-Committee A, *Report on a Single Insurance Market*.

Hughes, A. (1989), 'The impact of merger: a survey of empirical evidence for the U.K.' in Fairburn and Kay (eds).

Hughes, A. (1991), 'Mergers and economic performance in the UK. A survey of empirical evidence 1950–90', Bishop, M. and Kay, J. (eds), *Mergers and Merger Policy*, Oxford, Oxford University Press.

IFO (1993), *1992: The Stimulus for Change in Britain and German Industry*, April.

Immenga, U. (1993), 'Mergers and acquisitions between Germany and the UK: legal framework, ways and barriers in IFO.

Ingham, A. and Ulph, A. (1992), 'Estimating the capital stock of UK manufacturing industry using a vintage model', Treasury Academic Panel, October.

Institute of Grocery Distribution (1990a), *Grocery Market Information 1990*.

Institute of Grocery Distribution (1990b), *Food Manufacturing 1990*.

International Management (1990), 'Allianz's quiet coup d'etat', December.

Jenkinson, T. and Mayer, C. (1992), 'The assessment: corporate governance and corporate control', *Oxford Review of Economic Policy*, 8, pp. 1–10.

Keynote Report (1990), *Machine Tools: An Industry Sector Overview*, Seventh Edition.

Keynote Report (1992), *Machine Tools: An Industry Sector Overview*, Eighth Edition.

Kirner, W. (1968), 'Zeitreihen für das Anlagevermögen der Wirtschaftsbereiche in der Bundesrepublik Deutschland', Deutsches Institut für Wirtschaftsforschung – Beiträge zur Strukturforschung, Heft 5, Duncker & Humboldt, Berlin.

Kreinin, M. (1973), 'The static effects of EEC enlargement on trade flows', *Southern Economic Journal*, 39(4), April, pp. 559–68.

Kumar, M.S. (1984), *Growth, Acquisition and Investment*, Cambridge, Cambridge University Press.

Laudy, J. (1991), 'Financial Strategies' in Mayes, D.G. *et al.*

Leech, D. and Leahy, J. (1991), 'Ownership structure, control type classifications and the performance of large British companies', *Economic Journal, 101, no. 409, pp. 1418–37, November.*

Leibenstein, H. (1966), 'Allocative efficiency vs x-efficiency', *American Economic Review,* 56, June, pp. 392–415.

Littlechild, S. (1989), 'Myths and merger policy' in Fairburn and Kay (eds).

Lynde, C. and Richmond, J. (1993), 'Public capital and long-run costs in UK manufacturing', *Economic Journal,* 103, no. 419, pp. 880–93, July.

Lynn, M. (1991), 'Drugs companies in a fix', *International Management,* October, pp. 62–5.

Lucas, Robert E. Jr. (1988), 'On the mechanics of economic development', *Journal of Monetary Economics,* July.

Mason, G., van Ark, B. and Wagner, K. (1993), 'Productivity, product quality and workforce skills: food processing in four European countries', NIESR Discussion Paper (New Series) no. 34.

Matthews, D. and Mayes, D.G. (1993), 'The evolution of rules for a single European market in leasing', National Institute Discussion Paper no. 35.

Matthews, R. and Feinstein, C. (1990), 'The growth of output and productivity in the UK: the 1980s as a phase of the post-war period', *National Institute Economic Review,* 133, August.

Mayer, C. and Alexander, I. (1990), 'Banks and securities markets: corporate financing in Germany and the UK', Centre for Economic Policy Research, Discussion Paper 433.

Mayes, D.G. (1990), 'The economic effects of public expenditure', National Institute Discussion Paper, no. 168.

Mayes, D.G. (1993a), 'The implications of European integration for Australia', EPAC Discussion Paper, no. 93/01, November, Canberra.

Mayes, D.G. (1993b), Comments to conference on Conflict and Cohesion in the Single European Market, Newcastle Upon Tyne, November.

Mayes, D.G. *et al.* (1991), *The European Challenge: industry's response to the 1992 Programme,* London, Harvester Wheatsheaf.

Mayes, D.G. *et al.* (1993), *The External Implications of European Integration,* London, Harvester Wheatsheaf.

Mayes, D.G., Harris, C. and Lansbury, M. (1994), *Inefficiency in Industry,* London, Harvester Wheatsheaf.

Mayes, D.G. and Ogiwara, Y. (1992), 'Transplanting Japanese success in the UK', *National Institute Economic Review,* November.

Mayes, D.G. and Shipman, A. (1992), 'The response of UK retailers to the single European market', NIESR Discussion Paper (new series) no. 6.

Mayes, D.G. and Webb, D.C. (1993), 'Exchange risk as a barrier to cross border public procurement in the internal market', report by NIESR to the European Commission.

Mayes, D.G. and Young, G. (1993), 'Improving the estimates of the UK capital stock', report by NIESR to the Central Statistical Office.

MSI Databrief (1989), 'Machine Tools: UK'.

MTTA (1991), *Machine Tool Statistics 1991*.

MTTA (1993), *British Machine Tool Industry Basic Facts 1993*.

Nam, C.W. and Reuter, J. (1991), 'The impact of 1992 and associated legislation on the less favoured regions of the European Community', European Parliament, Research report no. 18.

National Freight Corporation (1989), *Contract Distribution Report 1989*.

NEDO (1985), 'Manufacturing Performance of the Process Plant Industry'.

Nerb, G. (1988), 'The completion of the internal market: a survey of European industry's perception of the likely effects', vol. 3 of research on the Costs of Non-Europe, Commission of the European Communities.

NIESR (1991), *A New Strategy for Social and Economic Cohesion after 1992*, European Parliament Research Report, no. 19.

North, R. and Mollett, S. (1989), 'Barriers to takeovers in the European Community', *Acquisitions Monthly*, November.

OECD (1990), *National Accounts*, vol. II, Paris.

OECD (1993) 'Methods used by OECD countries to measure stocks of fixed capital', *National Accounts*, No. 2, Paris.

O'Mahony, M. (1992), 'Productivity levels in British and German manufacturing', *National Institute Economic Review*, no. 139, February.

O'Mahony, M. (1993), 'Capital stocks and productivity in industrial nations', *National Institute Economic Review*, 145, August.

Otto, H.J. (1991), 'Obstacles to foreigners are nothing but a myth', *Financial Times*, 20 February.

Oulton, N. (1987), 'Plant closures and the productivity miracle in manufacturing', *National Institute Economic Review*, 121.

PEP (1965) *Thrusters and Sleepers: A Study of Attitudes in Industrial Management*, London, Allen and Unwin.

Peters, T.J. and Waterman, P.H. (1982), *In Search of Excellence*, New York, Harper & Row.

Plummer, M. (1993), 'Economic deepening and widening in Europe: implications for the Asia-Pacific rim', paper given to IDE Conference, Tokyo, June.

Pool, W.E. (1992), 'Insurance and the European Community', *The Geneva Papers on Risk and Insurance*, 17, 63, pp. 178–99.

Popper, K.A. (1950), *The Open Society and its Enemies*, London, Routledge.

Porter, M.E. (1990), *Competitiveness of Nations*, London, Macmillan.

Prais, S.J. (1981), *Productivity and Industrial Structure: A Statistical Study of Manufacturing Industry in Britain, Germany and the United States*, Cambridge, Cambridge University Press.

Prais, S.J. (1984) 'The stock of machinery in Britain, Germany and the United States', National Institute Discussion Paper no. 78.

Prais S.J. (1991), 'Vocational qualifications in Britain and Europe: theory and practice', *National Institute Economic Review*, 136, May, pp. 86–93.

Prais, S.J. *et al.* (1989), 'Productivity, education and training: Britain and other countries compared', NIESR.

Prais S.J. and Wagner, K. (1988), 'Productivity and management: the training of foremen in Britain and Germany', *National Institute Economic Review*, 123, February, pp. 34–48.

Pratten, C. (1988), 'A survey of economies of scale' in *Studies on the Economics of Integration*, vol 2 of research on Cost of Non-Europe, Commission of the European Communities, Brussels/Luxembourg, chapter 2.

Reuben, B.G. and Burstall, M.L. (1989), *Generic Pharmaceuticals – the Threat, Products and Companies at Risk*, Economists Advisory Group Report, 87IS02, March.

Rose, H. (1991), *The Question of Saving*, British North-American Association.

Salter, W.E.G. (1966), *Productivity and Technical Change*, 2nd edition, Cambridge, Cambridge University Press.

Salvadori, D. (1991), 'The automobile industry' in Mayes, D.G. *et al.*

Schmalensee, R. (1989), 'Inter-industry studies of structure and performance' in Schmalensee, R. and Willig, R.P., *Handbook of Industrial Organisation*, Amsterdam, North-Holland.

Sharp, M. (1991), 'Pharmaceuticals and biotechnology: perspectives for the European industry' in Freeman *et al.*

Shonfield, A. (1965), *Modern Capitalism*, Oxford, Oxford University Press.

Simon, H. (1992), 'Lessons from Germany's mid-size giants', *Harvard Business Review*, March–April, pp. 115–23.

Slatter, S. (1984), *Corporate Recovery: Successful Turnabout Strategies and Their Implementation*, Harmondsworth, Penguin.

Smith, A. and Venables, A. (1988), 'Completing the internal market in the European Community: some industry simulations', *European Economic Review, 32(7), pp. 1501–25, September*.

Smith, A.D. (1992), *International Financial Markets: the performance of Britain and its rivals*, NIESR Occassional Papers XLV, Cambridge, Cambridge University Press.

Smith, A.D. and Hitchens, D. (1985), *Productivity in the Distributive Trades*, Cambridge, Cambridge University Press.

Southall, S. and Winlow, M. (1992), 'A new civilization', *Post Magazine*, 6 February, pp. 12–13.

Städtler, A. (1992), 'Der EG-Binnenmarkt aus Verbrauchersicht', Versicherungsleistungen, mimeo.

Steedman, H., Mason, G. and Wagner, K. (1991), 'Intermediate skills in the workplace: deployment, standards and supply in Britain, France and Germany', *National Institute Economic Review*,136, May.

Steedman, H. and Wagner, K. (1987), 'A second look at productivity, machinery and skills in Britain and Germany', *National Institute Economic Review*, 122, November.

Steedman, H. and Wagner, K. (1989), 'Productivity, machinery and skills: clothing manufacture in Britain and Germany', *National Institute Economic Review*, 128, May.

Stevenson, R.E. (1980), 'Likelihood functions for generalised stochastic frontier estimation', *Journal of Economics*, 13, May, pp. 57–66.

Sutherland, P. *et al.* (1993), 'The internal market after 1992: meeting the challenge', report to the EEC Commission by the High Level Group on the Operation of Internal Market.

Times Books (1992), *The Times 1000, 1991–92*, London, HarperCollins.

Touche Ross (1990), *Piecing Together a Healthy Future*, London, Touche Ross Management Consultants.

Treadgold, A. (1990a), *Costs of Retailing in Contintental Europe*, Harlow, Longman.

Treadgold, A. (1990b), 'Only engagements so far', *European Retail*, September.

Treadgold, A. and Davies, R. (1988), *The Internationalisation of Retailing*, Harlow, Longman.

van Ark, B. (1990), 'Comparative levels of manufacturing labour productivity in postwar Europe', *Oxford Bulletin of Economics and Statistics*, 52(4), pp. 343–74, November.

Walters, A. (1968), *An Introduction to Econometrics*, London, Macmillan.

Weitzel, G. (1993) 'Retailing in the single European market: a comparison between the UK and Germany', in IFO.

Williams, P. (1991), 'Time and the city: short-termism in the UK, myth or reality?' *National Westminster Bank Review*, August, pp. 31–8.

Willamson, O.E. (1981), 'The modern corporation', *Journal of Economic Literature*.

Woolcock, S. (1993), 'Competition among forms of corporate governance in the EC: the impact on Britain', Royal Institute of International Affairs, mimeo.

Index

THE NATIONAL INSTITUTE OF
ECONOMIC AND SOCIAL RESEARCH
PUBLICATIONS IN PRINT

published by
THE CAMBRIDGE UNIVERSITY PRESS
(available from booksellers, or in case of difficulty from the publishers)

ECONOMIC AND SOCIAL STUDIES

OCCASIONAL PAPERS

OTHER PUBLICATIONS BY CAMBRIDGE UNIVERSITY PRESS

THE NATIONAL INSTITUTE OF ECONOMIC AND SOCIAL RESEARCH

publishes regularly

THE NATIONAL INSTITUTE ECONOMIC REVIEW

A quarterly analysis of the general economic situation in the United Kingdom and overseas with forecasts eighteen months ahead. The last issue each year usually contains an assessment of medium-term prospects. There are also in most issues special articles on subjects of interest to academic and business economists.

Annual subscriptions, £80.00 (UK and EU) and £100.00 (rest of world), also single issues for the current year, £25.00, are available direct from NIESR, 2 Dean Trench Street, Smith Square, London, SW1P 3HE.

Subscriptions at a special reduced price are available to students and teachers in the United Kingdom on application to the Secretary of the Institute.

Back numbers and reprints of issues which have gone out of stock are distributed by Wm. Dawson and Sons Ltd., Cannon House, Park Farm Road, Folkestone. Microfiche copies for the years 1961–89 are available from EP Microform Ltd., Bradford Road, East Ardsley, Wakefield, Yorks.

Published by
HEINEMANN EDUCATIONAL BOOKS
(distributed by Gower Publishing Company and available from booksellers)

THE FUTURE OF PAY BARGAINING
Edited by FRANK BLACKABY. 1980. pp. 256. £34.50 (hardback),
£12.95 (paperback) net.

INDUSTRIAL POLICY AND INNOVATION
Edited by CHARLES CARTER. 1981. pp. 250. £45.00 (hardback), £16.95
(paperback) net.

NATIONAL INTERESTS AND LOCAL GOVERNMENT
Edited by KEN YOUNG. 1983. PP. 180. £35.00 (hardback), £16.95
(paperback) net.

EMPLOYMENT, OUTPUT AND INFLATION
Edited by A.J.C. BRITTON. 1983. pp. 208. £40.00 net.

THE TROUBLED ALLIANCE. ATLANTIC RELATIONS IN THE 1980s
Edited by LAWRENCE FREEDMAN. 1983. pp. 176. £40.00 (hardback), £12.95
(paperback) net.